WHEN IN DOUBT
BE NICE

WHEN IN DOUBT
BE NICE

Love

Peter

LESSONS FROM A
LIFETIME IN BUSINESS

PETER MEAD

SILVERTAIL BOOKS • *London*

First published in Great Britain in 2014 by Silvertail Books Ltd
www.silvertailbooks.com
Copyright © Peter Mead 2014
1
The right of Peter Mead to be identified as the author
of this work has been asserted by him in accordance
with the Copyright, Design and Patents Act 1988
A catalogue record of this book is available from the British Library
Typeset in Ehrhardt Monotype by Joanna Macgregor
Printed in the UK by CPI Group (UK) Ltd, Croydon, CR0 4YY
ISBN 978-1-909269-06-4

For Sam – nothing would be possible without her,

And for my sons – I am truly blessed to have Billy, Ben and Harry.

CONTENTS

AUTHOR'S NOTE

This book was completed before the tragic, untimely and unexpected death of my beloved friend and partner David Abbott in May 2014. Ten days before he died I sent him a copy of the finished manuscript for his comments and, hopefully, his approval. A couple of days later, he sent me the following email:

Dearest Peter, I read the manuscript with great pleasure. It is wise, well-written, charming, and for me, full of fond memories. I hope it will help others to be as happy and successful as we were. With much love and congratulations, David xx

I replied:

Dear David,
Thank you so much for your note. I am more pleased than you can imagine with your response.
Thanks for everything.
Pxx

This was the very last contact I had with David. He was the greatest copywriter this town has ever seen and the spiritual leader of AMV. He was my and Adrian's best friend and we will both miss him more than we can say.

INTRODUCTION

Fifteen years ago I was interviewed by the media commentator Raymond Snoddy for *The Times*. Over tea and too many Silk Cut cigarettes in my office on Marylebone Road we touched on many different subjects, including my involvement with Millwall Football Club, London's Docklands development, Wembley and the NSPCC. Our chat felt more like a friendly conversation than an interview. We eventually got around to my career in advertising and shortly before we finished Ray asked me if I had any ambitions left. I replied that I had many but one in particular: I'd like to write a book which would show people that in business decent behaviour can bring commercial success.

This is something I have believed in for as long as I can remember and I explained to Ray how this approach played a huge part in my own career. At Abbott Mead Vickers our success was made possible first of all because in David Abbott and Adrian Vickers I stumbled across two truly like-minded partners. The combination of our bond of friendship and respect and our shared convictions about the way a business should evolve enabled us to shape AMV into the success it became. The three of us had an absolute coincidence of understanding of what doing the right thing meant and as a result we believed that if we always followed the objectives of doing great work and looking after the people who worked for us than there was a real opportunity to create a business which would endure and prosper. And we were proved correct, because over the past 37 years AMV has been everything we could have wished for. This book is my attempt to share the lessons we learned along the way in the hope people might find them useful in their own working lives.

I must stress here that do not claim to possess a magic formula which will enable anyone who reads this book to make their fortunes, nor do I claim to be some kind of guru who can make a brilliant businessman out of just anyone. I also know that my approach to management will not work for every manager in every company in every corner of the world. But what I do know is how David, Adrian and I built AMV. I know what worked for us, just as I know what didn't work, because we all make mistakes.

The book's title, *When In Doubt Be Nice*, is the unwritten mission statement that was at the heart of the agency from Day One. This view of the world is at the core of this book and is central to what I believe about advertising, business and life in general. It is the most important lesson I ever learned.

So, how did David, Adrian and I do it?

At the very start of AMV, back at the end of 1977, we set out to create an atmosphere that would be an enjoyable as well as fulfilling environment for all of us. Much has been written about company cultures, how they can be created and protected, what kind is more productive and so on, but for me, in the final analysis, company cultures have to emerge as a product of the people working within rather than being imposed from outside. It is created by choosing the right people and treating them in the right way. Then, once it is in place, the culture must be monitored, nurtured and even nudged, or else it can disappear through your fingers like fine sand.

When you are trying to create a company culture there is an enormous advantage in starting a business from scratch, as David, Adrian and I did. You have the ability to handpick your early disciples who are then fundamental in the creation of the next wave of employees who then become instrumental in influencing the next wave and so on.

6

From day one we made sure that fun was an important element in our particular mix. We laughed a lot. We played tennis, football, darts and snooker together. We worked hard but enjoyed ourselves as well.

We agonised over the people who joined us, using the Doyle Dane Bernbach mantra of needing them to be nice as well as talented. We tried hard to prevent bullying. We showered praise where it was deserved and the occasional admonishments when they were required. We reasoned that if we created a great place to work great people would want to come and work with us. Fortunately this turned out to be the case. The very best people in each of the advertising disciplines beat a path to our door. During the first decade of the agency's life only a tiny number of people left – and hardly any clients either.

Back in 1977 we did not start out with any specific aspirations, except to want to be the best. The best work, the best people, the best employer we could be, the best public company in our field and, latterly, the best partner for our American parent. Twenty years later we were the biggest advertising agency in the country, a position we have now held for more than fifteen years. In 2012 the *Sunday Times* 'Great Places to Work' survey ranked AMV as the best advertising agency in the UK to work for, a ranking based purely on what our staff relayed back anonymously to independent researchers. It was the second such award in the history of the agency and to me that validated everything we had tried to do since the very beginning of our company and was more precious than any craft award AMV had received.

When I started working on this book, my ambition was to pass on some of my life's lessons in the form of a book of business tips, all arranged simply and clearly. But in the end I decided to include much more than that, and so this has become what I call a 'buffet book', something that can be dipped in and out of and read very selectively, in the same way I do with the big, glossy coffee table books to which I am addicted. The first section of the book contains my favourite business tips – more than one hundred of the most useful lessons I have learned and the best advice I have been given over the years of my working life. The second section is my life story, included despite the words of a publisher who said to me early in the process that my formative years were of mild interest only to my family, and even they would be happy to wait for it to appear in a charity bookshop.

Whether or not that publisher was right, there is something in the book for 'Mad Men' fanatics, football fans and even hypochondriacs, but most of all, I hope, for people who are as intrigued as I am about the way companies work and flourish. So please feel no embarrassment about ignoring some sections – just as with the best buffet restaurant experiences, you always leave quite a lot on your plate at the end of the meal.

****

My approach to creating a successful business is rooted in my belief that we as a society these days have little left to believe in. One by one the cornerstones of my parents' existence, the institutions they took comfort from, have been eroded. The church, the judiciary, teachers, politicians, the media and the police have lost their roles in most people's lives and there has been little to replace the positive effects of their belief in the essential goodness, probity and stature of these pillars in their universe.

In my view people these days are thrashing around desperately looking for things to subscribe to with their emotions. I really became aware of this hunger for causes to believe in at the time of the death of Princess Diana. During the week following the terrible accident there was an astonishing outpouring of emotion. Of course a lot of it was a reflection of the affection that we held her in. But I would argue, over and above that, this was an event which allowed us all to join together and unashamedly demonstrate emotion on a giant scale. It gave us something to unite around and to believe in.

This paucity of things to bind us together is also the reason why football, for instance, plays such an important part in many people's lives. During the working week most fans have jobs working for companies they find it difficult to relate to and where their opinions are neither sought nor listened to. But when Saturday comes their opinions about their team are as valid as anybody else's and they can express themselves without fear – and certainly do so. Fans believe in their team, they share a dream with other fans and even when that dream is temporarily shattered by failure they still remain devoted.

This hunger for things to believe in is something that we can carry into our business lives. If we create a set of principles and beliefs that the people who work for us can subscribe to then the benefit to be reaped is enormous. I describe in this book the essential ingredients needed for running a people business. They resonated even in the hard place that is the City of London when we were a public company.

So if people do indeed need things to believe in and running a people business, I argue, is all about capturing an unfair share of people's heads and hearts, then the opportunity is there to encourage and create a secure and highly productive workforce. The following pages illustrate how I refined my beliefs, met like-minded people, most of all my partners David Abbott and Adrian Vickers, and created with them a culture which was comfortable, sustaining, more than a little exciting and ultimately hugely successful. I recognise that things are tougher these days, but would argue that in such circumstances the benefits of creating a working environment which is both principled and driven could be even greater.

Finally, I should also add that these musings are personal ones. I am not speaking for any other person or organisation and I recognise that neither I nor the companies I have worked for manage to live up to the highest standards all the time, but it is not for want of trying.

PART ONE

HOW TO BUILD A
WORLD CLASS COMPANY

122 BUSINESS TIPS

OPPORTUNITY AND STRATEGY

I've long believed that life is a mixture of opportunity and strategy, with opportunity being much more significant in the long run than strategy. The problem is, opportunity can't be legislated for – by definition it catches you by surprise – so you have to have a vague strategic plan to go forward with, in the knowledge that it will almost certainly get interfered with by opportunity but not knowing exactly when.

I learnt this lesson for the first time at the end of my school days when it was apparent that university was out of the question for me. My school had quite justifiably given up on me at the age of 16 and decided that I should talk to what was then called a Youth Employment Officer. This man, who sadly I never had contact with again, transformed my life. During our interview he asked what I would really like to do and I replied that I had no idea. Thoughts of being an airline pilot and other fanciful things were scuppered by my poor eyesight. However, an idea came to me. A few weeks earlier my father had bought our first record player, so my immediate response was to tell this man in my broad cockney accent that I'd like to join the promotions department of a record company so I could meet the stars. He looked at me rather quizzically and said, 'You mean advertising.' I knew nothing about careers in advertising but the Youth Employment Officer did and that mattered much more. He gave me three introductory cards to advertising agencies and I wrote to them immediately. Not long after that, two of the agencies offered me a job in their despatch departments. That one conversation ultimately led me to create, with David Abbott and Adrian Vickers, what Campaign Magazine once described as, 'the most successful UK advertising agency of all time'.

IF YOU DON'T BELIEVE IN IT HOW CAN I?

After my surprising and rapid rise through the ranks of my first ad agency, one day I had to go down to Hotpoint (a white goods manufacturer) whose offices were then very close to Buckingham Palace. The purpose of the meeting was to present for approval a relatively small advertisement that we had developed for one of their products for insertion in the Hong Kong newspaper the *South China Morning Post*. To my horror, the rather junior man who I should have presented the advertisement to was away sick and I was ushered into the large office of the Worldwide Marketing Director. I was terrified as I passed over the advertisement for him to look at because I had done no preparation at all for selling it to him. He looked at it and peered over his glasses and said, 'What do you think?' I told him that I thought it was all right. He then became quietly menacing and said to me, 'I never want you ever to come down here again with something that you think is "all right." If you don't think this is the best your company can produce and aren't prepared to say that in front of me, then I'm not prepared to give you the time of day.' It was a lesson I never forgot.

WHY DO PEOPLE CARE MORE ABOUT MACHINES THAN PEOPLE?

One day in 1960, in the early days of my career in advertising, the second floor of our eight-storey building was ripped apart and a huge room was created. After months of toil and expense, the magic day arrived when into the room was delivered the agency's first mainframe computer with, I suspect, all the capacity a BlackBerry has today. This gleaming monster was housed in a dust-free air-conditioned environment – the only place in the building that afforded such comfort. I remembered being astonished when passing by the area on the second floor and seeing the cool, gleaming, humming monster sitting comfortably there while the two people who operated it sat perspiring in the their little offices just outside. I thought if we can't treat our people as well as we treat our machines then we deserve to reap the whirlwind.

HOW AN UNDERSTANDING AUTHORITY FIGURE MAKES A DIFFERENCE

I hold a number of dubious distinctions in my life. I suspect the most public one is being chairman of a football club that was top of its division in December and relegated in May. To my knowledge, this is the only time it's happened in footballing history. The other distinction is that I was the first person to be declared redundant by my first advertising agency, S H Benson. For a working class boy this was an enormous shock, as well as being disappointing and a little frightening because I wondered if I would ever get such an opportunity again. I received the news as stoically as I could manage and went home trembling to tell my Dad. I arrived at our flat in south east London and rang the bell. He opened the door and said, 'What's happened? You look as if you've seen a ghost. You're as pale as a sheet.' I told him I'd just been given the sack. I was expecting anger but he said, 'Never mind, son, it's their loss. Come in and I'll make you a cup of tea.' That moment helped me realise how a level of understanding from someone you respect and admire can make all the difference when you are in a vulnerable state. My father's words helped me feel better very quickly and I got a new job within two weeks. With my redundancy pay after eight years at my first agency and my new salary, I can't remember ever feeling as rich or as satisfied. Thanks Dad.

HOW YOU DON'T HAVE TO BE DISTANT TO COMMAND RESPECT

In my third job in advertising I joined a newly formed advertising agency called KMP. I'd been there around 10 days when David Kingsley – the K – came up to me early one evening and said, 'Look, I've got to go home for a meeting now and there's a very important document being produced for a new business meeting. Is there a chance that you could bring a copy of it to my flat when it's ready later this evening?' Being a working class boy with a complete understanding of my place in the overall scheme of things, I said of course. I arrived at David's apartment just off Hyde Park at around 8pm with a copy of the document. I rang the bell, the door opened and there was David in jeans and sweatshirt. It was the first time it ever occurred to me that bosses actually wore jeans and a sweatshirt. I gave him the document and as I turned to go he said to me, 'Have you eaten yet?' I said, 'No, I'll have a meal when I get home.' He responded by saying that he and his wife were having spaghetti bolognese and he was sure they could stretch it to three so why didn't I come in and join them for dinner? From that moment on there was nothing I wouldn't do for him. That didn't mean that I thought he was an easy touch but I knew he was a human being. During the time I worked for him David remained an enormous source of inspiration for his intellect, industry and understanding of the human psyche. I would have run through walls for him.

THE DEFINITION OF HELL ON EARTH

A few years ago I went to a close friend's 40th birthday party and I found it a strangely muted occasion. Every conversation I started with anybody there began with them saying, 'Well it's the big one isn't it – the big four-oh.' As I had already passed that magic figure without trepidation, I found it very difficult to understand their concern. A couple of weeks later I was driving to work when things clicked and I began to understand what had happened that evening. Let me explain: I think the people at my friend's birthday party had found themselves forced to evaluate their own position in the cycle of life. The truth was that most of them had joined a company very early on in their working lives, married early, at say 22, had kids soon after and created a lifestyle in which he pursued his glittering career and she concentrated on bringing up the children. At around 40 he had worked out that he wasn't going to get any further in his career that once held so much promise. Indeed, he had young people threatening his position from beneath as well as seeing the odd younger person promoted over him. He had been institutionalised and probably emasculated by the environment in which he worked. He didn't have enough courage to leave and he told himself it was because he'd paid a lot of money into his pension plan and he had to hang on for the security that would give him in later life. He knew what he'd be doing every day for the next 20 or so years of work he had left. And each of those days would be tinged with fear and regret. When he went home in the evening, he went home to a different woman to the one he'd married so expectantly all those years ago. Indeed, the only thing they had in common now were the children, who were grown up and about to leave home to go to work or university. Thus he found himself increasingly forced back into a one-to-one relationship with a stranger and looking forward to 20 years of being together so they could earn the right to retire together. Truly hell on earth. The moral of this story is that relationships, both personal and professional , need constant evaluation and adjustment if the destructive force that is apathy is to be avoided.

WHY DEMOCRACY IS NO WAY TO RUN A COMPANY

When I set up my first agency at the age of 31, I decided that two things should happen. Firstly, I would have the biggest slug of equity, 33% (justified because I'd raised all the money from two wonderfully supportive people) and I would distribute the rest equally among the four partners I'd persuaded to join me in this venture. At the same time, I told them we would have a different structure to other agencies and we wouldn't have titles. Every decision we made would a democratic one decided by the five of us. There would be no boss – we would all be the bosses. We even decided that all our names should be in the title until we discovered that Byfield Mead Cruttenden Osborne Whelan was more than our poor unfortunate receptionist would be able to manage as she answered the phone a hundred times a day. My idea of trying to impose democracy forced people who wanted to be led into trying to be managers and it didn't work. Within three years those four people that I'd gifted with equity decided that they could dispense with my services. They came to my flat very early one morning and asked me to leave. A very successful fledgling agency withered and disappeared within ten years, a victim of a lack of clear management structure and an absence of clearly defined responsibilities.

LEADERS AND MANAGERS – THE ELUSIVE BLEND

From my experiences of lots of companies over the years, I've noticed a phenomenon. It's particularly true when dealing with companies that have been set up from scratch by a group of entrepreneurs. By definition, the next group of people they hire tend to be managers because founders view themselves, quite properly, as leaders. The mix works very well until there comes a time when the founders/leaders retire or leave the company. It's then left in the hands of managers, who were selected for management rather than leadership skills and it's enormously difficult to teach leadership. While leaders accept that they are not always brilliant managers, managers always believe that leadership is an attribute that can be acquired. But it can't. So many companies go through a painful period when managers try to be leaders when they're not and never will be. But I've noticed that the next layer down from those early managers quite often spawns a group of younger people who are restless to go back to the practices and beliefs that the original leaders of the business had. These people must be given their head, and more often than not 'leaders' will emerge.

COMFORT OF YOUR CONVICTIONS

A little while ago somebody was talking to me about a mutual acquaintance and said the problem with him was that he was a poor decision maker. At that moment the meaning of the expression 'courage of your convictions' became very clear to me. The truth is if you have convictions, both in the personal and business sense, then those convictions will probably account for 75% of any decision you're likely to make. That way you're only exercising judgement over 25% of any decision you take. So the expression is wrong, it should be called the comfort of your convictions. If, on the other hand, you have no convictions at all, you have no comfort at all and you have to use judgement to account for 100% of any decision. That is both tiring and dangerous and some of the time will definitely end in tears.

STICKS AND STONES AND ALL THAT

I've always felt that the expression 'sticks and stones may break my bones but names will never hurt me' was the most absurd expression in the English language. In reality, if I hit somebody and create a bruise, then that bruise, which was caused by a stick or stone, will disappear, probably within 48 hours. If, on the other hand, I used names or words or even silence to attack the same individual, the psychological damage might last forever.

WHY FEAR IS AN ABOMINATION AS A MANAGEMENT TOOL

Over the last 20 years we have been subjected to lots of fashionable theories about how to manage. One enduring one, sadly, has been called many things – re-engineering, maximising resource or rather more brutally, downsizing. The theory went like this: if you had ten people making 100 things, you could afford to get rid of at least three of them. The other seven would be so energised by this brutality that instead of making 70 items they would make 100 – making up the shortfall caused by the three people who had been 'downsized'. In reality what happened was that not only did the seven people not make the 100 items, they didn't even make 70. Why? Very simply, most of the time fear doesn't motivate, it paralyses.

A LESSON I LEARNT FROM AN ESTATE AGENT

When estate agents are buying or selling property, they often say that there are only three things that are important in the process: location, location, location. I absolutely believe that in a similar vein in business, and probably in life, there are only three things that are important: relationships, relationships, relationships. It doesn't matter how smart, how bright or how good you are, if you can't develop relationships you will make little progress either personally or professionally.

IS BIGGEST OR BEST THE TARGET TO AIM FOR?

When we set up Abbott Mead Vickers, we never aspired to be the biggest advertising agency, in fact the possibility never even occurred to us. The only sustainable ambition, in our view, was to want to be the best because that's the thing that keeps you striving day after day after day. The truth is this restless search and mission to be the best, to our enormous surprise, one day led to Abbott Mead Vickers becoming the biggest. As I said in a memo to everyone at the time, it's amazing how big you can get if you're not worried about how big you can get. That same memo said a big thank you from the acorns to the oak tree.

If you set out to be the biggest you will never be the best. If you want to be the best there is a real chance of becoming the biggest as a by-product.

FIND A FEARLESS FINANCE DIRECTOR

People over the years have often asked me, flatteringly, for help and advice when they set up businesses and over the years I think I've refined that advice down to a tiny number of things. One of the most important is to find yourself a finance director who isn't afraid of you, as soon as you can afford it. Far too many businesses set up by strong-minded, strong-willed and overly confident entrepreneurs ignore this. We found such a man, who is sadly no longer with us. James McDanell wasn't afraid of me, he wasn't afraid of David Abbott and he wasn't afraid of Adrian Vickers. He had complete confidence in his professional ability and as a result told us the unvarnished truth the whole time. He said to me at our first interview, when I baulked at how expensive I thought he would be, that if he couldn't make that much difference legitimately – i.e. cover his salary – within two months of joining us, then we should fire him. He transformed our business. His presence meant that we could all get on with doing our day jobs – the jobs that we were good at. David could write ads, Adrian and I could look after clients and James, who we could trust with our lives, made sure that the money took care of itself. It was an enormous liberation to have James McDanell and a tragedy that he died so young. Above all he believed in doing the right thing – he never talked about financial engineering or pushing the edge of the envelope. We could all sleep soundly at night.

REVERENCE AND THE WORKING CLASS

As a boy from South London, I grew up with what I often describe as a working class overdeveloped sense of reverence for the 'boss classes'. It was only later that I realised you can revere the boss classes too much. They have to prove their judgement and ability as well as the rest of us. Some of those things that I questioned early on but dismissed my doubts about, believing that greater minds than mine really were behind them, ended up going spectacularly wrong – the mergers of Time Warner with AOL and RBS with ABN–AMRO are just two examples of moments where greater minds than mine were definitely not at work!

WHAT ALEC GUINNESS SAID TO MARK HAMILL

Do you remember in Star Wars when Obi-Wan Kenobi said to Luke Sky-walker, 'Luke, listen to the force'? What I've always believed that to mean in business terms was, 'Trust your instincts.' Which is brilliant advice if you have great instincts but terrible advice if you have bad ones. Try to find out early whether your instincts can be trusted and if you're one of the fortunate few who do have good instincts, listen to the force.

THANK YOU JOHN D ROCKEFELLER, BILL BERNBACH AND BOBBY KENNEDY

When we started our agency we used three quotes. The first was from the patriarch of the Rockefeller dynasty, who once said, 'The ability to get along with people is a commodity like any other. The only difference is that I'll pay more for that commodity than anything else I purchase'. The second was from Bill Bernbach, probably the most famous advertising man of all time, who once said, 'I want a business full of nice and talented people. If they're nice but not talented there is no room for them but equally importantly, if not more so, if they are talented but not nice I don't want them around either.' And the third was Bobby Kennedy, with I think, apologies to George Bernard Shaw, who once said, 'Most people see things as they are and ask why? I dream of things as they could be and ask why not?' Not a bad trio of quotes to guide you through setting up a business.

PROFIT – PRINCIPLE OR CONSEQUENCE?

There has always been a belief in our company that if you do good work and look after your people success and money will follow. It has to be a consequence of what you do and not a principle of it. People everywhere would agree with that statement. They tend to say, 'Yes, you make money by doing good work and looking after your people.' By changing the order they change the effect – if money is the first thing they think of, then they're bound to compromise on good work and people. Good work and people (in either order) have to come first and second and the consequential success that should follow is both inevitable and deserved. However – and be under no illusion about this – you have to make money doing what you're doing to validate your principles and beliefs.

THE MENU PRINCIPLE OF MANAGEMENT

When the creative superstar, David Abbott, joined our tiny agency both Adrian Vickers and I felt a real sense of responsibility because he could literally have gone anywhere. So I determined that I would earn his trust by adopting what I subsequently called the 'Menu Principle of Management'. I would go to his office two or three times a day and run through all the issues that were of concern that day, which were mainly housekeeping. After a while he suggested that he didn't need to be involved in half of the things on the menu. Later during our relationship that became 80% of the things on the menu which he was happy to leave to me. Finally, the decisions we made were effortless. He trusted me to understand his attitude towards most of the decisions I took because I knew instinctively how he would react. It made day-to-day life in the agency very easy and enabled David to spend as much time as possible on what he did better than anyone else – great creative work and the big, important decisions.

THE UMBRELLA OF AFFECTION

The best partnerships have what we described over the years as the 'Umbrella of Affection' binding them together. We were all incredibly fond of one another which allowed each of us the freedom to criticise and bitch about the others, because we knew that the 'Umbrella of Affection' was inviolate and if ever push came to shove, the thing that would decide the way forward would be the way we felt about one another. That affection bound the three of us and also worked as a force field. Nobody could pick us off one by one.

BE A FATHER TO YOUR WORKFORCE

I have always found it amazing that people behave so differently at the office to the way they do at home. I remember once a colleague of mine saying that as he left his house in the morning he pulled on his 'office face' and as he drew into his drive in the evening he pulled on his 'home face'. I was astonished by this. I find it difficult enough to live with one persona let alone two. But it is obviously pretty widespread because if some Chief Executives behaved at home the way they behaved at the office, the NSPCC and most of the social workers in this country would pursue them for cruelty. It is a fact that we allow individuals to get away with reprehensible behaviour during office hours. I believe the same rules that apply to being a good father at home should relate to being a good boss during the day. An abusive boss should be treated every bit as seriously as an abusive parent.

THE RIPPLE EFFECT OF MANAGEMENT

There is a macho belief that decision-making is all and the great managers are separated from their inferior fellows by their ability to make decisions. This is partly true, but here are some words of caution. Firstly, making a decision in itself is only the start of the process because the decision then has to be managed. Any major decision will have reverberations and any manager worth his salt will clearly understand those reverberations before he makes, or at least before he announces his decision. It is what I call the 'Ripple Effect of Management'. It's a bit like dropping a large stone into a pond – you can be absolutely certain where the major splash is but you'd better know where the ripples from dropping the stone into the pond finish. If not, you will suddenly discover the bank of your pond is irretrievably damaged by those ripple effects. The effects of a poorly thought out decision will be equally catastrophic in your organisation. The words, 'I never thought of that', should rarely, if ever, be used by a good manager.

THE OBJECTIVITY OF IGNORANCE

In our business at least, where we deal with many different clients, we invented the expression 'Objectivity of Ignorance'. Rather than immediately immerse ourselves in a potential client's business, we like to retain the 'Objectivity of Ignorance' for as long as possible. It's the closest we get to being a consumer of that client's business and there is a magical time when your judgement is unimpaired by over familiarity or, much more importantly, political considerations and in which you can ask questions that you might later shy away from. It's a valuable period – don't waste it.

THE MYTH OF THE 'MISSION STATEMENT'

People spend hours, days and sometimes years, on putting together a 'Mission Statement'. I have sat in meetings where we've argued or at least discussed the meaning of a single word in a Mission Statement interminably. What normally happens is the process of producing the Mission Statement is so agonising that once it's written everybody breaths a heavy sigh of relief and thinks the job is done. In reality it's only just started – it's the Mission that's important and not the Statement. Walking the walk is infinitely more critical to a business than talking the talk.

THE CONFUSION OF ACTIVITY WITH PROGRESS

In the last few years I have used this expression more and more and it seems to be increasingly appropriate to the age we live in. I understand that email is real progress, but is voicemail? Or is voicemail just a way of distancing ourselves from one another and experiencing a disembodied irritation electronically as opposed to – shock horror – one person actually talking to another person? I think the most classic illustration of confusion activity that I have talked about happened a few years ago. For more years than I care to remember now, British Telecom ran an extremely efficient Directory Enquiries service. They changed the number every so often but 192 was something I knew would give me a good service and initially it was free – not surprisingly to persuade people to use the phone more. As the Regulator made their lives tougher, BT properly thought they should charge for this service. So it became a good, extremely reliable, inexpensive service. But a few years ago the Regulator came along and decided this was all too cosy and too efficient and looked too much like value for money. This was a monopoly, which was against the public interest he said. So he threw the field wide open for everybody. Where once we had a relatively cheap, extremely efficient service run though one provider, we now had a very expensive, deeply inefficient service run through about 20 different companies, many of whom went out of business within their first year of operation. We will never get back to that single, extremely efficient service that BT supplied. See what I mean about the confusion of activity with progress? And ask yourself as you finish your next meeting, what it achieved apart from deciding the date of a subsequent meeting!

OPTIONS – NONE OR TOO MANY

A few years ago a very eminent acquaintance of mine retired after a distinguished career at the highest level as a diplomat. We had lunch one day and he seemed agitated and confused. During the meal I discovered why. His seniority and success had made him the target of a number of different companies and he was bewildered by the choices facing him. It was then I created another definition of hell on earth, which is having no options at all, closely followed by having too many.

POLITICS – THE CANCER OF BUSINESS

I believe there is scarcely a company in the universe that doesn't have politics operating within it. I guess it is impossible to eradicate politics completely, but as I have suggested in the heading it is a cancer that can destroy companies. This is the root cause of trouble in business and countless non-productive hours are spent by people at every level in company politicking. Politics is like a virus, or, indeed, the cancer I referred to earlier, and it thrives in an environment caused by a vacuum. A vacuum created by indecision, weak management and a directionless company. That's the key point: politics in business are by and large the fault of the managers of business and not of the people who indulge in politics. Politics can be avoided by strong leaders who make and manage decisions and lay down a behaviour matrix for the company which all employees of that company can participate in and subscribe to. There are very few people who enjoy politics in their company. Quite often it's a product of despair and frustration, and it must be largely eradicated for any company to be successful long term.

AN UNFAIR SHARE OF HEADS AND HEARTS

When Abbott Mead Vickers became a public company, my role was to go and talk to analysts and fund managers in the City to explain the reasons why they should invest in our company. I wanted them to be secure in the knowledge that their investments were in good hands. I told them that I thought running a people business like ours was really simple because it was about capturing an unfair share of people's heads and hearts. I explained it in very simple terms – if the people in your company are spending 50% of their time feeling worried about their future, politicking or being psychologically bullied then the other 50% of their time is all the productivity you can expect to get from them and even that will be tainted. But if you can create a workforce where you can get a really good 75% of their head devoted to your company and at the same time twin that share of their head with a real affection for the company and what it stands for, then the levels of productivity you get in return are mind-blowing. It's really very simple.

COST CUTTING, THE MODERN PANACEA

Almost everything that is written about companies these days is fuelled by an obsession with discussions about costs. Costs have to be slashed, we are told. People have to get used to earning less money. People have to work harder. And most of all we are told that fewer people have to be used. I would argue that this view attacks the problem from the wrong end. As I have explained earlier, well-motivated, secure, valued people working for you will achieve productivity levels, which are often astonishing. The truth is you only need four well-motivated, secure, valued employees to achieve what eight insecure, frightened employees will achieve. The net result is the same – you will produce more with fewer people but the upside is enormous. And there is no downside.

STAFF RETENTION AND HOW TO DO IT

The other day I spent a long time talking to a company that I am involved with. They were very worried about their inability to retain their staff and had looked at all sorts of methods and advice about staff retention. Once we sat down and talked about the problem, it didn't take long to discover that their problem was not staff retention, it was staff recruitment. What they had been doing was not taking enough time and trouble over employing people in the first place. They had been allowing people to come into their company without clearly understanding what the company's objectives were, its method of operation, or even the job specification itself. They were confusing activity with progress (sound familiar). Not surprisingly they were losing a lot of people who felt they had been sold the wrong bill of goods when they started work at the company. They are now taking much more trouble over recruitment and I know that retention will immediately be better and importantly, recruitment costs will go down. For every senior employee who stayed an extra year, we calculated we would probably save in excess of £50,000.

BONUSES AND HOW THEY CAN BE DIVISIVE

I always found it strange that within companies bonuses often created politics and dissention instead of simply being rewarding for everyone who got one. We used to have a rule which said that everybody in the organisation was given the same percentage of their salary as a bonus. After all, if everyone didn't contribute towards the success of your organisation then they shouldn't have been there and if they did contribute to that success, they had every right to share in the rewards. Inevitably this system meant the most valued employees took home more money because they earned more money in the first place, but the strict rule meant there was a sense of fairness about the process and everybody was happy rather than feeling hard done by or wanting to argue about why their bonus should be more than anybody else's. Today this system has fallen into disrepair almost everywhere and bonuses are targeted much more narrowly. This is a great shame.

LITTLE THINGS MEAN A LOT

Over the years we have learnt that the principle of 'it's the thought that counts' is as important and useful in business as it is in one's personal life. Every company should devote a small budget and a couple of really concerned people to the simple job of making people feel better. For example, in our agency, every year on Valentine's Day morning every female member of staff would have a red rose on their desk waiting for them when they came into work along with a little note saying, 'Thank you from Abbott, Mead and Vickers'. There was one problem area I had after David and Adrian retired. Previously, when people had worked at the agency for ten years they were given a stainless steel Cartier watch as a thank you. This was changed a few years ago to people being given money in order for them to buy their own watch – the thought behind it was that this gave people ultimate flexibility. Although the sum matched what was spent on the Cartier watches, it missed the point, which was that most people given money would not indulge themselves by buying a watch to remember their company. Instead they would use that money to pay the sort of pressing bills that all of us face. Replacing the watch with money reduced the impact of the gesture which was intended to show somebody who had given ten years of their life to the company how valued they were. Even if they disliked the watch, they would always remember that they were given one. A confusion of activity with progress again, methinks.

THE NON-DECISION SOCIETY

Over the decades that I have been in business I have noticed an alarming trend. More and more people are being given the power to say 'No' and conversely fewer and fewer have the ability to say 'Yes'. I remember once sitting with the then chief executive of Millwall Football Club. We had built a brand new stadium, one end of which we had to devote to away supporters. That end was capable of housing 4,500 people but quite often the clubs we were playing would only bring 200 supporters. So we would be faced by an empty end to our stadium and relatively cheap seats behind the goal that our supporters could not use. I asked him to look at reconfiguring the stadium so that we could use that empty stand for our fans and re-house the away supporters elsewhere. He gave me a response that I haven't forgotten to this day. He said, 'Let me think why that's not possible'. There are far too many people in management at lower levels these days who spend valuable time and energy trying to work out why something is not possible instead of trying to make things happen.

REVERE YOUR CONSUMERS - IT'S YOUR ONLY HOPE

Over the last 25 years the ability for companies to distribute their products through a large number of different outlets has substantially reduced. The rise of supermarkets and retail chains, not to mention the internet, means the range of distribution channels available for most products has narrowed alarmingly, to the extent that in some cases no more than three major players dominate the distribution and sale of items in a product category. They become enormously powerful and quite often it is they who are deciding your marketing plan and not you. There is a way to fight this – and the way is to persuade consumers to demand your products. Years ago I remember a man called Derek Reeve, who was then running Walker's Crisps – a relatively new company which had grown remarkably rapidly by producing a better product which was competitively priced. One day they got a call from one of the large supermarket chains (not the one we have been involved with for decades) who told them that the way they supplied their product was no longer acceptable to the chain and the configuration had to be changed. The supermarket chain heard nothing back for four weeks and rang Derek Reeve himself to say that they hadn't had a response to their request to change the way Walker's Crisps shipped their product. He said they would need about eight months to adapt, to which the supermarket replied they wanted it done immediately. Derek said they couldn't do that and the supermarket bluntly told him if that was the case then Walker's Crisps would be delisted. To their surprise Derek said that would actually work out well for his company because they had a lot of small independent shops who wanted to stock their product and because of the high volume of sales through the supermarket Walker's Crisps were unable to meet their demands. De-list-ing would enable Walker's Crisps to supply all those small independents. Within a week the supermarket rang back and said they were happy to wait for eight months and in the mean time they would like Walker's to supply their product in the same old way. Of course, Derek readily agreed. The moral of this story is that the supermarket totally understood that if they didn't stock Walker's Crisps, their customers would go elsewhere. Oh and by the way, never refer to your customers as 'punters'. It shows a distinct lack of respect.

THE CURSE OF COMMODITISATION

We seem to have become a discount society, a society where everything we buy is defined by the price of that item. Most manufacturers are engaged in massively damaging price wars which ultimately take value out of their product and their service and leave their customers dissatisfied and with only a few more pennies in their pockets. The time has come to reverse the trend and a bit of thought can make the difference. People are tired of poor service, of products that don't deliver what they used to deliver, of call centres that treat them like automatons. I believe there is a huge opportunity to revert to treating people as individuals while at the same time respecting their privacy and gold to be made by people who take that view.

CREATIVITY AND ALL THAT

Ed McCabe, one of the greatest copywriters America has ever produced, said, 'Creativity is one of the last remaining legal ways of gaining an unfair advantage over your competition.' This is true of all of our businesses: creativity in the way we present our products to our consumers, creativity in the way we manufacture our products and creativity in the way we treat our people. There is no doubt that creativity is an outstanding weapon in the fight against commoditisation. Use it frequently and wisely.

RETAIL IS DETAIL

John Sainsbury famously said, 'Retail is detail.' The truth of the matter is that every business is detail. Once you have established your business's principles and beliefs and established the matrix around them, you have to worry about them on a daily basis. Every little decision you make must be judged against that behavioural matrix. A company culture takes an enormous amount of time to develop and unless it is nourished and worried about constantly, it will disappear through your fingers like fine sand.

ACQUIRING COMPANIES – BUILDING A GROUP

Once Abbott Mead Vickers became a public company, we had to decide how we would go forward. We believed we had a culture and a way of operating which would be attractive across a number of communication disciplines, so we set out to build a group. We started, however, by setting out what Abbott Mead Vickers the public company should be. We defined it as a greenhouse into which we would put fledging companies and allow them to blossom in the warmth of the Abbott Mead Vickers brand and culture. Once they had done that, we would encourage them to become little greenhouses of their own, retain their entrepreneurial spirit and use their greenhouse to grow other fledging companies. We decided above all that we would not extinguish the flame of entrepreneurial spirit present in the companies we acquired. Every acquisition had to be carefully thought out. It usually began with a call to me from somebody saying that they had never thought about selling their company, but they had had an approach which made them think about the prospect of capitalising on their efforts. Having had a discussion they would decide that the only company they wanted to sell their business to was Abbott Mead Vickers, or latterly Omnicom. I usually agreed to meet with them over breakfast for initial discussions. I did this deliberately and watched how they treated the waiters. While they could be really sycophantic to me, a clicking of fingers or an inability to say thank you to the staff, demonstrated they weren't the people for us.

If they passed the breakfast test, the next step would be to decide whether they were the best of breed, whether they were people we liked and whether there appeared to be a chemical attraction between our companies. We checked this out very carefully and what we did finally was to have a dinner with all the significant players from their business and ours. We would sit round a table for a few hours to check that critical chemistry. If that test was passed we would then begin the process of buying the company.

THE PARTY AND THE BALLOON

I had a very simple brief for our financial people – it was that everybody had to leave the party with a balloon. If one of the guys came back and said he had done a brilliant deal in acquiring a company for us, it would not be long before the acquired company realised that they had been short-changed. If that were to happen then the five year growth I had hoped for from that company would be much more difficult to achieve. If the company felt good about the sale, then it would be different. Hence the brief for our financial people: if everybody leaves with a balloon, the party will be long remembered.

INCREASING REVENUE VERSUS CUTTING COSTS

There is no doubt in my mind that increasing revenue is light years more effective at improving a company's health than cutting costs. In the short term-focused environment we find ourselves in, cutting costs is often the only option available to beleaguered managers. However, the trouble with cutting costs is that lots of companies cut through the fat into the muscle and into the bone, which means it is an act that can't be repeated for more than two or three years or else the company will die. On the other hand, if the focus is on increasing revenue and that goal is achieved, everybody will feel better. This transmits to potential customers and there is only upside.

YOU NEVER GET A SECOND CHANCE TO MAKE A FIRST IMPRESSION

Mae West, a very famous pre-war Hollywood movie star, is credited with this flash of insight. She also famously said, 'If you give him a free hand he will run it all over you' and even more famously, 'Come up and see me sometime.' But it was her line about first impressions which proved to me that behind the dizzy blonde persona, which obviously worked for her in the movies, she had a very good brain. Throughout the history of my active involvement in the running of our agency, Reception has always reported directly to me. I have always recognised the absolute importance of their role in our agency's life. Over the years we have had some great reception matriarchs. The first was a lady called Jan Elliott who spent ten or 12 years with us. Her nickname was Bubbles and she ran our frenzied little agency Reception with great aplomb. When she left, one of the greatest characters AMV BBDO has ever produced took over from her. Pascoe has been with us for well over 20 years and she has an effortless elegance and style which could be fearsome if it wasn't allied to a wonderful human manner and genuine concern for people's welfare. She and the team of Ingi, Karen and Swana are the first contact that prospective clients and employees have with our agency and I'm absolutely certain that over the years the impression given to visitors has made them more predisposed to like us. I know it's incredibly difficult to quantify but I suspect more than one piece of new business is down to Pascoe's wonderful welcome rather more than the strategies and creative work which followed it.

NEVER BE A SHOUTER

When people make a mistake they know they've made a mistake. When they have to face their boss and discuss the consequences of that mistake they are already embarrassed and sorry. They also feel that they've let their boss down and are eager to make amends. They feel guilty and are anxious to put the mistake behind them. If the response from the boss is sympathetic, understanding and all about putting the mistake right and making sure it doesn't happen again, then the guilt for making the mistake and the relief that it's been greeted in the right fashion intensifies the desire to make absolutely sure that person is never in that position again. We have to assume that they didn't want to make the mistake and so by definition it was an accident. If the understanding of that is not there and the person who made the mistake is shouted at and demeaned then the guilt and absolute desire never to repeat the mistake is replaced by anger. So in many ways the consequences of the mistake are exacerbated. In these situations understanding is an infinitely better management tool than condemnation.

THE ILLUSION OF INVOLVEMENT

There comes a time in everybody's business life when they have to move on, either upwards or sideways. From personal experience, I know this to be a very difficult time – handing over executive power and corporate responsibility is tough. But it has to be done cleanly, positively and without any room for doubt. If the inheritor of the power is a sensitive individual, they will feel that they should let the previous holder off lightly. They will include them on e-mails, if only to demonstrate a lack of brutality in the transition period. There are undoubtedly things that the passer of the flame can be useful on, but to give them the belief that they still have the power to alter decisions when that power has passed is not only unhelpful, but could be argued to be cruel. The belief that involvement is still at the highest level and can be exercised should be resisted at all costs.

'IN ORDER TO ENJOY THE RAINBOW YOU HAVE TO PUT UP WITH THE RAIN'

I know all of us in business would love a rainbow-filled existence because a rainbow means the sun is shining. Sadly life isn't like that. Putting up with the rain makes the rainbow even more enjoyable and in a business where you are one telephone call away from triumph or disaster, the healthy understanding that the only good thing about getting wet is that you'll be dry soon after is well worth remembering. I'd love to claim the quote as mine, but Dolly Parton said it first!

HOW VALUABLE IS CONSISTENCY IN MANAGEMENT

Some years ago there was a famous Russian psychologist called Pavlov. He ran a series of experiments using dogs (hence the expression Pavlov's dogs) in which he proved that it is possible to condition living creatures' responses to certain things. Pavlov managed to get his dogs to react to the ringing of a bell or another noise as if it were food – the dogs would hear the noise and start salivating even when there was no food presented. At those moments, they would naturally be rather confused and upset, and I expect that the more often this happened, the more unpleasant it became for them because they had no idea what the bell would represent. My point is that all living things look for consistency – if every time the bell rang the dogs knew they were not going to be fed, they would accept their fate but their spirit and personalities would remain intact. The inconsistency made the dogs' lives far too complicated for them to be happy.

I'm not suggesting that anybody in management anywhere runs their business using these techniques. However, quite often there is a great deal of inconsistency. You can create a dispirited workforce very rapidly if your responses to situations becomes erratic and unpredictable.

HOW USEFUL ARE MANTRAS IN BUSINESS

For many years one of the great American captains of industry had a mantra which was that every year he would cull the bottom 10% of his workforce based on a set of performance criteria. He trumpeted this rite of passage with great pride. Although it's difficult to argue with the success his company achieved, I would argue this mantra demonstrates a brutality that has no place in a caring society. This technique was neither humane nor commercially sensible. At the beginning of every year 100% of the workforce were worried they would finish up as part of the 10% at the end of the year. I know the argument is that this ensured all the staff were highly motivated but if like me you believe that in the long term fear doesn't motivate but ultimately paralyses, then an awful lot of productive energy is wasted.

In his retirement this feared captain of industry has become more reflective. He was recently quoted as saying that in order to create proactive relationships with the people who reported to you, you should find out what they're interested in and have casual conversations with them about their passions, whether it's football, TV, film, politics or anything else. This is such a reversal of his prior tough stance on people that speed bumps might have to be erected on his road to Damascus.

One of the other fashionable business mantras over the years was, 'If it's not broke, break it.' This always struck me as verging on the absurd. Whilst operating procedures and techniques need constant evaluation, the suggestion that just because something is working well it should be disrupted must be wrong.

SPORTING SAYINGS AND THEIR RELEVANCE

Very recently I was having a drink with an old friend of mine who had just lost his job as the manager of a Premier League football team. His demise smacked of unfairness and the way it was communicated left much to be desired. His wife, who was with us, said the immortal words, 'Oh well, that's football.' He immediately reminded her that he used that expression to me some twenty years before. He told her that my response at that time was to say that bad behaviour can't be excused by the use of a cliché. I find it sad that while football is characterised by use of the expression, 'Oh well, that's football' to cover a multitude of sins, our other great national sport lives or dies by the expression, 'That's not cricket.' Despite some recent events, bad behaviour in cricket is much less endemic.

BE CAREFUL WHAT YOU WISH FOR

I was recently having a conversation with my youngest son about what he wanted to do in his future working life. We were discussing life balances and I said I believed ambition is the enemy of contentment, because the pursuit of high targets can lead to the creation of a driven nature which may never be satisfied. The price of a really successful career can be very high.

SHOULD WE REWARD JOB CREATORS OR JOB DESTROYERS?

A few years ago I was fortunate enough to be playing golf on one of Scotland's great courses, Carnoustie. Because of my lack of both talent and knowledge, I would always have a caddie with me as I tried to navigate my way around this beautiful golfing torture chamber. As we walked round I asked my wonderfully patient, newly acquired friend how long he been a guide around the bunkers and heather here. He told me that he had been doing this job for around four years. I asked him what he did before and he said that he had been a middle manager in one of Scotland's biggest banks for 25 years. He went on to say that one Friday four years earlier, after he returned from lunch he was given a black plastic bag and told to clear his desk that afternoon. He was escorted off the premises by a security guard and never returned. I asked him if he'd managed to cope. He said that he hadn't and still took Prozac every day. The prime architect of the temporary destruction of his life was subsequently given one of the highest honours in this country can bestow. Before the inevitable demise of this great man, he had a reputation of being one of the great destroyers of people's hopes and dreams. Surely the people who should be rewarded are those that satisfy and help create those hopes and dreams, not those who destroy them.

THE PERILS OF EXPANSION

In my early career I worked for a really good company. The partners created and built a very powerful business which was very successful in a short space of time. Without allowing the company time to mature in its marketplace, they got a bit carried away and started to believe that they were masters of their own particular universe. One day one of their UK clients who was very happy with the work they were doing for them in their home market, suggested that their US business could be up for grabs if the partners opened a New York office. This was a very beguiling thought. They reasoned it couldn't be all that difficult to replicate their UK success in another market. They soon found out how difficult it was when after deploying some of their very valuable UK talent and a considerable amount of money they had to close their fledgling New York office after less than two years. The resulting loss was over £1 million and because this happened nearly 40 years ago, today that would be a hit of more than ten times as much, which is a lot of money. I believe that the expected long term success of the UK operation didn't happen because of this loss. It would have been assured if they'd stuck to their core business. Always examine the potential pitfalls of rapid expansion as well as the expected rewards.

BE GRACIOUS IN DEFEAT

The nature of the business that I have spent my whole working life in means that success or failure is only a telephone call away. By definition we are constantly presenting to win new business or defending our existing business. Many years ago one of our great British institutions, with a large prestigious advertising account, appointed a new chairman. He was tasked with shaking up the business which at that point had become a bit moribund. He needed to make, or so he believed, a momentous decision early on to demonstrate his 'new broom' credentials. He fired his existing advertising agency and appointed a new one. Though patently unfair, this is a risk that agencies face daily. The CEO of the fired agency held a press conference and attacked the unfairness and wisdom of the decision. The new agency that picked up the windfall from this major client had a disastrous first six months as custodian of the great brand. To this day I remain convinced that if the existing agency had remained sanguine about their dismissal in the face of such extreme provocation, the client would have come back cap in hand during that first six months.

Being gracious in victory isn't a bad tip either. When I was chairman of my beloved football club I made sure that on the odd occasion when we won an away game that we would, after the match, accept our hosts' hospitality and then leave as soon as was decent. This would allow no triumphalism on our part to pervade their boardroom but more importantly allow them to grieve in private.

RESENTMENT – THE MOST INSIDIOUS RELATIONSHIP KILLER

I've come to believe over the years that resentment is a very dangerous emotion. If not treated, it can destroy relationships more effectively than almost anything else. The biggest problem with resentment comes when it exists on both sides of an argument, when each side quite often has a kernel of justification for their feeling. This potential emotional volcano can lead to an irreversible breakdown. During the last recession I heard of a story involving a client and an advertising agency. The marketing director had been instructed by his board to pull his whole advertising budget for an unspecified period. He fought very hard and managed to get 25 per cent of the budget reinstated. The agency, which was counting on a spend of £8 million, was faced, in the short-term, with a £6 million shortfall. They complained bitterly about this, arguing that the client had committed to the larger sum and deeply resented the fact that they were faced with difficult decisions internally over the reduced budget. The client had put his job on the line to argue for the £2 million spend and resented the fact that the agency did not understand the extent of his personal victory and the possible career threatening consequences of him pursuing his quest on their behalf for that money. After a number of very testy meetings and exchanges resentment on both sides caused a really healthy and productive relationship to be terminated. Months later, when emotions had settled down, both recognised the extent and the validity of the resentment on the other side but by then it was too late.

FEARED, LOVED OR RESPECTED?

There was a business forum some years ago which asked which of these descriptors was the most desirable in a successful business leader. This has been a live debate since commerce began. I remember reading about a new chief executive at one of the World's biggest corporations. It was said about him that, 'he was a brutal man of limited tastes.' His tenure of office was neither successful nor prolonged and he was succeeded by a much gentler man who was tagged as being really nice but not decisive. Not surprisingly, his appointment didn't work out either. The world is littered with tough men who were relentless in their pursuit of success. The late Steve Jobs of Apple was a classic example – a man who, it is said, would put aside the niceties of relationships for the sake of his business. I'm sure that the people who worked for him would express an element of fear of him as an individual but at the same time enormous respect for his crusade for perfection. Less talented or driven individuals then Mr Jobs should adopt his management style at their peril. Fear coupled with respect works only as long as things go swimmingly. If there is a downturn these people have no reservoir of goodwill (something I believe affection creates) to see them through rocky patches. Obviously the most important of the three descriptors is 'respected'. I've always believed that this characteristic, coupled with being liked by the people who work for you, is much more important and long-lasting than the energy and ultimate paralysis that fear engenders.

A long-standing mantra of mine is that respect should be earned before it can be commanded. Being given the benefit of the doubt from an early stage, through the use of affection as opposed to fear, makes that task a lot easier.

DIG DEEPER THAN WIKIPEDIA

Today more than ever before it's possible to take a view of somebody one's never met by desk research. In the old days anecdotal views would create assumptions about the character of a new acquaintance. But these days this has been added to enormously by the amount of electronic information available on most individuals. So person A will now go to a meeting believing he has a relatively clear idea of what person B is like. The problem is, he might be absolutely wrong. It seems to me that it's possible for people to carry on relationships based on web-provided views of each other which are often far from reality. Without accurate knowledge about each other, truly meaningful and productive relationships can't happen.

I suffered from this myself during all the years that I was involved with Millwall Football Club. The image of the club would lead to a view that anybody involved with it would be a bloodthirsty Neanderthal likely to resort to violence at the first opportunity. We had to attack this preconception as often as we possibly could. Fortunately their expectations were so low that to turn them was relatively simple – a conversation rather than a series of grunts usually did the trick.

MAKE SURE YOU ASSUME RESPONSIBILITIES IF YOU'RE PAID TO DO SO

In the early days of my first agency one of our clients was the Milton Keynes Development Corporation. Every Monday there was a gathering of the heads of department to discuss issues of the moment. This included the chief officers for architecture, finance, estates, construction and so on. The client was very enlightened and so I was always included as chief communication officer. I remember one particular meeting when the great CEO Fred Lloyd Roche threw open a particularly knotty problem to the assembled forum. One by one everybody was allowed to express an opinion. When we were all finished Fred thanked us and made to move on to the next item on the agenda. The chief architectural officer interrupted this move by asking if we were going to vote on the point we had just discussed. Fred asked why he thought he was part of a democratic process. Of course we wouldn't vote on it, Fred said. Having solicited all opinions, Fred himself would make the decision. This might be affected by what the others said but Fred was paid to decide their next move forward and that's precisely what he did. Management by committee doesn't work. In most instances the buck should stop with the guy who earns the most bucks.

PASS PRAISE ON

It's always been my practice to pass on nice things that a third party has said to me about somebody we both know. It's a terrible waste telling me how great somebody is because in most instances the person under discussion is unaware of his standing. Obviously if the praise is given and I'm told not to reveal it I won't. But for the most part it's just forgetful behaviour on the part of the praiser to the praisee. Something that could make an enormous difference to a person's life doesn't get communicated – how sad is that?

HOW CAN YOU TELL IF A COMPANY IS IN TROUBLE?

Analysts in the City used to say that they wouldn't invest in companies that had a fountain in reception and a company helicopter. I'm sure that's a sensible tactic but I think there's a much simpler illustration of the cultural health of an organisation. At one stage in my Millwall negotiations I had an appointment to see the chief executive of a very, very large financial organisation. He had his own private office in the giant granite building where his bank had its headquarters. I arrived rather early for my appointment and casually started reading some magazines that were scattered around in the reception area. I was reading an issue of Newsweek and was horrified to read about an outbreak of hostilities in the Middle East. I thought that that particular confrontation had ended but here I was reading about it again. It was early in October and it was only when I turned to the front cover of that particular issue that I discovered that it had a cover date of June. The article I was reading happened three months before and the problems had been resolved by late September. I thought it said an enormous amount about a company that should have valued relevance and precision above most things that nobody cared enough to keep the magazines in reception up-to-date.

AFFECTION AND NOSTALGIA MAKE GREAT MARKETING WEAPONS

Within all manufacturing companies there are discarded and disregarded jewels. When we first began working for Smiths Crisps they had a very expensive new product development operation – I think there were at least 30 products being developed for market test. The last time I looked in any meaningful statistics only about 5% of any new products become winners. Smiths had long been famous for a product that could be described as 'salt and shake'. The unflavoured crisps came in a pack with a little blue bag of salt. There was a great deal of latent affection for this particular product because people remembered it fondly from their youth. We reintroduced it and it was a roaring success. It required none of the excessive costs and manpower needed to sweat a new product onto the marketplace and I seem to remember it had the highest margins of any product in the portfolio at that time. Now that salt is only just below arsenic on a list of substances that are bad for you, it might not work so well today but there are literally hundreds of products gathering dust that could be reintroduced and bring about the twin rewards of joy and profit. Old product development should be treated with equal importance as new product development.

VALUE WHAT YOU DO

A few years ago the then Chief Executive of one of our major clients retired and I took him out for a farewell lunch to say goodbye. At the end of the lunch I thanked him for being such a great client. He gave me a puzzled look and asked me what exactly I meant. I said that he'd been tough but that always brought good work out of us and supported us at times when the people who worked for him tried to rein us in. He said that I had misunderstood the relationship. He carried on by asking me how much difference I thought the work we had done over the years for him and the company had made to his business. Before I could answer he said the benefits that his company had had from the relationship was incalculable but could be measured in tens of millions, if not hundreds of millions of pounds. There are too many people in business generally who don't value what they do enough. How can you possibly get a good return for your efforts if you can't quantify the difference those efforts make?

CUTTING COSTS – FORGET THE PAPERCLIPS

There comes a time every so often in a company's life when costs should be reviewed. This is particularly appropriate when jobs are under threat. It happened to us at the end of the 80s, a time of severe recession. Clients were slashing their expenditure and we had to take a good long look at all our ancillary costs to see if savings could be made to protect our workforce. In the agency we have a breakfast bar which doubles up as a subsidised bar in the evenings. The concept is really quite simple: if anybody arrives before nine o'clock they get a free breakfast and in the evenings, in order to per-suade people to stick together and develop relationships, the bar sells beer more cheaply than any pub in the local vicinity. During the quest for aus-terity our Deputy CFO came to me and said that he had worked out a way of saving £15,000 a year. This was a relatively chunky sum and my interest perked up. He then went on to say rather triumphantly that if we closed the bar we would make this relatively significant saving. What he failed to understand, until I gently explained it to him, was that by getting people to work early in the morning and making them happy with a free breakfast and then helping to develop relationships in the evening because people spend a lot of their time talking about work, the bar was infinitely more valuable than the sum he had named. The value of a fully motivated workforce is not worth putting at risk for minor savings. I heard of one takeover in the advertising business where the first thing the new owner did was to cancel the free orange juice that was available twice a day. I'm not sure how much money he saved but the effect on staff morale of this being his first public act could in my view have been disastrous.

FIND A SINGLE SOURCE OF ADVICE AND STICK WITH IT

A number of small companies recently have asked my advice about how to grow their business and what direction they should take. There is hardly anything more rewarding than being asked for advice by fledgling companies. The trouble was that not only did they solicit my opinion but they asked three or four other ageing entrepreneurs for advice as well. It's absolutely sensible to get more than one outside view of your business and its prospects. However, the likelihood of four or five mentors agreeing on the way forward is so remote that only confusion will result. Spend a lot of time finding a single source of advice that you can trust and stick with it.

NEVER LOSE YOUR SENSE OF WONDER

Many years ago a couple of fruit farmers in California were growing pears. They were great pears, juicy and succulent and they gave the farmers, Harry and Fred, a very good living. A trend emerged around Christmas time when people would buy pears as presents. One year a relatively large customer asked if the pears could be boxed to enhance their value as gifts. In the ensuing years the demand for boxed pears increased enormously and the margins on boxed pears far exceeded those obtainable from normal loose pear sales. Harry and Fred had an increasingly profitable and growing business. One day they decided they could intensify this growth using advertising. They went to New York and met with advertising's great guru of the time, one Raymond Rubicam. His agency Young & Rubicam was the hottest thing in town. Intrigued by Harry and Fred, he agreed to meet them. Sensibly they bought pear samples with them and Raymond thought they were the best pears he'd ever tasted. However, he was concerned that the cost of an advertising campaign might be too high so he suggested that the agency present a media plan before doing any creative work to ensure that the capital cost was acceptable. Two weeks later another meeting was convened in New York and the media schedule was presented – top of the list of candidate magazines was probably the most influential business magazine in the world. Fred, wide-eyed with a sense of awe after looking at the schedule, said, 'Imagine Harry and me selling our pears in Fortune.' This little parable has stayed with me throughout my career. For me what it represented was a very down-to-earth view of business success in that Harry and Fred did not believe their own publicity or ever got above themselves. A sense of wonder makes sure that you're always grounded, grateful and surprised at a level of success. We use Fred's words often in our business. I remember the first time that David and I turned up for a meeting in the board room of one of Britain's biggest toiletries manufacturer after they'd appointed us to handle the advertising for two of their major brands. I turned to David and said, 'It's a Harry and me selling our pears in Fortune moment.' This attitude meant that we never took anything for granted.

FINDING GOOD PEOPLE – A GRIND AS WELL AS A TALENT

If I look back on the success of our agency the single most significant contributing factor has been the quality of the people we've recruited in our quest to be the best and finding them is a talent. My experience is that you know whether somebody might not be right almost as soon as you begin an interview – it usually takes about 30 seconds and feels instinctive. By extension, if the interview goes on longer than planned then it's also likely that the person in front of you will be interesting as a potential addition to your happy band of brothers. After using your talent to work out who might be a contender, the grind begins. You should then expose the potential employee to as many people as possible whose judgement you respect. Eventually you will narrow the field down to your chosen candidate.

As in every other area of leadership and management, someone has to make the final decision. In recruitment I've always found it really useful to have input from people I trust before the final decision is made.

HOW DOES BECOMING A PUBLIC COMPANY AFFECT THE ORGANISATION?

I have always found it rather strange that a company which builds itself by behaving in a certain way throughout its formative years suddenly feels it has to change once it becomes a publicly quoted stock. The disciplines required to be a successful public company in terms of financial management, operating procedures, ability to grow and competitiveness within its marketplace remain exactly the same as they were before the IPO. Obviously there are prescribed governance requirements but those, in my experience, are not very onerous if the company was already managed properly. So if the company was well-run and successful before going public then the City will just want more of the same, which will include a clear strategy going forward and consistent financial performance. We took the view that we should treat the City in the same way as we behaved towards our biggest clients in that we should develop a relationship with our major shareholders, give them no unpleasant surprises, make sure that they were fully informed and talk to them often. Financial institutions have money to invest. Indeed, they need to invest. And so companies who perform well are much sought after by institutions who have large portfolios of companies in their investment vehicles. For a fund to be able to be confident in any of their investments is an enormous relief. We found that telling the truth works really well in the City, particularly if related to a reasonable performance.

At the end of our first year as a public company I went up to Scotland to visit with a potential investor, one of the giant Scottish insurance companies. This was my second visit following a series of trips to Glasgow and Edinburgh I did following the public launch. On arriving in this particular institution I discovered that the fund manager I'd spoken to 12 months before had left. His successor informed me that following my meeting with his predecessor a note was left on the file saying that, 'Mead seems to care more for the welfare of his staff then his shareholders' and he asked me to comment on this. I replied that it was an absurd distinction but, if forced, I would argue that the people who work for our agency have to be foremost in our thoughts but at the same time there was an absolute coincidence of interest in looking after our people and looking after our shareholders – if our staff performed so would our share price. Two weeks later that institution bought a sizeable chunk of equity in our company.

CREATIVITY AND PROCUREMENT CAN THEY EVER BE HAPPY BEDFELLOWS

Sadly over the years creativity is finding itself more and more commoditised. The true value of the magic of great creativity seems now to come second to its cost. I'm reminded of the apocryphal story: centuries ago, the Pope was having a procurement meeting with Michelangelo. It went like this...'So, Mike, we have this project that I want you to quote on. It's this big Chapel ceiling that looks a bit dull. The cardinals and I thought that some sort of painting would liven it up. If you're interested perhaps you can send in a quote with your hourly rate and how many hours you think it will take to paint the ceiling. As well, would you estimate the cost of paint and brushes and turps etc. We've also asked eight other painters to quote so it is competitive and cost will be a critical element in deciding who gets the job.'

PROCUREMENT AND COMMON SENSE

John Ruskin wrote the following about paying for work:

'It's unwise to pay too much, but it's worse to pay too little. When you pay too much you lose a little – that's all. When you pay too little, you sometimes lose everything because the thing you bought was incapable of doing the thing it was bought to do. The common law of business balance prohibits paying a little and getting a lot – it can't be done. If you deal with the lowest bidder, it is well to add something for the risk you run, and if you do that you will have enough to pay for something better.'

Over decades we in the advertising business have not placed enough value on the difference that great creative work can make. Because by and large we operate in unquantifiable arenas, we have not made out compelling enough cases linking creativity with effectiveness. The IPA through its Effectiveness Awards have tried as hard as anybody but the essential link between the two has not been established. The ability to charge a premium for the very best has fallen away and it's our own fault.

NEVER GET BEGUILED BY THE PROCESS

There was a time when as a public company we were expanding our group. I was told that a very good company in our sphere of operations had fallen on hard times and was available for sale. After spending some time with the management I became very interested in them as a candidate for acquisition by AMV. There were ten subsidiary companies operating under the holding company that I was in talks with. The process of interviewing everybody, as well as the due diligence required, took weeks and it became overwhelming. We finally got to midnight on the day that we were supposed to be signing the purchase agreement and every one of our conference rooms was full of people with their advisers. As discussions went on I finally had a chance to sit and reflect on where we were and I realised that the goalposts had moved and we were a long way away from buying the company that offered the opportunity I saw in the first place. In the time since talks began, we had been allowing the deal that we thought we were doing to be diluted by all sorts of things. Just in time I understood that we had become immersed in the process not the end result. I called off the proposed deal that evening. Some people were upset with me, especially those who had already started to emotionally spend the money they thought they were going to receive, but I knew I was being sensible so it was OK. It was following this experience that we introduced the acquisition process I described earlier.

The closest analogy I can think of this was during my early days in advertising when one of my great friends met and fell in love with a girl who was due to get married three months later to somebody else. She felt the same about him but the wedding machine had taken over. It ground on until the morning of the wedding. Guests from out of town had arrived, presents were being given, everyone was getting ready. But in the nick of time she had the courage to tell her father she couldn't go through with the wedding because she had met someone else. Just as in my case, she was not popular for calling off 'the deal' but we were both right – it wouldn't have worked out in the long term.

TENACITY IS A MANAGEMENT TOOL

The lazy approach to management is a shrugging of the shoulders and acceptance of inevitability. For a long time at AMV we had a belief that we should never re-pitch for a piece of business we already had. We argued that the chances of winning the re-pitch were remote and we wanted to avoid a double hit on staff morale. This seemed sensible until the new management of the company, Farah Ramzan Golant and Ian Pearman, were faced in the early days of their tenure with re-pitch requests from three of the company's biggest clients. They could have stuck to our earlier mantra and declined to re-pitch but instead the whole company refused to accept the inevitable, competed hard and won all three. The outlook for the company was transformed by their tenacity. They were right and I was wrong.

PEOPLE BECOME A FLEXIBLE OVERHEAD

Sometime early in the 90s it became very fashionable for public companies to announce to the world that their staff had become a 'flexible overhead'. It was argued that in the event of a downturn in company profits, revenue could always be swelled by taking people costs out of the profit and loss statement. We always found this view abhorrent. I remember hearing a story about a senior man at another agency who, having been promoted way beyond his capabilities, was told on a Friday afternoon that after 15 years his services were no longer required. He decided not to tell his family of his plight at the traditional Friday evening dinner where they all gathered. He argued that he didn't want to spoil the occasion and might not even tell anybody until Sunday evening so as not to ruin their weekends. He said he finally found himself incapable of carrying this out and told everybody at the Friday dinner and said, 'We all sobbed together.' We determined that wherever we could we would not be a party to destroying people's lives in this fashion.

Every year just before Christmas we had a party for everybody's families. The first year this took place it was my turn to dress up as Father Christmas. I was to make a dramatic entrance into the atrium on the ground floor using the glass wall climber lift. Shortly before my descent, David and I stood on the sixth floor peering down at the excited faces of the waiting kids. David said quietly that if ever we thought about playing ducks and drakes with people's lives we should remind ourselves of those children gazing expectantly up at us. Those were innocent lives we had no right to disturb. During our time as an independent agency we never declared anybody redundant.

Of course, I am talking about much easier times. The tyranny of 90-day reporting of results and the seemingly endless assault on margins has made life almost impossibly difficult for the modern manager. As a public company in the eighties and nineties we had to report our figures (audited) just once a year so there was always time to absorb a financial body blow.

THE VALUE OF TIME

From the early days we had a rule that the agency would always close at 1pm on the Friday before any bank holiday. This would enable our people to get away a bit early and avoid the horrendous traffic jams that occurred just prior to any holiday weekend. We always added the proviso that clients still had to be serviced and invariably found that people who had work to do would waive the right to this extra half day. One of the companies we acquired heard about this procedure and followed my insistence that it should be applied to their staff as well. They then rang me and said that they had run a spreadsheet outlining how much complying with my request was going to cost in lost productivity. They, of course, had not taken into account the goodwill that this gesture generated and I argued persuasively and insistently that this goodwill was vastly more valuable in the quest for greater productivity than any of the costs that they calculated. On our 20th birthday as a present to all we added a week to their holiday. I'm convinced that these gestures contributed enormously to us having the lowest number of people per million pounds billing for most of the life of the agency.

THE SQUARE PEG AND THE ROUND HOLE

No matter how much trouble you take in hiring people you will make mistakes. There was a popular myth around that we at AMV, in the old days, never fired anybody – sadly this wasn't true. However careful you are in the interviewing process and when doing due diligence on candidates, every so often you would find yourself with someone in the organisation who didn't work out. Our view was always that the responsibility for things not gelling was at least as much our fault as the individuals because we would have spent a lot of time persuading that person that our company was the right place for them. In truth the company was probably 60% responsible for that person being employed. Once the square peg in a round hole situation has been reached the situation should be corrected promptly but as kindly as possible. We were always very generous with both time and money in allowing the person under question to leave with their dignity intact.

THE WORSHIP OF ACHIEVEMENT

Sometime during the 80s the booming world created an environment where achievement became all and the means of that achievement were either subsidiary or didn't matter at all. I suspect that banking misdemeanours, phone hacking and other modern day scandals are a direct result of not worrying about the means but focusing only on the achievement.

THE BALANCE BETWEEN MICRO AND MACRO MANAGEMENT

My fervent belief is that having appointed managers, my role was to let them manage. By definition management is a succession of small decisions – really large ones rarely happen – and if you can't trust your people to handle the day-to-day then they shouldn't be in place. Empower your managers to deliver and if they don't deliver, replace them. Micromanagement will suffocate them and will quite often lead to formulaic lowest common denominator yardsticks. If this is your management belief in the years to come you will be employing programmable robots to carry out your instructions.

BEWARE OF SUCCESS

In my experience at the start of any new venture the participants are bound together by a common fear of failure. Importantly, this allows the subjugation of egos and avoids that familiar virus – resentment. If you're not very careful a modicum of success can destroy the togetherness that fear of failure engenders and turf wars can break out based on individual levels of recognition for that success. Surprisingly then, it is success that can split an organisation asunder if great care is not taken.

MAKE SURE YOUR COMPANY CAN SURVIVE WITHOUT YOU

It is the unalienable right of everybody to decide where they want to work. In good times the market often creates better opportunities elsewhere which offer the prospect of individual self-advancement. However I do believe that the very top managers of companies have an obligation outside of normal parameters. That obligation means that their freedom to change their career path has to be tempered by their responsibility to the people who work for them in their current role. Before they move on, the absolute imperative is that they have created something which can survive without them and in some instances indeed flourish with a fresh injection of top management. Until that point is reached self-interest should be secondary.

DON'T DRINK THE KOOL-AID

Once you start believing your own publicity and embracing stuff that is written about you as the truth, then you are in trouble. There is a chance that you start behaving in a way that is driven by outside perceptions of you rather than reality. I would argue that many of the more sensational failings in business were contributed to by people being seduced by what the world was saying about them. The very best leaders retain a healthy level of scepticism and insecurity about themselves which results in them constantly evaluating their achievements through honest eyes rather than through the inevitably superficial and poorly informed view that the rest of the world propagates about them.

THE DANGERS OF LANGUAGE

Over the last few years some terrible mistakes have been caused by inappropriate use of language. The word 'bonus' for instance has lost some of its meaning. The reality is that for many companies a bonus which should be given as a reward for extraordinary performance is nothing more than deferred consideration. There would be much less furore about rewards and incentives if the inflammatory word bonus was not used so indiscriminately. One of my abiding thoughts about the problems of 2008 in the finance sector was that somebody used the term bailout to describe bank restructuring which involved government loans to ensure financial health. I think the emotions raised by the general public believing that they were bailing out bloated financial institutions would have been far less extreme if a more constructive term had been used.

THE VIOLENCE OF POLITENESS

This is not an original thought of mine – it came out of the discussion I was having recently with a very successful businessman. When I've talked previously about 'when in doubt be nice', I haven't mentioned that there is a danger. This sort of behavioural pattern should not get in the way of either constructive discussion or disagreement. Situations do occur when the overriding desire to be nice and polite prevents a free interchange of thought and feeling. Great care must be taken that a smiling and nodding response does not shield a seething inside. The internal feelings of frustration can quite quickly develop into resentment and once that takes hold all could be lost.

THE GOLDEN GIFT

When the advertising and communication business is working at its very best it creates for the products or services it represents the golden state of the benefit of the doubt. In the early days of our work on Volvo we created that benefit of the doubt, although it must be said we were helped enormously by the cars' performance. If your Volvo wouldn't start in the morning there was an inclination to believe that maybe the atmosphere was damp, such was the aura of reliability we helped to create around the brand. On the other hand, lesser models performing in the same way would be vilified and held totally responsible for the lack of performance. However, benefit of the doubt is a fragile ally. Once it is proven to be misplaced all hell can break loose. The sentiment destroyed can lead to a complete revisiting of all occurrences in the past where the benefit of the doubt was given and a very damaging re-evaluation can take place.

THE BENDING OF THE TRUTH

There are an increasing number of people who outline a fictional version of events and then a short time later convince themselves those events really did take place. These are very dangerous people to deal with because they have a complete belief that the lie that they knowingly told in the first place has suddenly become the absolute truth. This mode of behaviour was heavily featured in a celebrated biography and labelled as 'reality distortion'. It makes it very difficult for employees to work for managers who they know are guilty of bending the truth.

INSIGHT FROM A GREAT MAN

Jonathan Sacks, the Chief Rabbi and a man I respect enormously, said very recently, 'Trust depends on the virtues of self-restraint, steeped in a culture embodied by its leaders and embraced by individuals.'

IF YOU HIRE PYGMIES YOU WILL FINISH UP WITH A SMALL COMPANY

This old David Ogilvy quote might not be allowed in this politically correct age. Obviously he wasn't being literal but he was suggesting that if you hire people with small minds and talent to match you will never create a great company. Managers often forget they are only as good as the people they surround themselves with and if any manager is insecure there is a risk they will hire people who they believe offer no threat to them and people who offer no threat will offer very little value either.

I make no apologies for referencing Steve Jobs and Apple yet again: in a much-acclaimed book called 'Apple' written in 1997, the respected Wall Street journalist Jim Carlton outlines the failure of James Scully to pick really good people after the board dismissed Jobs. Apple had been designed as a home for the very best who, although they suffered indignities, recognised the special environment they were in. That whole mood crumbled under Scully to a point where Carlton wrote at the conclusion of his book, 'In short the real question of Apple is whether it has any future at all.' He went on to say, 'Can anyone stop it? Maybe Steve Jobs can. But the odds are good that he can do more than slow the fall, perhaps giving Apple a few more years before it is either gobbled up by a bigger company or finally runs out of customers.' If Mr Carlton is still around he will be mildly embarrassed to read those words. What Steve Jobs did on his return was to look around amongst his people, pick the best ones and allow them their head (as much as Steve Jobs allowed anybody their head). Sir Jonathan Ive designed the curvy iMac which reversed the downward trend in Mac sales and the rest is history.

No matter how brilliant you are you are only ever as good as the people who surround you. Jobs made a mistake when he championed Scully. But after his return he found the very best people, ones who could challenge even him, and that led to one of the greatest companies in history being created.

THE CLEAN WHITE SUIT

In the musical South Pacific Rodgers and Hammerstein created the story of a group of American servicemen defending a Pacific island. There were only a tiny number of women on the island, a situation which became a constant source of complaint from the troops. In the song 'There's Nothing Like A Dame' there was one memorable line in the lyric, 'There's nothing to put on a clean white suit for.' This only referred to the lack of ladies to impress but I believe it is a life lesson. If business life gives you nothing to put on a clean white suit for then you are doomed. Most early retirees give up putting on any suit at all and their days become mildly pointless. As Henry David Thoreau once said, 'None are so old as those who have outlived enthusiasm.' Life and commerce are driven by the desire to put on the white suit.

THE ACCESSION TO THE THRONE

There comes a time for lots of people when they are promoted to a level where they acquire responsibility for the welfare and advancement of others. All too often those who have been given the stripes of power assume that people's attitudes towards them and the way they behave to those people should change without any more than a piece of communication having been sent to their new constituency. Of course people's attitudes would have changed – but not in the way the person in power thinks or perhaps wants. Those people will be looking for indicators that the promotion has been deserved and will hope they have got somebody as their superior who they feel able to follow. This is a time when the newly anointed have to recognise one absolute truth: respect has to be earned before it can be commanded.

DON'T BE AFRAID OF YOUR COMPETITORS

I have come across many examples over the years of companies with enormous respect for their competitors. Indeed, the whole world is based on competition in one form or another and it makes a great deal of sense to constantly monitor your competitors' activities. In an ideal world you learn lessons from their mistakes before you make them yourself. But all too often companies become obsessed with the success that their competitors are enjoying. This obsession can lead to an unhealthy aping of competitive activity, quite often before that activity is deemed a success or failure. I have seen many a marketing plan over the years that might have been written by the marketing director of the competition rather than the company itself. If you have found a way of satisfying your customers in your company and its method of operation then build on that. It's often been said that business life is about building a better mousetrap. It might be more sensible to find a way of getting rid of mice completely. Lateral thinking is enormously important and not always obvious. Henry Ford once said if he'd relied on research he would have spent most of his life trying to breed a faster horse instead of creating a mass-market alternative form of transport.

THE LESSON FROM SEBASTIAN COE

From the early days of our company I used an analogy which involves Sebastian Coe, now Lord Coe. At the height of his running career he was the consummate athletic figure of his generation. He glided across the track with powerful elegance. But I drew inspiration from the way he won his races rather than how he ran. At the final bend of the race Coe was normally in the lead. His competitors would be bunched behind him gathering their strength as they thought he would be vulnerable to attack as the race neared its end – the problem any front runner faces. At the moment when he sensed that the competition was about to try to overtake him, Coe had the ability to accelerate again and break both their resistance and their hearts and to move away from them and win. I think this is a really good lesson for companies. Getting in front is one thing. Staying there and accelerating away is the only way of maintaining your pre-eminence.

ANOTHER LESSON FROM BILL BERNBACH

Much has been made of Bill Bernbach's influence on the advertising profession in the 60s and 70s. Alongside the great creative work he generated from his agency he had a firm belief in the way his company should operate and conduct itself. Although in those days people thought that there was an arrogance to DDB, Bill advised anybody presenting a piece of work to a client to have in his pocket an imaginary piece of paper on which the words, 'Maybe he's right' would appear. Bill argued that a good idea doesn't mind who had it as long as it sees the light of day. He also said that a principle isn't a principle until it cost you money. Principles are easy to adopt in good times when they don't involve pain. The only true validation of principles comes if they are maintained when the going gets tough.

THE RESPONSIBILITIES OF POWER

Never ever do things just because you can. When you accede to a position of authority those little indulgences you used to enjoy become unacceptable. Your time is literally no longer your own. You are in the spotlight and you should be setting standards of behaviour. If people are waiting to see you and you are late, they have no choice but to sit there and wait. It's because you have the power to keep people waiting that you shouldn't and it's because you don't have to explain yourself that you should.

WHAT MOTIVATES THE PEOPLE WHO WORK FOR YOU?

The very best company chiefs have an ability to read the people who work for them and understand that there is no universal rule for working out what motivates people. But demonstrating care for people as individuals is often powerful. I recently read the history of 'Saturday Night Live', the enormously successful New York TV show. After it had been running for a year Chevy Chase, the star who had become extremely popular, said he was going to leave to make movies. This was a hammer blow to all concerned. He did indeed leave but in an interview many years later admitted, 'And you know if Lorne (his boss) had put his arm around me and given me a hug and asked me to stay then I probably would have. But he didn't.' People are motivated by different things. Some need driving on while others need a Chevy Chase-style arm round the shoulder. But almost everybody needs to feel wanted. On the other side of the process it's often fear of rejection that stops most people from saying what they really mean. Maybe that was the case with Lorne all those years ago – what a waste.

HOW TO FIND OUT THE REAL TRUTH

The problem with being at the top, or near the top, of any organisation is that people try to guess what it is they think you want to hear and tell you that as opposed to simply telling you what you need to hear. From very early in my career I learned to listen to really junior members of the organisation, the ones who worked at the coal face. As long as their anonymity is respected and they're not placed in a compromising situation, they can be sources of information which is critical to the health of the company. Recently I've had experience of an individual who revels in a reputation as a really nice person. However any really junior employee when quizzed about him will suggest that that niceness is only skin deep – a weapon to be used for personal benefit. This person's pleasantness does not extend much past people who can be of immediate use. It reminds me of the 'be nice to waiters' anecdote that I've covered earlier in this section.

A DEFINITION OF THE DIFFERENCE BETWEEN LEADERS AND MANAGERS

Some 20 years ago I read what I think is probably still the best definition of this difference. It was that leaders are those people who tap into the human psyche and motivate and inspire it while managers use that inspiration to run efficient, decent and consequently profitable businesses. If you ever discover the very rare individuals who can fill both functions you must protect them, cherish them and keep them at all costs.

BE A GOOD LISTENER

Many years ago when AMV was partnering SMS in New York we helped on a campaign they were producing for a giant computer company called Sperry. Regrettably, like most of the big mainframe computer manufacturers Sperry no longer exists. At that time, however, it was pitting itself against the might of IBM – The Big Blue. The dominance in the marketplace that IBM had created had made it somewhat unpopular with its customers. The feeling among them was that it had become too big for its big blue boots and there was a sense that IBM was doing people a favour by allowing them to buy their product. That meant there was a niche for a rather more sympathetic approach to potential buyers. We decided to position Sperry as the computer company that listened to its customers' requirements rather than shoehorning those requirements into available products. We embarked on a companywide program aimed at teaching people at Sperry the importance of listening. The campaign theme was, 'We understand how important it is to listen.' It was successful and for a time actually halted the Sperry decline. That concept of 'understand how important it is to listen' remains as true today as it ever was. My experience from sitting in probably thousands of meetings over the years is that at least half the participants weren't listening to what other people said and were spending their time thinking of what they themselves were going to say next. The irony is that at least half the people wouldn't listen to them either. When reviewing the contents of meetings I've often been astonished to discover how few people had been listening intently. Many problems that occur could have been nipped in the bud by lending an ear to what was going on.

Incidentally, you will know you have become a good listener when somebody says he has just shared something with you which he had never told anyone before. It's happened to me a few of times and it's a wonderful compliment. There is an old and I suspect apocryphal story involving Samuel Goldwyn, one of the early Hollywood moguls, whose favourite subject of conversation was allegedly himself. It is said that during one lunch, after dominating the first 30 minutes with a monologue praising himself, he turned to his lunch partner and said, 'How rude of me to dominate the conversation. Tell me, what do *you* think of me?'

HOW TO BE A BOSS AND A HUMAN BEING AT THE SAME TIME

On days when I don't have a business lunch, I make a point of getting my own sandwiches. Before my trip to the local sandwich bar I ask if I can get anything for anybody else. There is nothing particularly special about this, in my view. I've always thought that it was totally unacceptable that I would ask somebody to go and get me my sandwiches in their lunch hour. They would have to bite into their precious free time just to make sure that I was fed. On many occasions travelling on British Airways, the more mature airline staff would tell me about the days when Lord King and Lord Marshall ran the business. They told me stories of how Colin Marshall would roll up his sleeves and help out getting passenger food ready in the galley once the plane was in the air. One of them told me proudly of the time that Colin spotted that a door was slightly loose, found a screwdriver and repaired it. His presence and charisma underlined the fact that he was the boss but his ability to get stuck in and help out meant that the people who worked at BA would follow his lead anywhere.

THE MESSAGE NOT THE MEDIUM

In the digital age we are told rather pityingly that we are dinosaurs if we don't understand how deeply significant the digital revolution is and how it has transformed all our lives. The depth and importance of this transformation could be discussed at great length but one eternal truth applies. My partner David Abbott once said, 'Crap that travels at the speed of light is still crap when it gets there.' I would argue that now more than ever before the quality and creativity of the messages we expect our consumers to pay attention to has never been more important – it is certainly much more significant than the vehicle that delivers it.

SONY AND THE BETAMAX FACTORY

A really important battle in the early days of video technology was the fight between Sony and the other Japanese manufacturers. In a battle reminiscent of the struggle between Apple and Microsoft for operating system supremacy, Sony produced the Betamax system while others decided to go with the VHS option. Although clearly superior in terms of size of cassette and speed of take-up, Sony failed to persuade enough manufacturers to adopt Betamax as their standard. There came a time when Akio Morita, the legendary head of Sony and as much an architect of its success as Steve jobs at Apple, had to admit defeat. He held a press conference to announce that Sony would be abandoning Betamax manufacture and using VHS on its recorders in future. A member of the press corps reminded him that he had a factory where 3000 people produced the Betamax product and asked if that meant that all these people would be declared redundant. Mr Morita indignantly responded that it was not a failure of the workers in the factory that had led to Betamax's demise; they had produced a superior product, beautifully manufactured. They were not at fault so there was absolutely no reason for them to be held responsible. He simply said that he would find something else for those people to do within the Sony empire.

WHAT WE LOOK FOR IN A LEADER

One of our relatively recent Prime Ministers believed that the way to appeal to the electorate was demonstrate his 'ordinariness'. He reasoned that this would create a 'he's one of us' feeling and enthusiastic support from voters would follow. In my view this was a major miscalculation. People need to be led by extraordinary people. Winston Churchill, arguably the most famous leader the UK has had, was a Nobel Prize winner for literature, a war hero, a member of an aristocratic British family established for centuries, a man of enormous personal charisma as well as being aloof but brilliantly witty – by any measure an extraordinary man. I've said before that the man in the street wants to believe that decisions affecting his whole life are being made by an intellectual capability way in excess of his own. The same criteria apply to those running his professional life.

OBLIGATIONS TO EXCELLENCE

At one stage in the life of our agency a client was proving very difficult. We had work turned down and the relationship was becoming increasingly fractious. On one of the many occasions that David and I sat over a cup of tea in his office I suggested the time had come when we should resign the business. David countered by saying that we had no right to resign because we had not produced good enough work. He agreed that the time was difficult and that a parting of the ways was almost inevitable but that shouldn't happen until we produced a campaign that we were really proud of. We would not earn the right to quit until we had satisfied our obligation to do great work. Soon after that he did produce a great campaign and – surprise, surprise – the relationship with the client got better almost immediately which meant we didn't have to resign it. It would have been all too easy to take the easy option of quitting while we were behind. Talking about resignation reminds me of Brian Clough's great thought in his biography. He had an unseemly spat with his employers and resigned on the spot. It was a decision that briefly gave him satisfaction but that turned to regret very quickly. He said in his book that if anybody feels like resigning they should sleep on it and if they wake up the following morning and still feel like resigning they should go back to bed.

HOW TO STAY AHEAD

Like, I suspect, most people I was highly cynical about the London Olympic Games in 2012. I was convinced we would win no medals and Central London would come to a grinding halt because of traffic overload so I went abroad for the whole two weeks of the Games. Of course, my holiday was completely dominated by my desire to get in front of the television set at every possible opportunity to get involved with the wondrous event it turned out to be. I will talk elsewhere about the cycling team's performance but their coach Dave Brailsford, when asked why his team performed even better than in Beijing four years earlier, said that it was a myriad of small changes and minor improvements made because he and his team were constantly re-evaluating everything in an effort to improve. This is a great lesson for businesses: constant attention to detail and minor adjustments ensure that a team is delivering at its optimum level.

LET'S DO IT FOR CAV

I'd never been a great follower of the Tour de France and it was only when I was watching at the end of the first significant weekend of the 2012 race that I began to take a real interest after my son, sadly a great devotee of Lance Armstrong, explained to me the mysteries of the Peloton. I was enthralled by the majesty of the event and delighted by Britain's success. But my overwhelming feeling was of admiration for the teamwork and selflessness of the Team Sky riders. There were two points during the race when management suggested that Bradley Wiggins, the race leader, should be nursed through two stages. He responded that was unacceptable and that he and the rest of the team wanted to make sure that another of their members, Mark Cavendish, would win another sprint stage in addition to the one he had already won. All of them pushed themselves to the limit to ensure Cavendish was positioned to win at the appropriate time. This subjugation of their personal egos and ambition for the good of the team and Cavendish in particular was breathtaking. It's not only business that can learn from this. I'm reminded of JFK's inaugural speech when he urged people to ask not what their country could do for them but what they could do for their country. If we could foster this thought in our businesses and, probably more importantly, in our society then we would be in much better shape.

THE CHARGE OF THE LIGHT BRIGADE

From the early days of the agency David and I had a rule when we were talking to prospective clients: if he wasn't prepared to do creative work for these particular prospects and I wasn't prepared to handle the account then we shouldn't expect anybody else in our agency to do it either. I've always believed that we should not ask anybody in business to do anything that we weren't prepared to do ourselves. During the Crimean War Lord Cardigan and his command team sat on their horses while ordering the best cavalry in the world to make charge after charge on the murderous machine gun emplacements of the enemy Russians. From his safe position he saw the cream of his command mown down. My view is that if Lord Cardigan wasn't prepared to ride his own horse at the front of the charge he had no right to expect people to sacrifice their lives in futile endeavour.

HOW OLD IS TOO OLD

There's an old expression which says 'If he's good enough he's old enough'.
I have always subscribed to this but with the proviso that experience is a
very valuable addition to talent. As I'm getting rather ancient myself, I also
believe that as a society we discard experienced and talented people far too
easily simply because they've reached a notional age which would suggest
they're past it. People should be continued to be judged on their ability to
do the job, not their age. I was much comforted recently to read that the
new chairman of one of our major financial institutions was well past the
age where perceived wisdom suggests that he should be put out to grass.
Wisdom based on experience is a much overlooked weapon in management.

LEARN HOW TO TAKE YES FOR AN ANSWER

Across the years I have presented many pieces of work to clients. On a number of occasions the first glimpse of the creative treatment has met with instant approval. For some of my junior colleagues this wasn't particularly acceptable because they had spent a great deal of time marshalling arguments and justifications for the work and wanted to ensure these were not wasted. On the odd occasion I have seen defeat snatched from the jaws of victory by advocates spending so much time explaining why a particular path had been adopted that the client started to question their first impression. In my view, the second somebody says 'yes', that's the signal to pack the art bags, click the briefcases and beat a hasty retreat.

ANOTHER NIGHT AT THE DORCHESTER

Over the years, AMV has been very fortunate to win a number of awards which are usually given out during a slightly drunken evening in the Great Room at the Dorchester Hotel. Typically, the evening has a star presenter who almost always has terrible trouble with agency names and has to struggle manfully to announce the winners and then to wait patiently while people struggle through a crowd of some 1,200 to get to the stage to receive their award. All of us who have spent a lot of time in the business get to be the chairman of some award panel or other. There was one year when I was chairman of the Campaign Press Awards. The host for the evening was Jimmy Tarbuck, who had become an acquaintance of mine. He introduced me as 'living proof that Snow White and Dopey had sex' – as far as I was concerned too many people laughed out loud for comfort. But there is a serious point to make about awards and particularly those creative ones that are judged by other creatives from across the spectrum of agencies. The ads that are produced specifically in order to win awards and which then do so stand out a mile but fortunately they are few. It's a lovely experience to stand up and receive an award but the real benefit is that the more awards we won, the more the very best creative people wanted to work for us. It is said that clients pooh-pooh the industry's award structure but certainly over the last 20 years many clients I have shared a table with have been just as excited as we were that our work was being recognised.

The best award in the agency's history, however, had nothing to do with the trip to the Dorchester. This award was a US import. For many years in the States, the 'Hundred Best Companies to Work For' award was the annual accolade that all companies strove for. The mechanism was simple – the company compiling the awards would request complete access to every member of staff and would then ask them to fill in a questionnaire based on a well-researched set of criteria that laid out the parameters of what made a company good to work for. All employees and their comments remained anonymous. The award came to the UK and, with hundreds of other companies, we were asked to participate. The scheme over here was run by *The Sunday Times* and the publication of the results were eagerly awaited. In the inaugural year of the awards AMV was voted the seventh best company in the UK to work for. We were way ahead of any other company in our business and this was a source of great pride to us all because it was our employees who had voted for us.

Here's a word of warning for those people who don't take enough care to understand the implications of this award. A couple of years ago a major operation in the UK decided that it would be a good idea to enter. Not only did it not win a place in the top hundred but the feedback from staff demonstrated that it would have been a prime candidate in a race for the hundred worst companies to work for. The results demonstrated an astonishing lack of connection with the company's staff and an inability to understand how badly management was failing.

SLICING THE CAKE

Every newly formed company has a nucleus of founders. These are people who shoulder the pressure and in many cases the financial risks of trying to fulfil the dream of being their own boss and of building something which they hope will endure and prosper. The very best entrepreneurs will recognise they can't do it alone and to ensure the organisation's success should spread the potential rewards within it. This is not only fair but commercially sensible because people who have a piece of the action are much more likely to engage and give of their all rather than feeling that they are constantly pushing themselves to make a tiny number of people rich. Over the years I have had many conversations with people who were interested in selling their companies. Those who came to me and explained that they owned 90% of the equity failed to capture my interest. It meant that they had not used the weapons of inclusiveness and equity to attract the very best people to drive their business forward.

CARELESS TALK COSTS LIVES

This was a famous wartime expression trying to persuade people that indiscreet asides could be very dangerous because the enemy might be alerted. In a somewhat less physically dangerous context, I have sat many times in crowded restaurants full of people in my profession where somebody in a loud voice was discussing sensitive details about their clients or new business prospects with their colleagues without being aware of the proximity of a competitor. It's particularly important when you're sitting next to a table occupied by a lone person waiting for their guest. If you are that lone person it's almost impossible not to be interested in the conversations of those surrounding you. Apart from consuming the highly calorific bread roll and butter you've got nothing else to do. Important as it is, this is not the main point of this particular topic. As a manager or even more importantly as a leader you are likely to have tens of conversations every week with the people who work for you. It's impossible to remember word for word every one of those conversations but of one thing you can be certain: the person you've had a conversation with will not only remember every single word but the manner in which it is said, from every inflection to your body language. Be very careful how you dispense information and be doubly careful of any promise you make during these conversations. A really good memory is an invaluable leadership tool.

YET ANOTHER GREAT THOUGHT FROM A CLERIC

I have already quoted the Chief Rabbi Jonathan Sacks a number of times. I first heard him speak at a meeting of the 30 Club, a gathering of the great and good in communications, which took place over dinner at Claridges. Several things he said had a really profound effect on me but the most moving quote of all was his belief that, 'Everybody has the right to equal access to hope.'

A BURDEN ADVERTISING PEOPLE HAVE TO BEAR

For many years lots people who work in advertising have tried to suggest is a profession rather than a business. In my view they are wrong and it is indeed a business. Why do I think this? It seems to me that one of the definitions of a profession is that practitioners in that profession can issue relatively uncontested opinions. Doctors, lawyers and accountants, for instance, accumulate deep knowledge over a long period and the manifestation of our trust in them depends on our belief that they have earned the right to show us the way forward. This is not true of advertising. Despite the many years that the best people in our business have practised, everybody believes that they are an expert and there is no guarantee that opinions formed over decades' experience will be respected or given authority. A young marketing man will vigorously express a point of view on the way a piece of work communicates with its audience without fear or favour. At the same time the very best clients understand that a lifetime of putting together meaningful and successful campaigns to consumers should mean that the author of the idea has a more valid opinion than those with less experience. It's sad that this is a rarity and ironic that the very people who often kill great ideas because they think they know what they're talking about would not dream of contesting an opinion from a young doctor, lawyer or accountant.

INDULGE ME IF YOU WILL

Many years ago I spent a lot of my early life delivering special letters to the giant Beecham organisation which sprawled across a number of buildings on the Great West Road. Macleans toothpaste was in one building, Lucozade in another and so on. They were, and are, one of the great British advertisers coveted by all advertising agencies. They have consistently spent money heavily on marketing over the years and despite a couple of changes of ownership they still do so today. There came a point in the history of AMV when we were asked to present for some of their brands and it was a seminal moment in my journey from despatch boy to agency principal because we won some of them. One day I was having lunch with the marketing director when he asked me who were the most important people in our agency. With absolute conviction I said everybody in our agency was important and to choose one group as being more important than others would be invidious. He said that he took the point but could I be invidious and indulge him with an answer. I said that if forced I would choose the creative people. We were a company that made a living out of delivering ideas that changed things. Central to that was the quality of the message that we created for our clients. That being the case, the people who ultimately put down on a blank sheet of paper thoughts that would create business for our clients had to be first among equals. They were indeed the geese that laid the golden eggs. It wouldn't matter if everything else we did was perfect. If we couldn't deliver results throughout creative work we would not succeed.

RAMBO AND URIAH HEEP

I was once in a large meeting with a major UK retailer. The whole board was present and we were receiving a presentation from a highly respected forecasting unit about the consumer who we were likely to face in the 21st century. He went into a great deal of detail about the demographics, tastes, characteristics and requirements of this critical constituency. At the end of the presentation about the consumer I asked what we expected of the 10,000 people who worked for the organisation, mostly in its shops? What imaginary uniform that they put on when they came to work every day? How did we expect them to represent the company? The personnel director turned to me with a rather pitying look on his face and said, 'You should understand that we deal in high turnover low cost personnel.' This didn't really answer my question but I concluded he meant that because he took the view that the staff were expendable and replaceable, there was no point in trying to give them any directions on how to behave when faced with customers. I felt then and still do now that this was a policy of despair. I've often made it clear to the people who worked at AMV that I would not want them to be Rambo in attitude but I didn't want them to be Uriah Heep either. A pride in working for the company should not translate into either obsequiousness or arrogance. Quiet confidence and an understanding of what our company represented and how important our customers were was the way forward.

BLACKADDER AND BALDRICK

The social order portrayed by Rowan Atkinson and Tony Robinson should not be a blueprint for any employer/employee relationship. The brutality, derision and contempt heaped on the unfortunate Baldrick is not what the enlightened 21st-century industrial relations should look like. However, beneath the obvious comedy of the situation a critical truth exists: Blackadder could not survive without Baldrick. When applied to any organisation it should be understood that this mutual dependency is critical. Businesses cannot survive without people whose ambition is limited to being the best at what they do no matter at what level they operate. Any company needs great footsoldiers who have no desire to be generals but just want to get the job done. These people should be cherished and looked after just as much as the highflyers because without them nothing is possible.

SIT BACK AND LET OTHERS DO IT

After we became a public company we had the ambition and the where-withal to expand our offering to clients. The communication process with consumers is wide and diverse and we reckoned that we should be represented in all the main disciplines with only two provisos. The first was that the company we became associated with should be best of breed and secondly they should share our beliefs and principles, particularly in the area of how people should be treated. The strategy we adopted was clear. We would expand vertically in the significant areas to increase our relevance to our client base. Typically, we acquired companies set up and run by entrepreneurs and once we'd bought the companies it always seemed to me to make sense to make great use of the entrepreneurial spirit that they possessed. So in every instance I urged the new members of our group to expand horizontally. They knew the best other operators in their area of expertise more clearly than I ever could. Giving them the mandate to acquire companies in their chosen field who would report to them had the twin effect of giving us potential new areas of revenue but also allowed to them to carry on in the mindset of entrepreneurs. They are a rare breed of animal and need to be nurtured.

THE TITLE RACE

No, for once I'm not talking about football. For many years British business resisted the temptation to follow the American route and have a myriad of job titles spread through the upper echelon of businesses. For many years 'chairman' and 'managing director' were the only two titles of any note. However, over the last decade or so UK management has given in. Business cards now carry a bewildering array of titles which by and large are bestowed either to smooth an ego or to negate the need for a salary increase. When I ran AMV all those years ago I resisted the temptation to have associate directors, in those days a very fashionable titbit to offer people. I reasoned that if I made a whole bunch of people associate directors, on their appointment they would immediately start a campaign to be made full directors while the rest of the organisation would aspire to an overnight promotion to associate director. Rather than solving any problems, in this case expediency would have created a whole lot more. This is another example of the ripple effect, something which managers of people absolutely must understand if they are to be successful.

I'M SORRY WE'VE MADE A MISTAKE

The very best companies quite often are defined by the way they handle mistakes or complaints or deficiencies in their product offering. I've recently had experience of trying to get an expensive Swiss watch serviced only to find it had to be sent back to Switzerland, the process could take months and it could result in a hefty bill which would add insult to injury. In contrast, a little while ago a product made by a manufacturer called Bowers and Wilkins – an iPod dock with a speaker and amplifier called a Zeppelin Air – that I had purchased some years before developed a fault. There was no question that its warranty had expired and there was more than a hint that I might have been responsible for the malfunction. When we telephoned them to explain the fault and to ask for guidance they could not have been more helpful. They sent us transit packaging so we could return the product to them and within two weeks of receiving the errant item they repaired the fault and serviced the rest of the machine. It was returned completely free of charge with a letter of apology from a senior person at the company. A really classy company behaving in a high-class way.

NOT A BAD WAY TO DEFINE YOUR CAREER

There are many things that I have to be grateful to David Kingsley for – particularly his lessons on how people should be treated. Close to his desk he had a framed cartoon from *The New Yorker* magazine. It depicted two executive types having lunch. The caption underneath was one saying to the other, 'What I really want is to do my bit for mankind and get a piece of the action.' As long as you go about it in the right way there is absolutely no problem at all in aspiring to get 'a piece of the action'.

PART TWO

**A WORKING LIFE IN
ADVERTISING
AND A FEW OTHER
DISTRACTIONS**

INTRODUCTION

This whole book exercise started as a self-indulgent trip down memory lane primarily for my family's benefit. My father died very young, way before I married Sam and had my three sons, and I wanted to chronicle my early days and give them a colour of his life too. My memories from all parts of my life are set down on these pages exactly as they are in my head but I understand that the mind becomes very selective as the years go by (as Admiral Crowe, a past Chairman of the US Joint Chiefs of Staff, once remarked that as he got older, he had increasingly vivid recollections of events that never took place) and I suspect that many of the reminiscences in the book suffer from a condition called 'rose tint'. It has not been my intention to upset anybody or claim credit where none was due. I apologise if I have done either of those things. Equally, these views are mine and mine alone.

CHAPTER 1

ondon in 1956 was a tremendously exciting place.
The city was just emerging from its post-war
agony: rationing was ending, the huge project to repair the damage done
by German bombs was nearly finished and brand new council houses and
flats had finally replaced the rubble and mess which had lingered depress-
ingly since 1945. Eleven years on from the end of the war the economy was
growing, unemployment was shrinking and a new sense of optimism was all
around. Colourful clothes were becoming trendy again and everyone was
listening to rock 'n roll, the new music sensation. I was sixteen years old
and this was the London I started work in, a vibrant city of opportunity
and hope.

I am a Londoner through and through. I was born and brought up in
south London and at the age of sixteen still lived with my parents in our
council flat in Peckham. I had not done well at school and my academic
progress was such that university was out of the question, so I had no choice
but to leave and start working. The question I faced was, what would I do?

Shortly before school ended I was sent to talk to a Youth Employment
Officer, a man who went into schools to help find jobs for boys like me, ones
who did not have the qualifications to go to university. There were plenty
of jobs around and the YEO, a friendly middle-aged man, was relaxed and
positive about my prospects and seemed genuinely interested in helping me.

During the interview he asked me what I wanted to do with my life. In my broad Cockney accent I replied that I had no idea. Thoughts of being an airline pilot and other fancy things had been scuppered by my poor eyesight and beyond that I really was at a loss. I assumed I would end up working as a printer, like my uncles, or cleaning windows, like my father. None of my family had ever worked in an office.

And then I had a thought. A few weeks earlier my father had bought our first record player and so I said I'd like to join the promotion department of a record company so I could meet the stars, people like Frank Sinatra who I had recently become a huge fan of. It was at that moment that this man, this stranger who I am sad to say I was never in contact with again, transformed my life. He looked at me quizzically, considered my words for a few seconds and said, 'You mean advertising.'

I didn't know exactly what I meant by 'the promotion department' but I didn't think I meant advertising, because I had no idea what it was. But the man seemed sure of his assessment and he gave me three introductory cards to advertising agencies, telling me to write and ask if they had any opportunities for someone like me. I thought I might as well do as he said because I had nothing to lose, no expectations to fall short of and I knew that there were plenty of other jobs around anyway if nothing came of my letters. Not long after I wrote, two of the agencies, SH Benson and J Walter Thompson, called me in for interviews and then offered me jobs in their despatch departments.

As I said above, that one conversation with a kind, encouraging and imaginative Youth Employment Officer transformed my life. I cannot overstate the importance of that meeting. It gave me my opportunity in advertising and set in motion a chain of events which led me to create with David and Adrian what *Campaign* magazine would later describe as, 'arguably the most successful UK advertising agency of all time'. It is amazing what a bit of kindness and encouragement can do for people. My only regret is that I never had the chance to thank him.

****

My parents, William Mead and Harriet Easto, married almost nine months to the day before my birth. I came into the world on 22 March 1940, in St. Olav's, a gloomy hospital in Bermondsey, in those days one of the tougher areas of south London. The indigenous population were mainly dockers and stevedores who worked on the endless expanses of the London Docks, the transformation of which I would play a part in many years later. St Olav's has hosted some notable births over the years, including a certain Maurice Micklewhite, better known as Sir Michael Caine. The hospital itself, provided the wind was in the right direction, was within the sound of the Bow Bells, which makes me officially a Cockney.

As this was pre-NHS, I'm not sure how my parents paid for my entrance to the world. Money was not very plentiful in the newly established Mead household. William Mead, Bill to everybody who knew him, was the victim of an unfortunate life-changing circumstance. He was born the first of three children in straitened circumstances in Southwark (an early adopter of what we know today as gentrification, but sadly not at the time my father's family lived there). His mother supplemented my grandfather's small wage by selling vegetables on the doorstep of the family home in Swan Street, SE1.

Having had not much of a formal education, my father's big opportunity came in 1925 when somehow he gained an apprenticeship to an antique dealer in the Kings Road. We never really discussed what happened in detail but, as I understand it, he was doing rather well until the general strike of 1926 was called. The owner of the antique shop gave him an ultimatum: either he carried on working or he would be fired. My father, sadly, had no choice because there was no way a working-class boy from south London could resist the order to strike – the social consequences would have been dire. And so he was given the equivalent of a P45 a day after the strike started. That was my father's one real chance, his big opportunity in life. Jobs in the Kings Road for south London lads were not exactly plentiful, so after a succession of menial jobs he became a window cleaner, which was how he earned his living until he died.

Harriet Mead was, for some reason I've never discovered, known as Addie, a much more comfortable name to have in non-pretentious south London. After leaving school early she had fun for a while and ended up meeting Bill Mead in a pub close to the Elephant & Castle and almost equidistant from their homes in SE1 and SE17. The attraction was instant and they married 18 months after they met.

They were very different individuals. Bill was an imposing man of about six feet, always smartly turned out, somehow managing to afford to shop in the Fifty Shilling Tailor outlet in the Walworth Road, part of a large chain which subsequently became the Burton Group. What I admired most about him was he was afraid of nothing and nobody when it came to defending what he thought was right and while many of his contemporaries turned to a life of petty crime he resisted the temptation to break the law for easy money. He was a private man but was fiercely proud of the fact that we never went hungry.

Addie was truly a saint on earth. Her whole life from as long as I can remember was devoted to my sister and me, along with anybody else who had a problem or had fallen on hard times. Nothing was ever too much trouble for this gentle, truly nice lady. I can't remember ever hearing her complain about anything. She, like most working-class mothers of this generation, had a part-time job in Boots the Chemist on Stamford Street, close to Waterloo Station. We did not have much but if she had a Shilling and somebody she barely knew needed sixpence she would hand it over without another thought. She was tiny, barely over five feet tall, and although gentle by nature had the resilience of high tensile steel when necessary.

When I blinked my way into the world, the Second World War had already been going for six months. The portents were not good but the courage demonstrated by the Meads together with most of their contemporaries was truly astonishing. It is easy to forget that they lived with the very real fear that goose-stepping Germans could, in the not too distant future, be marching on London.

Bill had very poor eyesight, a genetic failing he passed on to me. This impairment stopped him from joining the armed services and instead he became a fireman in London. As I'm sure an examination of the statistics would demonstrate, this was every bit as hazardous as being in the front line. His luck changed a bit when he was given the task of being resident fireman for some of London's theatres and the Coliseum in Saint Martin's Lane was where he spent most of the war. Only minor damage was caused despite everything lethal and German that landed on London during that time.

My father was a little showbiz himself. Family and war stopped him indulging in a great passion of his – ballroom dancing. He was, by all accounts, pretty good and won some minor competitions, although not with my diminutive mother. Sadly, unlike his poor eyesight, he did not pass his twinkle-toed ability on to me. I think it was a source of sadness that, despite lessons at Arthur Murray's dance school in Lewisham and trying to adopt the often-quoted life rule, 'Dance as if nobody's watching', I was never poetry in motion. Years later we would huddle around our tiny TV set with a large oil-filled enlarger (concave in shape, it epitomised the phrase 'goggle box') watching every episode of the new BBC programme *Come Dancing*, with very stiff couples in evening dress performing the waltz, foxtrot or quickstep while Dad gave expert commentary. The highlight of the show was the formation dancing competition, a sort of synchronised swimming by penguin lookalikes on dry land.

For the first few years of my life we lived in Larcom Street, not far from the Old Kent Road in south London, in one of those neat little rows of houses that I suspect were built around the turn of the century to house domestic servants or early graduates from the workhouse. Pay levels for wartime fireman must have been pretty dire because when the four of us left our little house in Larcom Street, when I was three, it was to move to an even smaller place in Cole Street, close to the now trendy Borough High Street. About two miles from London Bridge and not far from Lant Street, Charles Dickens' boyhood home, the area did not escape the ravages of the Blitz. But miraculously our home, 4a Cole Street, a two-and-a-half room flat, remained unscathed but I do remember daily trips to our local air raid shelter. Looking back now it's difficult to believe that anyone felt safe in those concrete boxes from the destructive might of the German Air Force. Nonetheless, we survived and we were lucky because many of my parents friends perished as South London took hit after hit from the Luftwaffe. The area was a prime target because of its close proximity to the docks and the main railway line that ran out of London Bridge Station.

Life in Cole Street, as you may have gathered, was not tranquil. However, it was fun. Dolcis, a giant shoe shop chain in those days, had a warehouse on the other side of the road from our flat. It was big and not a pretty structure but it had enormous recreational value to us as it provided two sliding shutters about the same size as a full-size football goal. These shutters were very useful to us as we set about developing the ball skills which might give us an escape route from our circumstances and lead to us playing for Millwall, our local team.

These two green goals were our Wembley Stadium at the end of the Dolcis workers shift. We would play every evening until it got dark, ball after ball crashing into the iron shutters. I shudder to think what today's health and safety disciples would make of all of this, let alone the noise abatement officials. I am convinced that the four or five of us who were resident members of Cole Street United would have all been given ASBOs.

Dad always joined us whenever he could. He was quite a handy footballer, quick on his feet from ballroom dancing and tough in the tackle. He usually dominated proceedings, not difficult when the people playing against him were between seven and nine years old. His crunching tackles and thunderous shot usually meant he and I prevailed, often helped by my diminutive sister Pat, an early trailblazer for women's football, who, at five years old, blonde hair flowing, had to be avoided at all costs when playing otherwise a nasty pain in the shin was almost certain to come your way.

The living accommodation itself in Cole Street gave real meaning to the term rudimentary. The two-and-a-half rooms comprised a sitting room, one bedroom and a half-room which doubled up as a kitchen, washroom and a once-a-week bathroom. Personal hygiene in south east London, although slightly better than in medieval times, was not top of everybody's agenda. There were two ways to scrub your body clean in those days. One entailed a visit to the local municipal baths with an attendant cost which put off lots of families. The second and more widespread route to cleanliness was the galvanised tin bath. Rarely seen these days except on things like the *Antiques Roadshow*, these handy devices were around five feet long, around three feet high and two-and-a-half wide. Lots of water had to be heated in the big pan over the fire. The hot water was then transferred by the bucket load into the tin bath. Six or seven buckets were needed to get the water to a level which would cover enough of the body to make a scrub down possible.

In the Mead household there was a pecking order for this Friday evening ritual: Dad first, Mum second, my beloved sister Pat third and then it was my turn. Because of the effort and cost of fuel everybody used the same water. Dad obviously did very well with first crack. But the temperature and colour of the water deteriorated quite rapidly and by the time I finished my turn I could well have been dirtier than when I started.

The other element of the modern bathroom, the loo, was housed outside in the communal yard. Not surprisingly for most of the year it was freezing cold and constipation came as a blessed relief for us. There was an early example of recycling connected with this outside torture chamber: instead of soft fluffy loo paper, the *Daily Mirror* was used, though arguably it was unfit for purpose.

The four of us slept in the same bedroom – Mum and Dad had their bed and Pat and I slept head to toe in a small bed almost within touching distance of our parents. Under those circumstances it is hardly surprising that the family did not get any bigger.

As time passed in Cole Street, the threat of Wolfgang or Hans being caught up in the traffic in Piccadilly dramatically receded and in 1945, like everybody else, the Cole Street gang had a street party to celebrate us winning the war. There was no fatted calf or roast suckling pig but sugar sandwiches and lemonade went down a treat.

It was about this time that I joined what was to be my intellectual home for the next six years. Joseph Lancaster Primary School in Harper Road was a late Victorian purpose-built school. Richard Rogers or Norman Foster would not have been inspired to a future career in architecture by the building. It was tall, made out of grey bricks and had a forbidding prison-type facade. The enclosed playground was the scene of the usual playground fun, beating skittles out of each other but always making up at the end of the bout.

They were really fun times and only made possible because they were pre-health and safety. Interestingly, discipline in class was a given. Most of us came from homes where there were no books at all and were very keen to learn. A lot of us were very keen readers, however, because of our devotion to four weekly comics that were solely text. In the absence of television, the internet, computer games and any other modern entertainment, they were the best things available to us by some distance. *The Rover*, *Hotspur*, *Adventure* and *Wizard* chronicled the over-the-top lives of a whole host of characters and were wonderful stories, very skilfully written, and they finished with a cliff-hanger every week. My favourite character was Alf Tupper, the 'Tough of the Track', who had the odd habit of consuming fish and chips before every race. There was a lot of 'fried stuff is good for you' propaganda around in those days and when Roger Bannister finally broke the four-minute mile in Oxford a few years later, many of us Alf Tupper disciples knew that our hero had beaten him to it years earlier, fuelled by a big piece of cod and double chips.

My love for the written word started with those four weekly fantasy trips. Years later, when my two eldest sons showed no sign of a similar love of words, I tried to get them back copies of these important publications, only to discover that past editions fetched considerable amounts of money and had long since ceased publication, their demise sadly hastened by the introduction of comic strips – illustrations with speech bubbles.

It was during this period that I first fell in love. The lady in question was Joyce Dawson. A dark-haired vision with sparkling eyes who was also a very good teacher. Whether or not she was married was irrelevant. At least ten of my classmates were also in love with Miss Dawson and we spent endless hours dropping pencils under our desks so that we could peer through towards the front of class hoping to get a glimpse of her wondrous legs. I remember her more vividly than any teacher I've ever had.

A couple of decades ago I developed a new way of looking at life or, if I'm honest, mortality. I compared life to going away on a holiday which was two weeks long. I was sitting reflectively at the end of a really good first week, comforting myself with the fact that there was as much left of the holiday as I'd already had. This was a really nice thought to dwell on.

However, rather disturbingly, I realised that if I related this principle to life itself there was nowhere near the same level of comfort to be had, given my age. Even in this advanced era of medical science I recognised that I did not have as much time left as had gone before. Maybe I was two thirds through my tenancy on earth. Chillingly, it could even have been three quarters. I found this to be an unacceptable scenario.

So I decided to take a more lateral view to get me to a point where I might have as much left of my life as already gone by. This entailed aggregating all the really quality days that I had experienced. I went through my life in five-year chunks adding up all the quality days. There were some five-year periods when there was a paucity of quality days. The end result of this entire endeavour got me to a point where the sum of all those quality days added up to around twenty years. I then worked out that I could have at least the same again as I'd already had in *quality* terms. Perhaps, misguidedly, I found this reassuring and I took from it the lesson that you had to try and make every day of your life a quality day.

I've outlined this little aside now because my days at Joseph Lancaster gave me one of the best five-year aggregates that I can remember. Despite my unrequited love affair with Miss Dawson, those years at Joseph Lancaster were almost perfect. I was Head Prefect, captain of both football and cricket teams and smart in class. I used to finish in the top two or three of every exam every year, even with the deterioration in my eyesight, which I inherited from Dad and which I am sure was made worse by my habit of reading the latest of the weekly four with the torch under the bed clothes most nights.

I even used to win the odd prize at Speech Day. Sadly, I no longer have any of them except the Memorial Prize I got just before leaving. The school was named after a local boy who won a Victoria Cross in the First World War and the Premier Prize at Speech Day was given every year in his memory. It was a dictionary which I still have to this day and it was awarded for 'Continued good work and helpfulness'. These days I think it makes me sound like a smart sycophant.

Britain from the mid-forties to the early fifties was ravaged by the aftermath of war, a particularly unappealing example of which was rationing. Still, it was occasionally a period of great discovery. But never mind kiwi fruit or mangoes; our voyage of discovery of exotic offerings brought us oranges and bananas. And school meals lacked a little of the culinary skills that Jamie Oliver's crusade delivered way into the future. We supplemented Joseph Lancaster's food with takeaways from a very conveniently located fish and chip shop where, for three pennies in old money, a large bag of very hot, very greasy chunks of fried potato would satisfy even the most voracious appetite. There were no campaigns in those days aimed at preventing fat little five-year-olds from blowing up like barrage balloons. But it didn't matter because any calories we digested were immediately burnt off by endless games of football started in the playground and finished off by a good hammering of the Dolcis goals.

Rationing applied to sweets as well as anything else. I can't remember the exact amount we could buy on a weekly or monthly basis but it wasn't very much. To my eternal shame one day I was walking home from school and there lying on the pavement in front of me was an anonymous white envelope, inside of which was a whole six months' worth of sweet coupons. I rationalised my not taking this to the local police station in two ways. Firstly, boys from the Borough did not have a nodding acquaintance with the local constabulary and secondly, as somebody once said, it was temptation beyond endurance – my flesh is weak when it comes to Cadbury's Dairy Milk and Dolly Mixtures.

Talking about all things sugary reminds me of an incident close to the end of the Second World War when Dad was working at the Winter Garden, like the Coliseum a grand Theatre close to Covent Garden. Dad had moved there from the Coliseum at a time when there was a play or musical being performed. He developed a relationship with the star of the show, a fairly famous film star who took to the theatre when the celluloid jobs dried up.

She was one of those flashing-eyed beauties, the most famous of whom was Margaret Lockwood. She obviously took a shine to Dad because we were all invited to visit her at her palatial apartment in Park Lane. For the refugees from 4a Cole Street it was luxury the like of which none of us had seen before. Light, airy, large rooms, each one bigger than our entire flat, took our breath away. We perched rather nervously on the edge of silk covered uncomfortable chairs sipping tentatively from the finest bone china teacups a pale green fluid that was served after we all asked for tea. It was my first introduction to Earl Grey and I dislike it today almost as much as I did then. None of us had the courage to suggest that in our case tea meant a thick dark liquid so strong and sweet that you could almost stand your teaspoon up in it.

Apart from the wonders of her bathroom, all white and shiny, and the mirrors that were everywhere, the undoubted high spot of the visit was when she served us a plate full to overflowing of a dark brown sweetmeat which turned out to be vanilla fudge. My sister and I devoured it down to the last piece. In direct contrast to Earl Grey, I've loved vanilla fudge ever since.

My parents told me later that following the trip to Park Lane our film star friend asked if she could adopt me but my parents declined to pass me on to a life of luxury and endless vanilla fudge in Park Lane. They properly wanted to protect me from having to drink endless gallons of Earl Grey on those shiny wooden chairs.

The story has a tragic ending because some years later, still childless, our film star fell in her bathroom and cracked her head fatally on the side of the bath. My only memento, apart from the love of fudge, is a book where she penned an inscription, 'To my Little Prince with all my love...'

Our star must have helped nourish my lifelong passion for film. Cinemas in those days were enormously popular. During a five year period the two biggest cinemas in Europe opened in London, The Gaumont State in Kilburn and the Trocadero at the Elephant & Castle. When we were small, Mum, wearing the longest coat she had, used to smuggle Pat and me into the Troc. We would shuffle along under her coat, terrified of discovery or of tripping as we mounted the stairs to the One Shilling & Ninepence seats. Once the ascent was completed we would emerge in the darkness like moths from a chrysalis and watch the film. We were brazenly in place by the time the lights went up and the interval organist appeared, although on one occasion my dear sister, who often courted controversy, said to an usherette, 'My mum didn't pay for me!'

As we got bigger the flat in Cole Street seemed to get smaller and Mum made endless trips to the local council to try to get us re-housed. Post-war a massive municipal rebuilding programme was underway but the chances of us escaping from the outside lavatory always seemed tantalisingly distant.

CHAPTER 2

1948

At the age of eight my lifelong addiction to Millwall Football Club began. In those days your football affections were transmitted directly from your father. Mine had been a lifelong fan and would regale me with endless tales of trips made following his team to faraway, romantic places like Sunderland, Derby and Stockport. My addiction was profound indeed because forty years later my great friend, James Macdannell, sadly no longer with us, who was finance director of Abbott Mead Vickers, accused me of having a mistress who was getting in the way of us running our advertising agency. I was initially outraged at this suggestion of infidelity. But then he revealed the name of the alleged mistress – it was Millwall Football Club. Such was my devotion to the cause.

On match days we used to get a bus from Borough High Street which took us to the Elephant & Castle and on to the Old Kent Road heading towards New Cross. The Old Kent Road in those days absolutely deserved its £60 rating on the Monopoly board. It was shabby and full of tatty pubs and cafes.

We would get off the bus at Ilderton Road and then had a short walk past different timber merchants and newly built estates to the Den – the

156

fearsome home of the lions of Millwall. We always stood behind the goal on uncovered terraces with a man called Henry Hall who was smartness itself as far as we were concerned. He lived in Epsom, a leafy suburb full of expensive houses, and was 'something in sales'. His main claim to fame, however, apart from his very snappy attire (he was easily the best dressed supporter behind the goal at Ilderton Road) was his Jaguar. It was dark green, smelled of leather inside and was a one-off in the dodgier parts of Millwall's rubble strewn car park. Our other constant chum was Jimmy, a newspaper seller at London Bridge. In those days he had the *Evening News* and *The Star* as well as the *Evening Standard* to sell. Each of these had a special Saturday afternoon edition which came out within half an hour of the end of matches and covered the results and reports of all London teams. Not surprisingly, just before the final whistle of every game Jimmy would leg it back to London Bridge in order to serve his eager patrons who were desperate to read about something they just spent an hour and a half watching.

At half-time there was a rush to the stalls that sold cups of tea, scaldingly hot Bovril, greasy burgers and hot pies. Apart from the prawn sandwiches in the executive boxes little has changed then.

There was no segregation of fans of different teams in those days and as far as I remember there was very little thuggish behaviour, except, perhaps, when the hated enemy Crystal Palace visited the Den. When the crowds got really big, shutting off not only the view of the game itself but any glimpse of the sky from this eight-year-old, I was passed over their heads of the fans and deposited right at the front, from where my view was unobstructed. If the significance of being a football fan – having something in your life which allows an escape from the drudgery of working from Monday to Friday – is important now it was even more so then. But enough of that for now, I will return later to the significant episode in my life that was Millwall Football

Club, where as a director I found myself fighting financial forest fires with tumblers of water.

Our weekends in Cole Street were defined by Millwall's performance on a Saturday afternoon. If we won, a general sense of euphoria emanating from Dad infected the family as well as most of South London; if we lost he found it difficult to speak for twenty-four hours, and if the defeat was humiliating, even longer. It was only after the final inquest in the Monday newspapers had been and gone that we returned to some normality. Pat and I knew to not to push our luck until Monday evening if Millwall had lost the previous Saturday.

Pretty much every Sunday we made a pilgrimage to East Lane which ran from the Old Kent Road through to Walworth Road. It was south London's answer to the much more famous Petticoat Lane which operated on the outskirts of the City. I guess the market was about a mile and a half long altogether and packed cheek by jowl with stalls selling almost everything. There was one particular stall that drew me like a magnet every Sunday. It sold the exciting and colourful American comics immortalising the adventures of Superman, Batman and others. As far as I can remember the first of these superheroes was Captain Marvel, who transformed himself into a lean mean fighting machine by uttering the immortal word 'Shazam!' Clad in blue and red, he then flew through the pages correcting wrongs and rebuilding the world every three or four weeks. These comics were a lazy escape from the more challenging (no pictures) *Rover, Hotspur, Adventure* and *Wizard*.

There was always a shortage of ready cash in the Mead household, so I only got an American comic from Dad every two or three weeks, and only if Millwall had won the previous day. This irregularity massively heightened my sense of joy whenever I did get hold a copy of the latest epic adventures.

From a very early age I understood that anticipation was almost as good as realisation. I can't remember Pat's favourite stall but I'm sure there was one where gifts to her were dispensed with equal frugality. On the rare days when we both achieved our objectives of leaving East Lane with our favourite items, we felt truly blessed.

Life at Cole Street was now spiced by my new addiction to Millwall. One Saturday in every five Henry would arrive in his bottle green Jaguar outside our door and we would, rather grandly, sit in the back to be whisked to the Den in glorious comfort. These really were happy times, augmented every so often by my father taking me to New Cross Stadium where greyhound racing happened every Thursday and on Saturdays when Millwall were playing away.

There was no National Lottery in those days or even betting shops on the High Street so Bill Mead, in common with most of my uncles and working-class men in general, gambled outside the law. Most days Dad would write out a little betting slip in his very elegant handwriting using a Parker 51 fountain pen, which I suspect must have been given to him as a gift from the time when he put out fires in Theatreland. I quickly came to understand that for the small-time gambler winning, although relatively important, was subsidiary to being in the game.

My father's demeanour hardly changed if all of the horses he bet on that day finished last. The only legal gambling was on the racecourse itself or in the case of Thursdays and Saturdays at the rather tatty New Cross Stadium, where lots of men in flat caps and trilbies scurried from bookmaker to bookmaker to get the best odds on 'Camberwell Flyer' or another romantically named greyhound.

I've always thought that greyhounds were pretty miserable looking animals. They were paraded around the stadium, and then shoved into little boxes six abreast released at the moment a totally unbelievable mechanical hare passed by – the gates of the boxes went up and the chase was on.

I saw little of Dad when he took me with him on his gambling outings. He would park me by a convenient crash barrier, although the sparse attendance meant that crashes or crushing were a very unlikely event, and he would always come back and stand with me while the races were on. I grew used to the ritual of him tearing up his betting slip after each race, soon to be followed by him disappearing again while intently studying the published odds for the next race.

He made sure that I was comforted by a couple of cups of hot tea (proper tea, not Earl Grey) and a sausage roll. After eight races the floodlights around the track dimmed and the Stadium, now strewn with torn up bookies cards and dreams, disgorged its customers and the evening was over. We walked back to the Old Kent Road through the gloomy streets of south London and got the bus back to Cole Street.

I look back on those trips to the football and dog racing with my father with enormous fondness. They were the times that really bonded us. Dad used to get up at 3am every day to go to work cleaning the shop windows in the West End – he had to be finished long before the shops opened each morning – and so I hardly saw him during the week. But I treasured our weekend or Thursday night trips. It is true what they say about fathers and sons in those days, that there was no real emotion shown in either direction. But that didn't stop us from bonding. Dad taught me to box, we played football together and the fact he took me with him to the football and the dog racing meant a huge amount to me. By having me with him he made me part of his world and that made me feel very special, as did knowing at the dog track that he always made sure he came to stand with me for the actual races. The joy of him coming back after placing his bet meant far more to me than the anticipation of the race about to start. They were really good times.

During my time at Joseph Lancaster we had one school trip, or 'school journey', as they were called in those days. Out of season the school negotiated terms with a place near Great Yarmouth called the Hopton Holiday Camp. It was pretty basic stuff and for a week we were housed in dormitories. It was the first time away from home for all of us and I would wake in the night to hear boys gently sobbing with homesickness. Although it was only a week Mum still sent me food parcels. Beautifully wrapped in brown paper, they contained cake and sweets and I was the envy of Dormitory B. For a while I was the most popular boy in town as I shared my goodies.

We had a couple of organised outings during the trip. The first was to the Smiths Crisps factory near Great Yarmouth. Men in hairnets took us on a guided tour where we saw huge machines slicing potatoes at unbelievable speed. The potatoes were then moved into giant vats of cooking oil, bubbling and smoking away. A great roaring sound came from them as the raw potatoes were shovelled in. A minute later the newly fried crisps came out onto a production line to cool before being wrapped. We were allowed to taste some of those crisps straight out of the vat and they were easily the best I've ever tasted. Fresh and crisp, they were like nothing I'd eaten before. Many years later I worked on the Smiths Crisps account and we were never short of delicious samples but I never tasted crisps as good as that day on our school journey.

The other notable trip was to allow us to go shopping in Great Yarmouth to buy little gifts for our loved ones. After a cursory look around the shops the lads descended on Woolworth's, or FW Woolworth as it was known in those days. Traditionally a giant of the High Street, the store in Great Yarmouth was no exception. It dominated the row of shops in which it was situated. As it was the outlet of choice for day trippers and holidaymakers as well as the local population, it was always packed with people. At that time FW Woolworth was the ultimate store. It called itself a 'variety store' and variety was not an understatement. Everything you could possibly think of was in stock. But it was never tacky, nothing like a penny store, just a really good shop. Woolies' had a way of treating with dignity people who couldn't afford to go elsewhere. You didn't feel you were demonstrating your penury by shopping there.

As I discovered on that trip it was a treasure trove and having looked amongst the various choices on the scent counter I chose 'Soirée de Paris' a noxious little number in a purple bottle attached to a white card. All the gifts in FWW were attached to little white cards, which would allow prompt payment and easy wrapping.

I suspect Woolworths must have had a huge reserve in their accounts every year to cover pilferage. That reserve would have been particularly appropriate on the occasion that Joseph Lancaster's gang of Fagin apprentices hit the store.

I did not participate in this orgy of looting, but not for any high-flown moral reasons. I was terrified of being caught and having to explain to Dad what I'd done. My other contemporaries at the school appeared to have no such inhibitions (this was years before the introduction of CCTV or electronic theft detectors) and like a swarm of locusts they descended on the open counters and stuffed their pockets full of swag before we made our way back to the train station to return to Hopton. But such was the extent of the shoplifting-fest that halfway back to our holiday camp the police stopped the train and boarded it. The booty was hastily dispensed with, through the windows and out onto both sides of the railway tracks which, now covered in FWW's white cards, gave the effect of a snowstorm in mid-summer. I think the police decided that it was not worth fingerprinting everybody to try and discover the culprits but we were all given menacing stares by large policeman with red faces. One or two of the more adventurous would-be villains kept a little of their haul stuffed down the front of their underpants. They were hailed as heroes on a return to the dormitories.

My white card containing the small vial of 'Soiree de Paris' finished up on the embankment even though I'd paid for it. I don't think receipts were given in those days and I had a terrible fear of being the only one who, having paid, would still get caught up in the maelstrom – I did not feel like being made an example of that day. A decade or so later I decided to buy some perfume again, this time for my great friend Jenny Armstrong. Around Christmas time I was wandering up and down Regent Street. Surrounded by Christmas lights and storefronts covered in fake snow I made my way to the London outlet of a large French store called Galerie Lafayette. It was about as different from Woolworths in Great Yarmouth as possible. In those days thick carpet was laid throughout the store and elegant counter units were manned by languid, haughty-looking Frenchwomen imported to intimidate unsuspecting English innocents into making a purchase.

Hermes, the great French fashion house, had just launched a new perfume. It was called 'Caleche' and was being sold in a giant bottle which I guess held around 150 ml of scent. I rather casually asked one of the po-faced French assistants how much it was and she replied, 'Rather more than you can afford Monsieur'. This was a brilliant sales technique because, although she was absolutely right, I dug deep into my pockets and purchased the giant bottle. They did gift wrap it for me though.

But back to holidays. As a family we combined holidays with a bit of work in the giant hop fields of Kent. When the picking season was ready we would get on a train from London Bridge and travel down to Paddock Wood. As I remember it, Paddock Wood was like a town that time had forgotten. The High Street was full of small shops, bakers, butchers, a fishmongers, newsagents and compact grocery stores. There were two or three pubs and the ever present fish and chip shop and tea shop.

The hop farms covered enormous acreage and ten or fifteen families would come down and pick the green, rather abrasive crops for hours on end every day. We slept in dormitories which were comfortable, if a little basic. Meals were provided and in the evening we were transported to various quaint country pubs, where there was beer and snacks for the grown-ups and lemonade and crisps for Pat and me and all the other kids. My memory of this time is pretty hazy but tinged with affection for the locals who were kind and generous. The countryside in the Garden of England was a welcome change from dusty London. Mum and Dad made some life-long friends and visited Kent quite often outside the hop picking season.

Most weekends the whole family would decamp to Nanny Mead, my grandmother. Her home at 61 Swan Street would become the focus of attention for the whole clan. Nanny Mead was a formidable woman, stocky with steel-grey hair she dominated everyone she came into contact with. I remember my paternal grandfather, who was also called Bill, as a gently rotund silver-haired, long-suffering and kindly man. It seemed to me he lived in the shadows of this powerful woman, constantly smiling benignly and speaking only when he was spoken to.

I never saw him hug my father or, for that matter, anybody else. I once saw photographs of him as a very young man in army uniform. Unlike many of his contemporaries he had survived the First World War. The photographs showed him with horses. I suppose he may have been in the cavalry and he carried on working with horses after he came out of the Army, driving a Brewers Dray behind two huge stallions. Maybe his experiences during the Great War caused him to be the introvert he was. He died when I was quite young.

Christmas was a particularly significant time in Swan Street. Despite having a blowout lunch in Peckham at four o'clock after watching the Queen's Speech, Dad would gather us all together on Christmas Day and march us, literally, off to Southwark. It was a pretty long walk, only occasionally relieved by the luxury of hailing a passing taxi. On arrival at the senior Mead household a vast display of food awaited us. Ham, pork pies, pickled onions, mustard sauce, bread and potatoes sat on a groaning table. Refusal to participate in the second feast of the day was not an option. There was not a hint of a piece of lettuce or tomato anywhere. Protein and carbohydrate were the working class ingredients of choice. The event was made tolerable by a second round of present opening. In addition to our gifts, Nanny Mead gave Pat and me half a crown (12.5p in today's money but worth so much more in those days) every time we visited her. Needless to say we spent a lot of time in the company of this awesome woman. She was the godfather of the family – tough as old boots, she dispensed kindness and wisdom in a generous way. The only proviso was that her view would prevail. There was no room for argument with Don Eliza of Swan Street.

There was a time when, incredibly, my Mum stood up to her. Nanny Mead said to Mum rather forcefully that she should have told off Pat for something more harshly than she did. Mum, although a peacemaker by nature, was fiercely protective of her role in our lives and fought back, disagreeing strongly with her mother-in-law. And then Nanny Mead slapped her face. We were all there and it was a horrible moment. The result of this was a stand-off between them which lasted for two years and during it they didn't speak at all, a situation which was profoundly tricky for everyone. Mum, however, always encouraged Pat and me to visit Swan Street every weekend and always turned up at the Christmas festivities although a barrier remained between them. Dad, being a typical man, took the path of least resistance and stayed well out of it. After a while they did call a truce and the level of involvement was re-established. However Nanny Mead's influence on our upbringing was severely dented.

CHAPTER 3

1951

I *was eleven when another series of momentous events shaped my life.* I became the first member of my family in living memory to pass the 11+ exam, which was so central in defining the future of young South London children. I found it laughably easy and was not surprised when I was told that I had passed, along with about five or six other Joseph Lancaster alumni. Mum especially was very pleased. My passing the exam was not a great surprise because I was doing well at school but it was rare in our neighbourhood and the progress of her children was what Mum's life was all about and so she had the quiet satisfaction of being able to downplay it. 'I can't imagine how Peter passed the 11+ but he did,' was how she would have told people, using plenty of understatement.

And so the hunt for the next school began. There were some good grammar schools in south London – Haberdashers, Aske's, Alleyne's and Wilson's were great schools to aspire to. Young hopefuls had to go and have an interview to try and persuade distinguished-looking, elderly headmasters that they were suitable candidates to enter their establishments. Mum and Dad took me to these various interviews. With me scrubbed up as much as possible, with the help of the tin bath, off we went.

I can only really remember my interview at Wilson's. Founded in the 1600s it was a statuesque red brick building on Camberwell New Road. To either side of the school, with its large two-level playground, were very elegant gently sloping roads full of beautiful Victorian and Edwardian houses. The area itself, stuck between Vauxhall to the north, Southwark to the south and Peckham to the east had slid down the social rankings in the years following the war. Its centrepiece was Camberwell Green which, if I remember rightly, was less a Green than a traffic accident waiting to happen. Three or four major roads converged at an incredibly busy junction and in the evenings, gangs of moody young men gathered to plot their next altercation.

Like many mini centres a theatre dominated. The Camberwell Palace, all neon and light bulbs, sat on the road leading from Camberwell up towards Brixton and beyond. It had seen better days but around this time a resurgence was underway, fuelled by a blonde lady of indeterminate age called Peaches. She shocked the local Women's Institute but thrilled boys of sixteen or so by standing bare breasted on the stage. A recent edict from the Lord Chamberlain's Office had made it legal for stage performers to be semi-naked, providing that they always stayed absolutely still under the lights. Four or five years later, when I reached the age of consent – by which I mean the consent of the bouncers on the door rather than any legal sexual threshold – I saw Peaches. The years had not been kind to her but it was still a hormone-rattling moment for me.

The headmaster at Wilsons Grammar School was a tall and rather frightening man, Mr J S Lee. He had white hair and a very dusty demeanour. Even at my now advanced age I feel uneasy in the presence of headmasters and I remember being particularly apprehensive about Mr Lee. Unlike the rather cuddly Mr Wearne at Joseph Lancaster, the headmaster of the grand institution that was Wilsons was inscrutable and stern. Before my interview I was aware that the half hour I was about to spend with him could turn out to be a crucial time in my development and so I was nervous.

The interview didn't go well to begin with. I think he had some trouble with my deep cockney accent – he didn't understand a word I said for the first five minutes. If not a wave, I was beginning to feel a heavy stream of despair beginning to flood over me. And then a miracle happened: he asked me about the last book I'd read. It was Treasure Island by Robert Louis Stevenson which by chance was a favourite of his and as I'd not only read the book but had also seen Robert Newton's portrayal of the evil anti-hero Long John Silver on the silver screen at the Trocadero, I was able to have an animated conversation with Mr Lee about Jim Hawkins and the gang. We left the interview feeling mildly confident and this feeling was justified two weeks later when an embossed envelope telling me of my success came through the rarely used letterbox in Cole Street.

As I will illustrate later, for my education it was only downhill from there.

This great day was followed soon after by another less impressive white envelope telling us that the family could be re-housed if we accepted what was called in those days the Council's 'offer of alternative accommodation'. Mum's endless trips to the Council's headquarters, where she would queue up time after time in line at the Housing Department, had borne fruit at last.

The offer was for a three bedroom flat in Collinson House on the newly built Lindley Estate in Peckham. Our appointment was for a week's time and I can't remember my parents ever being more excited by anything than that piece of Southwark Council letterhead. We believed it would be the start of a whole new way of life.

Collinson House was at the apex of the Lindley Estate. Radnor Road defined the right-hand boundary of the Estate while the busy Commercial

Way, which ran between Camberwell Road and the Old Kent Road, was immediately in front. To the left was Peckham Park Road which ran down to the Old Kent Road opposite the Odeon cinema, which many years later was famously torn apart when Bill Haley's ground-breaking music 'Rock Around the Clock' was featured in a Glen Ford film called 'The Blackboard Jungle'.

The day of the appointment came and wide-eyed and trembling with anticipation, the four members of the Mead family were shown by the Council Housing Officer into a lift on the ground floor which whisked us up to floor three where number twenty sat just to the left of the lift doors. The shiny new key opened the Yale lock and we entered what I can only describe as paradise. To the left of the front door was the toilet, separated from the next room alongside which housed a white and gleaming bath, a hand basin and the mirror. Among its other luxuries the flat included a boiler with hot water coming from the taps and our levels of personal hygiene rocketed from that moment.

On the right-hand side of the corridor which dissected the flat were three bedrooms. The master was at the end of the corridor. One back and only slightly smaller was bedroom two and just by the front door was bedroom three which today would be considered a box room. In line with the traditional pecking order in our family, (which I never quite understood) guess who finished in the box room? It was only large enough for a single bed and a built-in wardrobe in the corner but that space more than accommodated my rather meagre clothing collection and other bits and pieces. On the left-hand side of the flat, past the bathroom, was a kitchen with work surfaces, a new gas cooker and a large sink. This led into the living room, a good size with double doors at one end which led onto a small but blissful balcony which overlooked grass lawns and a community centre. This building incorporated a large hall on the first floor, a laundry full of newly invented washing machines and pram sheds on the ground floor which played an important part in the estate children's voyages of sexual discovery.

It is impossible to overestimate the joy we all felt about our new accommodation. Our lives were transformed. I have moved home on many occasions since then but nothing has come even close to the feeling of delight that we all felt at transferring from Southwark to Peckham. Collinson House rapidly became the centre of our universes. Cole Street United, the main players who were apart from us, Tommy Smith and Kenny Mallardet, disbanded. The Dolcis nightwatchman must have breathed a heavy sigh of relief – no more goals flying into the top corner. But maybe Tommy and Kenny found new playmates and peace did not descend after all. I would never know either way.

Almost my last act in Cole Street saw me flying over the top of the handlebars of a bike when the chain snapped and the bike stopped suddenly and I didn't. Another trip to Guy's Hospital followed, but this time to the dental department because my quick trip across the handlebars finished with a landing on my two front teeth. This was the beginning of an enormous amount of time spent over the years with dentists of all descriptions. The sugar sandwiches finally took their toll.

That first trip, with bloodied mouth and busted front teeth, was rewarded by a certificate from the head dentist at the school citing 'bravery in the dental chair'. I think on reflection it was less courage than fear that made me sit deadly still while dentists and students probed with their instruments of torture. The drills they used in those days were hideously slow.

So here we were in Peckham and the grass that surrounded each of the blocks that comprised the Lindley Estate gave a real sense of space. The little houses in Radnor Road must have found the massive new development extremely disconcerting. Further on, they merged into a rag and bone yard, a bomb site and a pickle factory which ran half the length of the road with six-foot high walls topped with barbed wire. There were very few cars parked in the streets in those days for the simple reason that virtually nobody on the Radnor Estate could afford to own one. This gave us our new football stadium bounded on one side by the pickle factory and on the other by the grass fronted Radnor House.

Two bricks at either end of a one hundred foot run of road served as goals and Tommy and Kenny were quickly replaced by John and Ralph. The matches went on hour after hour, day after day. The only interruption came when our precious ball sailed over the barbed wire of the pickle factory and the guilty party had to take on a Colditz-type scaling of the wall and then attempt to cross the deadly wire. Almost all the injuries picked up in these games came from the barbs and many a pair of short trousers were ruined from the journeys into the pickle factory yard. As vinegar and onions were the prime ingredients of this particular manufacturing unit the smell, particularly on a summer day, had to be experienced to be believed. But it was still paradise.

The choice of Wilsons and the subsequent admission to that establishment couldn't have been more convenient. It meant a walk to school of about half an hour through what is now the notorious North Peckham estate. But psychologically the move from Joseph Lancaster to Wilsons was really bad for me. At the former, I was the undoubted cock of the North or King of the World – first at everything and teacher's favourite. I rolled up to Wilson's and never recovered from the shock of having at least sixty people who joined from a multitude of schools across South London who were every bit as smart as me.

My years at Wilsons were dominated by pretty fearsome teachers, one of whom stood out as the scariest by far. In his classes you could hear a pin drop, he would cane you on the backside without a moment's hesitation if you spelled a word wrongly and he appeared to take some pleasure in inflicting angry red wheals across our backsides. He dispensed capital punishment liberally and had a rather disconcerting habit of putting his hands down the back of our trousers while suggesting that we might have put exercise books down there to obviate the pain he was about to inflict.

He was also a housemaster and his particular house won everything on sports day, on speech day, on steeplechase day and even his cadet corps used to win all the battle exercises fought with blocked World War I Enfield 303 rifles. I've always believed that fear paralyses rather than motivates but such was the level of terror that he inflicted on his cowering charges that they were spurred into superhuman levels of achievement. There is no doubt that he went way beyond the permitted levels of educational brutality even in those days. If any poor, ill-advised boy complained to his parents and the result was an interview with the aloof headmaster, the consequences for that boy were dire once this teacher found out about his treachery. I remember it happened to a boy named Holder. The poor little sod was moved to the front of the class, whereupon the teacher said to the class with his voice full of sarcasm, 'Bit chilly in here today boys. Are you warm enough? Holder, are you warm enough? I must make sure you're warm enough. I don't want you to have to run to your mother again.'

His intention was to humiliate Holder by making him appear a mummy's boy because at our school that was the last thing anyone wanted. Your life would be ruined, and that was his intention and how he got his revenge. He made quite an impression on all of us.

If we were doing the totting up of special days that I talked about earlier resulting from my time at Joseph Lancaster, the harvest from the Wilsons days would be meagre indeed. I slipped from an effortless number one in most subjects to constantly battling, in football parlance, relegation. Like my team when Saturday came, I got relegated on quite a few occasions. I'm only mildly exaggerating when I describe my fall from grace as being from 1A to 5E over my stay at the school. My reports penned by weary teachers occasionally gave nuggets of comfort like, 'He is a very reliable right back in the school B team' and 'He has made a worthwhile table lamp in carpentry this term'. I was the despair of my French teacher who one term gave me six per cent for getting my name right at the top of the exam paper.

Sadly I made no lifelong friends at Wilsons. There were a bunch of us who hung together for a lot of the time, including three or four who huddled together for safety walking through the hazardous backstreets of Camberwell and Peckham on our way to and from school, but this mutual protection group did not evolve into an enduring bonding.

These were very difficult times in other ways too. From 12 or 13 onwards the boasts about sexual gratification began to abound during playtime chat. On reflection I suspect everybody was lying but for those of us whose connection with the opposite sex was completely non-existent their lurid tales of furtive fumblings played havoc with our sense of self-worth and confidence but above all highlighted our lack of knowledge. Some of this was alleviated by Mr Shakeshaft, our Biology teacher, but far too much time in lessons was spent dissecting rancid rats or frozen frogs and nowhere near enough exploring the mysteries of the opposite sex and what you did with what and to whom. Our sexual education – put together by fanciful descriptions of sexual conquests by young would-be Warren Beattys – only served to confuse and frustrate us even further.

As life in Peckham became the norm I thought it was time that I started to be employed. I was aware there wasn't much cash around in our family and

I wanted a bit of financial freedom for myself. My first job was as a paperboy for a tiny shop just off Peckham Park Road. It was a classic example of shops that were on every other street corner in London at that time. Newspapers cigarettes and sweets accounted for about three quarters of the stock. Rationing was over and for me it was heaven. Big glass jars full of things like sherbet lemons, buttered brazil nuts, toffee of all description and coconut ice filled the shelves of the little shop to bursting point. I loved them all.

There were many more newspaper titles to be sold and delivered in those days. The joy of living in Peckham as far as a paperboy was concerned was that the overwhelming preference was for the Daily Mirror, which made the job much easier. Sundays was dominated by the now-defunct News of the World followed by the middle-class powerhouse that was the Sunday Express. I would be at the shop around 6.45 every morning to pick up my bag and go on my way. Papers were much less hefty in those days – inserts and supplements were not even a twinkle in an advertising man's eye. In later years Charlie, the owner of the store, would have to appoint mini Arnold Schwarzeneggers to deliver essential reading but in those days an element of speed was more significant than strength in delivering pre-breakfast entertainment to our many customers. Every so often somebody would have in their order a mildly risqué publication like Tit-Bits or Reveille. This caused a pause in the frantic rush to push newspapers through letter boxes and a quick skim through what, by today's standards, were innocent shots of ladies in bikinis. Page 3 was a long way off.

It took about an hour to complete the news run. I would then hurry back to Collinson House and change into my black and gold uniform before heading off to Wilsons. The pay was not particularly generous but Charlie allowed the three or four of us hired as paperboys a few sweets from the four-for-a-penny box. His work clothes were a long brown coat, exactly the same as the one worn by Ronnie Barker many years later in Open All Hours. Although slightly brusque he was essentially a very kindly man and I have nothing but fond memories of him. Like many other corner shops he did not survive the advent of supermarkets which caused a culling of the many small newsagents like his.

There were great joys to be had as a paperboy. I loved the early mornings and the feeling of being the first person out onto the streets. This was especially so when it had snowed and I was the first person to put footprints in the fresh white stuff. There was also great satisfaction in the work itself and the feeling at the end of each delivery of a job being done. I would start with a bag full of papers and an hour later it was empty. The joy was in the finality of it and looking back I understand why I felt so happy walking back to the shop with an empty bag.

After about a year the milkman who delivered to us at home said that one of his chums needed help at the weekend. This was a busy time because not only were some minor groceries carried on the electric trolley but bills had to be paid on either Saturday or Sunday. The addition of this particular chore, twinned with having to climb endless stairs (only the Lindley Estate in our immediate vicinity had lifts) meant that Saturday and Sunday's milk rounds were very demanding for one man, particularly when it meant he spent an extended amount of time inside blocks of flats while the electric cart remained unattended and its precious load became potential prey for the magpie-like boys and girls of SE15.

Andy, the Co-op milkman who employed me, was again very nice. He would bring a flask of tea to work and we would have the odd stop for sustenance. We had a whole range of milks in those days. Blue, silver, green and gold capped bottles sat in wire crates stacked up on our state-of-the-art electric milk float. Gold Top was by far the most expensive milk we carried.

It claimed to be full Jersey cream milk and the cream at the top of the bottle was a pretty deep yellow colour. When Andy stopped and dispensed tea from his flask we always diluted it with a dash of Gold Top milk. The first couple of cups tasted great but the tea in the flask atrophied as the morning wore on and became pretty repellent by the time the last cup emerged, not steaming but tepid, from Andy's Thermos. During the round we each had at least two Lyons fruit pies from the stock that we carried on the float. Blackberry & apple and apricot were my constant choices and our snacks were delicious. I've never been able to replicate the magic of the sweet taste of the pies mixed with the richness of the Gold Top milk.

The round was pretty hard work especially in the winter. On really cold days when I met Andy at the depot some of the milk would have frozen overnight and quite often the frozen milk stood proud above the top of the bottle with its top perched like a rather stylish piece of headgear an inch higher than it should have been. It took most of the round for the milk to go back in the bottle and on really cold days it never did. Andy let me operate the float, which I'm sure was against every rule, but it meant that we were a quick and efficient team in dispensing milk, eggs and fruit pies and collecting money. We had very few bad debts and quite often picked up pieces of toast and other food direct from the ovens of our customers. For a tough neighbourhood everybody was very nice and it was only one or two deeply unpleasant dogs that we had to be careful of.

Back at Collinson House we added another form of entertainment to our small television set. It was a radiogram which, as the name suggests, was both a wireless and a gramophone. It was a very handsome piece of equipment. Made by Ferguson, it could play five records stacked on its turntable one after the other. These were the 78 rpm vinyl variety. Incredibly fragile they came in a brown paper sleeve and were pretty expensive. Dad bought the radiogram on Wednesday and on Saturday I prevailed on Andy to pay me then rather than Sunday so that I could hurry down to the local record store and buy my first ever record. The store was run by Fred Tipple who had the distinction of being the Chairman of the British Record Retailers Association and had racks full of the latest hits.

This was when I began another lifelong addiction, this time to Frank Sinatra. After a period in the wilderness following his unhappy marriage to Ava Gardner, he was a huge star again. His latest hit fresh off the presses was called 'How Little We Know'. The irony of this purchase crossed my mind fleetingly at the time but it soon passed. As I have outlined earlier, the radiogram and Frank Sinatra were to play a massively important role in my future, although I didn't know it at the time.

I was coming to the end of my time at Wilsons. Apart from some minor sporting achievements, I was by no means a star pupil. I had performed diligently for my House, under the leadership of Mr Massey, but, to be honest, I had not distinguished myself in any form of endeavour. It was obvious that I was not going to go on to university – there was no family tradition or money or academic achievement to suggest that this was even a possibility – and I was consigned to those groups of boys who had underperformed and were sent to classroom 4E to meet with the Youth Employment Officer, a Government-sponsored adviser who changed my life.

It was a source of small satisfaction to me that many years later Wilsons, having discovered that I'd been successful in my calling, asked me to be the guest of honour at Speech Day. Somebody told me unofficially that I was the third most successful pupil to emerge from Wilsons after Michael Caine and an eminent Professor in the medical profession who had had 'papers published'. I suspect that more diligent digging would have revealed a whole host of old Wilsonians who had been more successful than I was but I embraced without question my ranking in Wilsons' modern history.

In the end I left Wilsons with two O levels, in English Lit and Geography. But the most important thing I took away with me was given to me by the Youth Employment Officer in the meeting I have already described. This man with a twinkle in his eye was helpful and encouraging which was in keeping with the spirit of the times. Everyone was helping everyone else as the joy of post-war recovery spread. A generation of young men like me were leaving school ready to work and the country found itself with a workforce replenished for the first time since so many were tragically lost during the war. To be young, male and able-bodied was rare. Business was simpler then, too, with no human resources or health and safety to deal with. And so London was full of opportunities.

Mine came in the form of that Youth Employment officer giving me three cards and three addressed envelopes to send off to three of London's advertising agencies. One never replied, all too prevalent these days but rare in those better mannered times, but the other two granted me interviews. These were both arranged from the payphone down the road from our flat because we didn't have our own phone.

In the build-up to the interviews I wasn't at all nervous. They were by no means life or death: I didn't have a burning ambition to get into advertising and I knew there were plenty of other jobs out there if I didn't get one of those two. Also, while I had support from my family, I was under no pressure. I had never felt it was my destiny to work in the West End and none of my family had ever worked in an office but equally, my father had never dismissed it. Ahead of the interviews he gave me some general advice, telling me to say I was prepared to work hard, that I knew I hadn't worked hard enough at school and would work harder in future.

My first interview was at S H Benson. I met two people, Mr Frost and Miss Miller and they were very friendly. We had a fairly cursory chat and I wasn't sure what to expect in terms of a job offer or otherwise. The second was at J Walter Thompson in Berkeley Square. Now owned by Martin Sorrell's WPP Group, it was then part of a giant American chain that behaved in a quintessentially British way because it was far more intimidating. I was interviewed by an impressive woman in twinset and pearls in their Personnel Department (human resources as a term had not been invented yet).

Again, I was not sure whether or not to expect a job offer to follow. But there must have been a London-wide shortage of likely candidates for despatch boys in those days because JWT and Benson's both offered me exactly the same job on exactly the same salary: a position in the despatch department on an opening salary of £3.10 shillings a week, the equivalent of seven weekends on the milk round.

Choosing between the two was simple in the end. I preferred the atmosphere at Benson's anyway but my choice was confirmed in my mind when shortly after offering me the job JWT's stern interviewer told me that, 'Of course we have a staff canteen here but sadly on your salary you won't be able to afford to eat in it but you may eat your sandwiches in Berkeley Square.' I found this curiously offensive and being a rather stroppy south London Millwall supporter decided to go elsewhere. Decades later when Abbott Mead Vickers became the biggest agency in the country, one of the agencies we overtook was JWT. On reflection rather childishly, that day I got a Tupperware box of sandwiches and sat in Berkeley Square and ate them.

And so I had my first job in advertising, as a despatch boy for Benson's. That was my way in to the industry I still work in now, more than fifty years later.

CHAPTER 4

1956

My first day at Benson's dawned. On that first morning I was very nervous. Aged 16 I was excited simply to have a job, especially one in the West End, but at the same time it was a journey into the unknown for me. The two-bus commute that was to be my lot over the next nine years started in Peckham Hill Street, took me first to the Elephant & Castle on a number 63 bus and finished in Kingsway on a 177. The trip could take upwards of an hour and saw me pass through some of the tattier parts of South London. With so much more traffic around now the same journey would probably take two hours today.

SH Benson was housed in Kingsway Hall. The ground floor was a place of worship for Methodists while the rest of the building was full of advertising people – a quirky juxtaposition. Bensons was a very large agency in those days and lots of the iconic brands of the day were clients. Bovril, Guinness, Omo, Maclean's Toothpastes and Woodbine Cigarrettes were just a few of the heavy hitters who trusted their advertising accounts to the agency.

In the Copy Department there had been some notable literary figures and the most famous of these was Dorothy L Sayers who, as well as coming up with such notable ads as the Guinness toucan, invented Lord Peter

Wimsey, her upmarket sleuth. The despatch department, where I worked, was in the basement of the building. It was a very large area and accommodated quite a few people. There were three of us newly appointed despatch boys, nine despatch riders and a van driver, as well as Bob Louden and his team of parcel wrappers and stamp dispensers. This huge operation was made necessary by the way advertisements were printed in those days.

Once an idea had been approved by layers of people in the building and the client, a piece of artwork was produced which was then translated onto either metal or plastic blocks. Quite often mounted on heavy pieces of wood, these blocks had to be delivered to newspapers where they were translated once again onto large semi-circular printing matrixes and then onto the giant printing presses.

Fleet Street, which runs between The Strand and Farringdon Road in central London, was totally dominated by both the national and regional newspapers in those days and our job as the despatch boys and motorcyclists was to make sure that the blocks were delivered in plenty of time to get into the next day's newspapers. My role was to sit on the back of a very powerful Norton Dominator motorcycle driven by very masculine guys clad in full leathers and boots for whom helmets were not yet either fashionable or mandatory. These leader of the pack lookalikes drove the machines with a side box running the whole length of the motorcycle, in which the blocks were carried. The despatch apprentice's job was to jump off the motorcycles and zigzag down Fleet Street delivering the blocks to the multitude of newspaper offices on both sides of the road and in the small squares which fed off the main thoroughfare.

I more often than not was twinned with a rider called Bert, the most normal looking of all the motorcyclists. He lived in Lewisham and was very nice to us young faced would-be advertising men. Bob Louden planned the routes and dispensed each of the rounds to the nine bikes and of course every day it became a competition to see which pair could complete their round first. Bert and I were pretty nifty and we would expect to win on at least two of the three daily outings. When we finished our rounds we were still on call to deliver 'specials', usually letters to senior clients begging forgiveness for some mistake or other. Occasionally the specials demanded a trip to the Great West Road to deliver material to the giant Beecham Building and relating to one of the many brands based there which were held by Bensons at the time.

In between trips on the bikes, our job was to help wrap the hundreds and hundreds of blocks and other materials that were sent hot foot out of the Kingsway Hall basement every day. The place was dominated by the smell of the glue from the brown paper, which was dispensed ready for immediate use in great streams from a machine which covered one side wall. At the end of each day it wasn't unusual for hands to be covered in paper cuts and crusted glue from the brown adhesive, which I came to hate.

Health and safety didn't exist back then and I never quite understood why the refugees from motorcycle heaven were fully clad in protective clothing whilst us lads had no such safety features at our disposal. Arguably we were much more at risk sitting on the back of the bike hanging on for grim death while the powerful motorcycles roared up and down, quite often on just two wheels.

I did about six months in despatch and made some really good friends. Bob the boss and Bert in particular became great mates and the latter would occasionally take me home to Lewisham where he lived and let me ride his small motorcycle around his tiny garden. This was absolutely forbidden fruit for me because my father not only would not allow us to have a motorbike but even forbade us from having pushbikes after the unfortunate contact my teeth made with the front wheel of my bike a few years before. I thought I was a natural on a motorbike until one day I came off while negotiating a flowerpot in Bert's small plot and grazed my hand and arms quite badly. At home I had to hide the injuries for a few days to avoid having to offer an explanation of how they occurred.

One morning as I was preparing for the first trip of the day to Fleet Street Bob took me aside and said rather gravely that Personnel wanted to see me. Gilbert Frost was the Personnel Manager for the whole of Bensons and was ably assisted by Joyce Miller, who reminded me a bit of the delectable teacher I fell for at Joseph Lancaster ten years earlier. Miss Miller greeted me at the door of her office and ushered me in. She uttered the dreaded words, 'We've been keeping our eyes on you,' and the thought flashed across my mind that I was about to be sacked. Maybe a block hadn't been delivered on time or Arthur, the hairiest and most Marlon Brando-lookalike of all the despatch riders and who was slightly jealous of my relationship with Bert, had complained about me. Either way, I was out. My next thought was how I was going to explain to Dad that I been given the sack.

So I was truly astonished when Miss Miller told me that I was to be promoted to office boy from Monday of the following week. I was to go to the International Department – in those days it was called the Overseas Department – and report to Clive Wilcox the Deputy Department Head. One minute I was expecting the worst and the next she said I was, in fact, about to make a massive leap upwards. Until this moment my future held the possibility of becoming a despatch rider, then maybe a van driver with the vague promise of becoming a manager in the despatch department at some point in the future, all of which were warehouse-type jobs in the basement of the agency. You didn't see the real bit of the company from where we were. Despatch boy was not even in the same universe as being an office boy.

I had been a semi-failure at grammar school and yet now I was being given a real job, one which involved more than sitting on the back of a motorbike.

The really odd thing was that my promotion just happened. I didn't ask for it, I hadn't applied for the job and I didn't even know there was a vacancy up there. But they chose me anyway. This moment showed me two things which would be hugely important over the rest of my career. The first was that I could win people over, which gave me confidence. The second was that there was no glass ceiling above me. I had made my way into a part of the agency which I thought I'd never get near. This fired my ambition and made me wonder what else I could achieve if I really put my mind to it.

Around this time in South London the Teddy Boy era was rapidly taking hold. I mentioned earlier the riots at showings of a Glen Ford film 'The Blackboard Jungle' featuring Bill Haley's worldwide hit 'Rock Around the Clock' and the two had a profound effect on the youth of the UK in sartorial terms. So on the Saturday before my new job started I went to Peckham Rye Lane, which was full of rather flashy men's shops, and kitted myself out with a new outfit before having a fashionable 'DA' haircut. This particular style resulted in the back of your head looking like the rear of a duck. You've probably now worked out what DA stood for.

My new wardrobe consisted of a full drape, powder blue, black-flecked sports jacket which reached down to about an inch above my knees. The trousers were absolutely skin-tight drainpipes in a shiny black material, so tight they almost cut off my blood circulation. The effect was completed by a rolled collar shirt and a Slim Jim tie. At the end of the drainpipe trousers pale blue socks ran into thick soled black "brothel creeper" shoes.

I took my purchases home very proudly and performed a fashion show for the family. Mum look shocked and Pat broke down into hysterical laughter but Dad just nodded and said, 'You saved the money so you should be able to buy what you like.' It was not the first or last time that he demonstrated a level of understanding which I've tried to carry through to my dealings with my own sons. Obviously I looked ridiculous but needed him to allow me to make my own mistakes. At the time I was so proud of my new wardrobe that I would have slept in it, except that the top half was too floppy and the bottom too tight to allow for more than robot-like jerky movements.

Yet another Monday morning, when butterflies chased one another around in my stomach, arrived and I reported to Mr Wilcox on the first floor. He lifted one eyebrow as far as it would go at my appearance but again allowed me to enjoy my fashion peccadilloes without saying anything negative. I suspect that both Dad and he knew that my affection for this outrageous look would pass and some sense of normalcy would return pretty quickly. In fact, it happened sooner than any of us thought possible. On the Wednesday of my first week as I was bending down to complete my first round of filing in giant grey-fronted cabinets there, was a sound like a rifle shot and the black shiny drainpipes split from waistband to crutch. I thanked God for the full drape pale blue sports jacket which hid both my bottom and embarrassment for the rest of the day. The only part of the brave new fashion statement which survived for more than ten days was the Brylcreem-covered DA hairstyle.

Around six of us worked in a pretty large general office. The Department Manager, Charles Cruttenden, an imposing man of some 6'4" in height had his own office in the corner. He ruled the Department rather imperiously and had on his desk a buzzer. Each of us had our own code and mine was three dots followed by a dash. When we heard our message we rushed to be of service. One of my tasks was to serve him morning coffee and one morning early in my employment I tripped on his meagre piece of carpet and to my horror saw the cup of scalding hot coffee head towards

4 Babmaes Street,
London, SW1 6HD

32 Aybrook Street,
London, W1M 3JL

191 Old Marylebone Road,
London, NW1 5DW

151 Marylebone Road,
London, NW1 5QE

Four offices in 36 years – all of them have been very lucky for us.

Remember when agencies used to have philosophies?

When individuals dug deep into their past and said "This is what I believe in?"

Remember how agencies grew up around such disciplines? How the men who gave their names to an agency also gave new insights to the business?

Men like Raymond Rubicam, Leo Burnett, Bill Bernbach and David Ogilvy.

Today, it's unfashionable to have a philosophy. "Our philosophy is that we have no philosophy." How often have you heard that said?

Yet how can you start an advertising agency without a philosophy?

What is it that makes a group of people jump out of safe, secure jobs if it isn't the desire to make their own little mark on the pages of advertising history?

THE SILLY SEASON.

At this agency we have a philosophy and it's born out of our concern with much of the advertising we see around us.

The correct marketing credo seems to go something like this.

"Most products are pretty much the same these days. The consumer is now much more sophisticated and cynical. We live in a world conditioned by television, where people react to impressions and images more readily than to information."

In this environment it's become fashionable to talk about the need for advertising to "add value" to the product.

People are encouraged to "like" a product because advertisers are not sure they can make them "want" it any more. If they say anything too directly, the cynical, sophisticated audience will turn off. What everyone needs, it seems, is the customer's goodwill.

So the argument runs.

It's a seductive platform, because the planks that go to create it are in themselves sound.

But it's led, we believe, to a basic and dangerous misunderstanding and a whole raft of silly, undernourished advertising.

Of course, advertisers need the goodwill of the consumer, but we delude ourselves if we believe goodwill alone can sustain a brand.

It can't

When we ignore this fact we do at our peril. We run ads to be liked rather than to sell. We become complacent. We neglect product improvements and competitive activity. We hide behind the "entertainment" value of our commercials. We go for the popularity stakes while the real stakes are so much higher.

NEW CONSUMERS DON'T HAVE OLD LOYALTIES.

Those products that have the goodwill of the consumer do not have it by divine right.

If the advertiser fails to give the consumer continued reasons to buy (both in his advertising and in his product) then the goodwill will soon evaporate along with the sales.

Most of the brands that have remained at the top over the past twenty years have had three things in common.

They have consistently improved their product.

They have kept their customers informed of such changes.

They have maintained a competitive share of voice.

Nobody can trade on goodwill for long. Not even Cadbury's Dairy Milk chocolate. (Welcome back glass-and-a-half of milk).

Yet week after week we see costly new advertising campaigns of quite stunning emptiness.

Advertisements that are downright silly.

Radio commercials that play games.

Television spots that are parodies of movies and situation-comedies. (Not to mention salesmanship.)

If today's consumers are so smart, why are we treating them like morons?

THE DEFEATIST CLIENT.

Sadly, we've noticed that more and more clients are taking this attitude too. The factory visit isn't demanded anymore. Briefs start out with an admission that there's nothing to be said about the product. Everyone is looking for the "Big Idea"– the magic show business/advertising gimmick.

Hallelujah!

Claude Hopkins, Bill Bernbach and David Ogilvy all produced advertising with ideas.

They built bridges between products and users, but beneath the wit charm and friendliness of their ads were always solid foundations.

The ads said something meaningful; something that gave a long term value to the product or the client.

Has the world really changed that much? Were there no "me-too" products in the thirties, fifties and sixties? Or is this lack of faith in substance merely a premature defeatism? A kind of intellectual laziness?

We believe it is.

BACK TO BASICS.

Information isn't redundant today. It just takes more craft to make it interesting. It takes people who are still excited by ads. People who won't let an ad go through the door if it doesn't contain a nourishing idea.

We have such people.

At Abbott Mead Davies and Vickers we'll help you define what advertising can do for your product. We'll help you position it with a long term strategic base. Then we'll try and say what has to be said like it's never been said before. (That's the real "added value.")

Of course, we don't believe in dull advertising. There's no virtue in being right if you're invisible.

But come what may, we're not going to write flab. We're not going to write whimsy. We're not going to write thin advertising.

BRANDS IN DANGER?

We've prepared a list of endangered brands. Brands that have stopped giving the consumer a reason to buy. Brands that, we believe, are living dangerously on historic loyalties.

Maybe one of your brands is on that list. Maybe you're worried about it too.

Come and see us. Soon.

We've got a lot of energy, a lot of ideas and a lot to prove.

And according to another management philosophy, that's always a good time to do business.

Nobody should start an advertising agency without giving it a lot of thought.

Abbott, Mead, Davies and Vickers. 19 Bruton Place London W1 01-493-5042.

This appeared in Campaign in December 1977. Take time to read David's copy – it's brilliant and could run today.

Watch out Colletts, we're only £34 million behind you.

Abbott, Mead, Davies & Vickers Ltd. 19 Bruton Place, London W1. 01-493 5042

How old are Abbott, Mead and Vickers?

In recent articles about the new agencies we've been surprised, flattered and bemused to find ourselves grouped with agencies like BMP, as a kind of benchmark for the youngsters.

Surprised, because AMV itself is not yet five years old. (Watch this space for our birthday announcement.)

Flattered, because it's always nice to be grouped with good creative agencies like BMP and TBWA.

But bemused because though we're definitely established we're far from being establishment.

We have six creative people on our board who still work at the drawing board. Our media department is still as aggressive and inventive as the day we started the agency back in 1977.

And our account men and planners still believe the business is all about good ads.

So please, please, don't put years on us before our time.

Or one of us at least will have to go back to the Grecian 2000.

Abbott Mead Vickers/SMS Ltd., 35 Ryknield Street, London WC1H 7JE. Telephone 01-486 6122. Telex 8817.

We believed in advertising. In all, we bought about 12 double page spreads in Campaign and a 96 sheet poster on the Brompton Road.

J.R. Hartley became everybody's favourite author.

At Sainsbury's if we don't sell our mince in a day, we don't sell it.

The best mince is fresh mince.

So all our ground beef and mince beef has a sell-by date of just one day.

What we don't sell in a day comes out of the cabinet as a fresh supply goes in.

Does this mean we waste a lot of mince?

On the contrary.

It seems when people know you sell good lean mince at good keen prices, they can't wait to buy it.

Not even for a day. **Good food costs less at Sainsbury's.**

Guess what Sainsbury's new canned grapefruit tastes like?

In its own little way our new canned grapefruit is something of a milestone.

It's vacuum-packed. (As far as we know, the first on sale in Britain.)

The outcome is grapefruit that tastes uncannily like the fresh fruit.

But taste isn't the only advantage. With vacuum-packing, we're able to put much more

grapefruit into the can.

On average, 25% more fruit than with traditional canning methods.

You can buy our new 'flavour seal' grape-

fruit, unsweetened in pure juice or in a syrup.

Either way you get more flavour and more fruit.

Good food costs less at Sainsbury's.

Sainsbury's have a peach of an idea for Parma ham. But it isn't peach.

What is it?

Well, its taste has been described as a mixture of apricot and pineapple. Though many believe it better than either.

Originally from the East, it's been grown for at least 4,000 years.

John Fryer, a famous traveller in the 17th century, wrote of this fruit.

For taste, the nectarine, peach and apricot fall short.

When ripe, the flesh is juicy, golden and truly delicious – especially with Parma ham.

(It's the kind of starter that's bound

to start a conversation.)

But you can also use it in fruit salads or as a purée to add to ice cream.

Or if you like, in a mousse.

Mystery Mousse

1. Take three of our fruits and blend the flesh into a purée with the juice of 2 lemons (or limes) stirring in 2 oz. of caster sugar as you go.

2. Next, dissolve one envelope of gelatine in two tablespoons of hot water, cool, and add to the purée.

3. Finally, whisk up 2 egg whites and fold in with ¼ pint of whipped double cream.

Put the whole mousse in a dish and chill for at least 2 hours.

It couldn't be simpler or more refreshing.

Having whetted your appetite perhaps its only fair to satisfy your curiosity.

The fruit in question is the mango.

Available all year long at

Sainsbury's – the biggest greengrocer in the country.

And the bravest.

Good food costs less at Sainsbury's.

David Abbott and Ron Brown transformed
retail food advertising with this campaign.

Ian McShane

Kiri Te Kanawa

Catherine Zeta Jones

Beautifully written, painstakingly shot, this campaign by the master was the forerunner of many others.

"I never read The Economist."

On the edge of a conversation. One of the loneliest places on earth.

The Economist

It's lonely at the top, but at least there's something to read.

The Economist

As good as it gets.

"Frustrating"

"Bakers"

"Missing Trains, Missing You"

"Not Talking for Long"

The late Bob Hoskins with a selection from the
'It's good to talk' campaign.

This ad was voted D&AD best of all in 1984.

Chivas Regal is always twelve years old. Rarely thirteen.

Because I've known you all my life.

Because a red Rudge bicycle once made me the happiest boy on the street.

Because you let me play cricket on the lawn.

Because you used to dance in the kitchen with a tea-towel round your waist.

Because your cheque book was always busy on my behalf.

Because our house was always full of books and laughter.

Because of countless Saturday mornings you gave up to watch a small boy play rugby.

Because you never expected too much of me or let me get away with too little.

Because of all the nights you sat working at your desk while I lay sleeping in my bed.

Because you never embarrassed me by talking about the birds and the bees.

Because I know there's a faded newspaper clipping in your wallet about my scholarship.

Because you always made me polish the heels of my shoes as brightly as the toes.

Because you've remembered my birthday 38 times out of 38.

Because you still hug me when we meet.

Because you still buy my mother flowers.

Because you've more than your fair share of grey hairs and I know who helped put them there.

Because you're a marvellous grandfather.

Because you made my wife feel one of the family.

Because you wanted to go to McDonalds the last time I bought you lunch.

Because you've always been there when I've needed you.

Because you let me make my own mistakes and never once said "I told you so."

Because you still pretend you only need glasses for reading.

Because I don't say thank you as often as I should.

Because it's Father's Day.

Because if you don't deserve Chivas Regal, who does?

The top ad won a top award while 'Father's Day' is one of the most famous drink ads ever.

AN 18 YEAR-OLD VOLVO AND TWO OF ITS CONTEMPORARIES.

IF THE WELDING ISN'T STRONG ENOUGH, THE CAR WILL FALL ON THE WRITER.

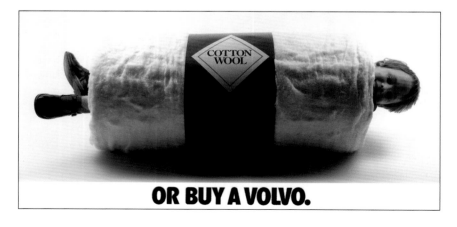

OR BUY A VOLVO.

Three of the very best pieces of work for Volvo.

Volvo Eggs

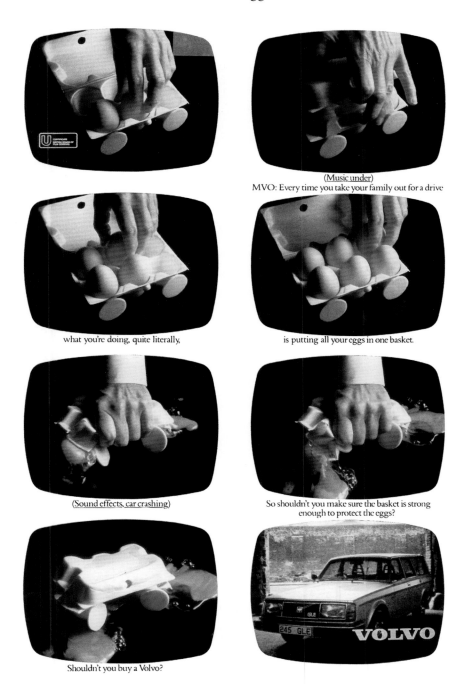

(Music under)
MVO: Every time you take your family out for a drive

what you're doing, quite literally,

is putting all your eggs in one basket.

(Sound effects, car crashing)

So shouldn't you make sure the basket is strong
enough to protect the eggs?

Shouldn't you buy a Volvo?

This was a test commercial David wrote to persuade Volvo to use
TV advertising. I think it cost £500!

Guinness Swim Black

This is such a great commercial produced by
Tom Carty and Walter Campbell.

Guinness Surfer

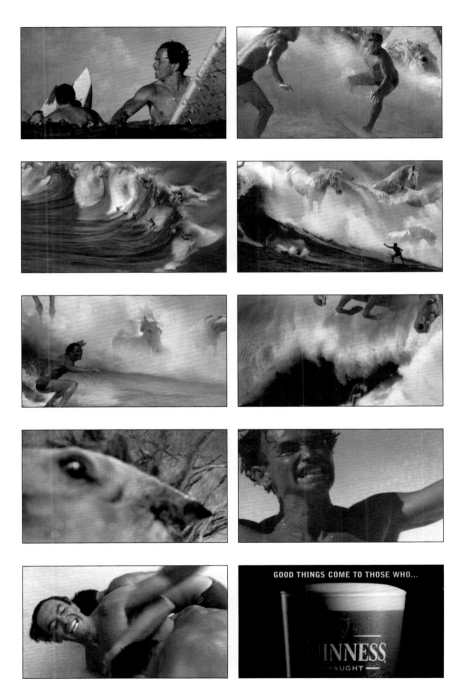

Voted best ad of all time on Channel 4 / Sunday Times
100 Greatest TV Ads.

David Abbott 1938-2014

his shirt front and MCC tie. Despite him probably having second-degree burns he was very gracious. Like Don Draper in *Mad Men* he always carried a clean shirt in the drawer of his desk. So far as I can remember that was his only similarity to the character from the television series. I settled in quickly to my new role. I had resolved to be as nice as I could be to everyone at all times and to work as hard as I could.

Very soon after I joined the Department the agency moved lock stock and barrel to a brand new building, 129 Kingsway. It was on the corner of High Holborn and was positively luxurious after the religious mausoleum that was Kingsway Hall. Around this time the Department was completely reorganised. Messrs Cruttenden and Wilcox were both despatched to one or other of the many outposts of the Empire in which Bensons were represented. At around this time as well, I struck up a relationship with a flame-haired beauty who happened to be my boss. She handled overseas media in the Department and I had to make sure that the rate cards for thousands of indigenous newspapers were kept up-to-date.

She lived in Canonbury, a fashionable enclave north of the Angel Islington and south of Highbury Corner. Like all of us she lived with her parents so again privacy was at a premium. Once a week we would go to the movies but most times we sat in her sitting room at the end of a very long dark corridor, watching television and making idle chat. If the trip from Kingsway to Canonbury was relatively arduous the trip home at the end of the evening was even worse. All in, the journey was about two-and-a-half hours. Most evenings when I was at her flat before I made the long trip home she would see me to the door 30 feet away from her parents and allow me to kiss her chastely on one cheek only so the journey home was not only desperately long but also dominated by feelings of frustration.

She was a newly converted Catholic and struggled with all the tensions that came from being a young woman with normal physical yearnings who was totally constrained by the strict codes of behaviour that both the church and society in those imposed in those days. We went out for a while but the relationship was not progressing to my satisfaction, by which I mean no physical contact was on offer. To my astonishment my dissatisfaction was exceeded by hers and just before Christmas one year she told me that we could no longer see one another for that reason. But she still gave me my Christmas present which was the very latest Sinatra album, *Songs for Only the Lonely*. Unnecessarily brutal at the time, I thought, but life had to go on. We remained really good friends for a few years afterwards and I was an usher at her wedding but once again I was without a girlfriend.

Benson's new premises were on the sixth floor. A man called George Knight who had just stopped being a colonel in the army was recruited to run the department. As it became increasingly impossible for Britain to ignore the rest of the world, our status in the company increased dramatically. A new name was invented, Bensons Overseas Marketing and Advertising Service – BOMAS for short. My status changed too because I finished my stint as office boy and was made a junior executive. There I was joined by two university graduates, Richard Nixon and Nick Turnbull. We rapidly became a happy band of brothers helped by the wonderful Jennie Armstrong, for many years the wife of Peter Mayle of *A Year in Provence* fame, who was PA to the four of us.

It seemed appropriate that, given my immediate career path was going to involve overseas markets, I should experience the delights of Europe first hand, and so in the early 60s I took my first holiday abroad. Prices of air travel had just come down as operators looked for volume in the mass market. I and a posse of my chums from Peckham decided we would go to the fashionable resort of Benidorm on the lower east coast of Spain. Originally a fishing village on one of the great beaches of Europe, it had been developed unbelievably hastily with high-rise hotels and British fish and chip shops. We went in the very early days when it still had a lot of its fishing village charm, which was somewhat disturbed by the Guardia Civil who would, fully armed, patrol the beach to make sure that no women were offending public decency by sunbathing topless. We had flown to Alicante and then had a four or five hour coach trip to the resort. Sadly I'd never liked the taste of beer – its gassy bitterness has never been that attractive to me. So on the last night of our holiday, which until then had mainly been spent patrolling the beach fruitlessly looking for dinner dates for the evening, we went on a pub crawl during which my chums managed to consume eight litres of beer each. They insisted that even though I didn't like beer I should keep pace with them and get involved with the spirit of the occasion by drinking the firewater that was Fundador Spanish cognac (the rumour was it could also be used as lighter fuel or paint stripper.) Having consumed eight small brandy balloons full of this extremely toxic beverage, I was more ill that night than ever before. I suspect I probably had borderline alcoholic poisoning, but I know for certain that it was at least two weeks before I felt vaguely human again. It's probably why I've never drunk to that level of excess again.

CHAPTER 5

1959

Around that time I decided that regretfully the *Cockney accent had to go.* Advertising in those days was full of Bertie Wooster-type young gentleman. Most of them had degrees in the arts from Oxford or Cambridge and there were quite a few double-barrelled semi-aristocrats floating around the floors. It was indeed a 'hello Rodney, hello Charles' environment and my Cockney patois was increasingly out of place. So I set about doing a Professor Higgins on myself. It was difficult at first, particularly when I got home in the evenings when I was surrounded by the distinctive accents of south London.

I embarked on a period in my professional and personal life which became increasingly rewarding. The atmosphere in our department with Richard, Nick and particularly Jennie Armstrong was wonderful. The guys were of course graduates and ex-public school boys, however my degree in street wisdom and my training as an office boy and despatch boy stood me in good stead. I knew how the company worked, I knew people on every floor, especially the secretaries (the most important people to be on good terms with) and how it all ran. At the same time it was strange having my own desk and more than a modicum of authority, especially as I was 18 and my colleagues were university graduates and three or four years older than me.

I had my own accounts to handle, the big one of which was Vickers-Armstrong Tractors Ltd. It was on this piece of business that the first of my many early mishaps in my career took place. We used to buy colour double-page spreads in all of the world's major business magazines to extol the virtues of these giant tractors. It was subsequently discovered that Vickers lost a considerable amount of money on every one of these monsters they sold, but that only came as a useful piece of information which, at the 11th hour, prevented them from going into bankruptcy – victims of our good advertising and their own success in selling lots of these gleaming pieces of machinery.

Alongside the tractors they had a division called Onions Harvesting Equipment, Onions being the surname of the business's original founder rather than a vegetable reference. The first of my many subsequent problems having these ads translated into Spanish came when a worldwide magazine called *Vision* took an innocent phrase in the copy which read, 'Vickers-Armstrong Tractors and Onions Equipment For Harvesting' and translated it as 'Vickers-Armstrong Tractors and Equipment for Harvesting Onions'. This ad appeared throughout the Spanish-speaking world and it was one of the first times that my burgeoning career in advertising nearly came to an abrupt halt. Most of the problems that I encountered were to do with the translation of English copy into foreign languages. Unlike my educated colleagues, I had no grasp of any other language. Indeed, before my Cockney accent finally went the way of all flesh, it could have been argued that English was slightly alien to me as well.

Throughout my illustrious career as an office boy I ran errands for the senior people in the department as part of my duties. Acquiring commodities such as coffee, tea and cigarettes was an integral part of the life of an office boy. Around this time, inspired by George Knight, I took up smoking, a nasty little habit that has stayed with me for the rest of my life. In those days, however, pre-the American Health Department warnings and the *Reader's Digest* campaign, cigarettes were stylish and chic. Indeed at that stage Lucky Strike, one of the most popular American brands, was running a health centric advertising campaign with the headline, 'Smoke Luckies instead of eating sweets that make you fat'. The prospect of being both stylish like Humphrey Bogart (we all used to practice inhaling and exhaling our cigarettes in front of the mirror) and slim meant I didn't hesitate to swap Nelson cigarettes for calorie-filled vanilla fudge.

Packs of 10 cigarettes were the affordable purchase in those days and on an early day in my life as an executive I discovered I'd run out. The obvious thing to do next was to ask the newly appointed office boy to go out and get me some more. It was his job, after all. But I deliberated over this for some time before sending him out. The reason for my hesitation was that the new office boy might have been a couple of years younger than me but he had come to Benson's straight from Dulwich College and in every sense had an upbringing superior to my own. Coupled with that he was six foot four, all muscle and came from a very famous rowing family. In fact he went on to win either a silver or bronze medal at the Melbourne Olympics. He could have snapped any of my major bones with a tweak of his enormously large hands. However he recognised the pecking order in those days and without a hint of irritation came back with ten Nelson cigarettes in the pale blue pack. He went on to have a very successful career in advertising, becoming chief executive of one of Britain's biggest agencies some years later.

George Knight, having spent many years in the military, before embarking on a new career in advertising, believed in deploying his forces proactively. He wanted to take a rather more professional approach to the way we advised our growing number of international clients and he believed that

Richard, Nick and I should become experts on various parts of the globe in order to make both our clients and our creative people more aware of the massive differences in the way that various parts of the world needed to be advertised to.

As a first step he apportioned different parts of the world to the three of us. Richard got the Americas, Nick got Europe and I was given Russia and China (the rest of Asia would follow once I'd got up to speed with the vagaries of the Communist states that I'd been assigned). At this time, the world was in the middle of the Cold War. Nuclear paranoia was at its height and I remember at roughly that time seeing Gregory Peck in a film called *On the Beach*, from Neville Shute's book of the same name. The film followed the adventures of a submarine which had been submerged while nuclear holocaust went on above the waves. I remember leaving the cinema weak-kneed and fearful. I, along with the rest of the audience, had a horrible premonition that devastation wrought by the very two regions that I've been tasked with becoming expert in was just around the corner.

As for my research into my new territories, you must remember that this was way in advance of the internet age and I couldn't just sit in front of a monitor and drink in all the knowledge that flashed up at warp speed, which meant gathering information proved difficult. I, of course, used the agency's press cuttings service to deliver me scraps of paper on a weekly basis with all the articles published about the countries but it wasn't enough to satisfy George's lust for expertise. I made more inquiries and for China I discovered that there was a publication available to Westerners called Peking Weekly. As this was a totally Government-controlled medium the information gleaned from its pages was tainted, to say the least. It was only many years later that I suddenly thought that anybody applying in the UK for a subscription to this rather colourful piece of propaganda from the land of flying daggers will almost certainly have been flagged up to MI5 or MI6 or maybe even both. I've often thought, under the Freedom of Information Act, I should go back and check whether I'm on some list of dangerous subversives which might have affected my ability to get a mortgage all those years ago.

As far as Russia was concerned there was no such publication available. Just as well, probably, because if *Moscow Monthly* was plopping through my letterbox at the same time as *Peking Weekly*, George Smiley and his boys would have found me almost irresistible. After some deliberation I decided that, to use George's expression, a frontal assault was required, so I rang the Russian Embassy and asked to speak to the commercial attaché. To my astonishment I was put through to a man called Ivanov. I explained the task that I been given and asked if it was possible to have a meeting to explore commercial opportunities for some of our clients in Russia. He agreed to meet with me and suggested that we had lunch. I thought that this was a great, if somewhat terrifying, proposition. Apart from a youthful battle with a rump steak at the Angus Steak House a few years before and my occasional foray into the Bensons canteen (a much more affordable catering operation than that enjoyed by J Walter Thompson in Berkeley Square) I had no experience whatsoever of the mysteries of eating out.

Mr Ivanov suggested that we should meet at the Strand Palace Hotel. Opposite the Savoy Hotel in one of London's busiest thoroughfares, I knew where it was because the Strand ran north of Fleet Street where I spent many hours delivering all sorts of material in my early days at Bensons. I arrived at the appointed time to meet with Mr Ivanov to discover, to my surprise, that he was accompanied by a very large gentleman who said very little but had gold front teeth. He could easily have been the prototype for all those Cold War villains that made Ian Fleming such a lot of money later.

We went into the dining room and sat down at a table laden with cutlery and I had no idea what to do with most of it. A rising sense of panic gripped me. But I thought quickly and decided the way to handle such a situation was to the order the starter that Mr Ivanov's minder had gone for, follow Ivanov's choice of main course and watch the way each of them attacked the food with the appropriate piece of cutlery before tucking in myself. This worked very well and my meal of prawn cocktail and steak passed without incident. I was especially grateful to Mr KGB for this, because I would never have attacked the prawn cocktail with a spoon unless aping him.

Feeling relaxed, I asked my guests if they'd like dessert as they had already demonstrated pretty healthy appetites and I wasn't surprised when they both said yes. As was customary in restaurants in those days, as I subsequently discovered, a dessert trolley arrived with all sorts of sweet exotica on display.

Amazingly, because we were in September or maybe even October, there was a bowl of strawberries on the trolley. For those of you under fifty this would not cause any surprise because these days out-of-season fruit is flown into our supermarkets from all over the world so the seasons in this country barely matter at all. But this was not the case in the late 1950s. I thought it was time to show a delicacy of taste and I ordered just strawberries while my newly acquired Russian chums tucked into sherry trifle and chocolate cake (Black Forest Gateau, to be precise). The desert orders arrived. My strawberries looked very inviting laid out on a dazzling white plate. Even I managed to work out that the desert spoon and fork – the only remaining cutlery on the table – were the implements of choice for this most English of dishes. I picked up my spoon to attack the strawberries when disconcertingly the waiter put down in front of me a silver bowl with liquid and slice of lemon inside. I was transfixed, were you supposed to drink the liquid, float the strawberries in it to gently wash them or ignore it completely? It was, of course, a finger bowl but these were not plentiful in the dining rooms of Peckham. Indeed I'd never seen one before in my life. Terrified of making a fool of myself, I left the plate of strawberries uneaten in front of me and murmured to the waiter that my eyes were bigger than my stomach.

I explained my discomfort to Richard and Nick when I got back to the office they fell about laughing but then gently explained the role of said silver bowl. I learned quickly, which was just as well, because in my role on Vickers Armstrong Tractors I was courted by highly paid representatives from *Time* and *Newsweek* magazines. My gastronomic education was completed by a rather elegant man called Michael Earleigh, the man from *Time* magazine and Nigel Smith from *Newsweek*, another ex-military man with a goatee beard that he constantly played with. They were both told that they should take clients out to lunch every day. Indeed they were admonished if a blank appeared in their diaries.

They only went to the finest restaurants and Nigel in particular took me under his wing. We had many meals at Simpsons in the Strand – a meat eater's paradise with carving trolleys with huge sides of beef, pork and lamb sitting below the silver dome of the mobile meat dispenser. Nigel taught me that it was absolutely essential that the carver should be tipped separately from the rest of the waiting staff. They were great days and the meal served in the middle of the day, which in working-class South London was called dinner, became a series of food adventures.

Over the years I've entertained clients often. Like me, a few of them demonstrated a real lack of knowledge of the art of fine dining. I remember two clients in particular, one of whom ordered prawns and when they arrived fully clothed, so to speak, attempted to remove them from their shells with a knife and fork. I gently explained that I found that a difficult process and always used my fingers. I demonstrated and at the end of the procedure I grandly washed my hands in the newly discovered finger bowl and used another recent discovery, the napkin, to dry them. The other poor client ran into a much more intransigent problem. Having ordered artichoke, which obviously he had never had before, he proceeded to tear off a whole leaf and started to chomp on it. Those of you familiar with this rather prehistoric-looking vegetable will know that the leaves do not melt in the mouth, to say the least. And so we sat there in a slightly uncomfortable silence for a few minutes while I worked out a way of telling him that the delicate tips of the leaves were the only bit that could be consumed. It was an 'emperor's new clothes' moment and could have been truly awkward but we moved on quickly and became good friends. Much later we laughed at that incident while trying to crack lobster claws with the absurdly difficult to use instruments restaurants supply with them.

Michael and Nigel were very patient in guiding me through restaurant rituals. Eating asparagus with your fingers, twirling spaghetti onto a fork so that you could eat it and breaking bread rather than slicing it into small pieces with a knife were just a few of the many exercises that they instructed me on. They also spent time teaching me about wine. Whenever I hear Michael McIntyre's sketch about wine in restaurants I laugh at how perceptive it really is. It's bizarre that a wine waiter who had spent many years training to be a sommelier would pour a little wine into a glass and ask you whether you thought it was fit to drink. As McIntyre astutely points out, for the majority of us red or white, perhaps burgundy or claret, is the limit of our knowledge. The only thing that we're really qualified to judge is the prices on the right-hand side of the wine list. The delicacy of the distinction between a Chateau Latour and a Petrus is infinitely less significant than their capital costs.

In those years the advertising world was very much like what you see on 'Mad Men'. The office was constantly full of smoke, there was a drinks cabinet in every office and very few women around who were anything other than secretaries. Like Peggy in the series and Dorothy L. Sayers, there was the occasional female copywriter but they were rare.

My favourite person in the whole department was Jennie Armstrong. It had nothing to do with her enormous blue eyes, sweet disposition and body to die for. Very early on in our relationship I asked her out and she responded by telling me that she would like to go out with me but she was madly in love with Richard Nixon, one of the other languid executives in our department who shared with his famous namesake an ever-present five o'clock shadow. I thought he could probably have grown a luxuriant beard in about 36 hours. Jennie's reply was a bit of a setback as I thought she was a goddess (although tall she was wonderfully feminine and really, really nice). But the story ended happily because instead of having a short-term love affair with Jennie we became soul mates. She went on to a very successful career in television commercial production, at one stage having Alan Parker and Adrian Lyne on her books as directors, both of whom went on to be enormously successful Hollywood feature film directors.

Both Jennie's parents had died when she was young and she had a very powerful sister called Patsy who still lived in the Midlands close to Stratford-upon-Avon where they grew up. Jennie lived in a flat in a part of the world both which was very stylish then and now, just off Harley Street. There were a multitude of beautiful women sharing the flat, all of whom were close to my definition of a dream woman. I got nowhere with any of them but became very close to some of them, especially the matriarch of the apartment Shirley Tufnell-Barrett and Lindsay Granger, the daughter of two very famous film stars Stewart Granger and Elspeth March. Maybe an interesting aside is that Granger's real name was James Stewart. Unfortunately another Mr Stewart had already claimed star status under that moniker so a name change was vital.

Shirley TB worked for a very famous fashion house in those days. Pre-political correctness it was called Sambo Fashions (yes, honestly) and it had a huge sub-brand called Dolly Rockers which became a real symbol of the swinging 60s. Jennie and I would often meet with Shirley at the Sambo Fashions headquarters in Hanover Square. The showrooms were always full of influential buyers from giant retail stores. The most important customer in those days was a lady called Jackie Rose who was the head buyer from Richard Shops and could make or break a fashion house based on her order for any one collection. For a boy from Peckham in his early twenties, it was sheer heaven. The house models (Cynthia and June) were both extraordinary pretty and nice, particularly Cynthia who lived in Acton with her antique dealer husband Mike, a member of the very influential in antiques Crowther family.

The matriarch of Sambo Fashions was a fearsome lady with a heart of gold called Renee Sherman (née Shaw) who owned one of Britain's most successful fashion retail outlets in Sutton, eponymously named. Her partner was a wonderful man called Sam. An immensely revered and respected man in the rag trade at that time he was effortlessly elegant, permanently tanned (from winter holidays at Sandy Lane in Barbados and summer stays at the Carlton in Cannes) and wonderfully approachable. He drank a bottle of Dewars whisky a day diluted with an Italian fizzy water called Apollinaris decades before bottled water became de rigueur.

He had one son Simon and an older stepson called David. Both had led very privileged lives – educated at expensive public schools always elegantly dressed and again tanned from weeks spent in the exotic places I've referred to earlier. They both became really close friends of mine and had a huge role to play in my formative years. Fifteen years later Simon went to America, married a California lady and started his own sportswear business. Tragically he died from an aneurysm at the age of 35 while playing squash. A picture of Simon and me still sits in a prominent place in my study today.

In turn I met Tony Charles, Gerald Bernard and Jimmy Rhodes, all Crown Princes in rag trade Royal families. All swarthily handsome, impeccably turned out and not short of the folding stuff. They initiated me in the ways of rich young men, taking me to all sorts of "in" discos where I demonstrated once again that my father's ability on the dance floor had not been passed down. While they glided effortlessly, performing dances like the Twist or the Madison, I made polite chat to the coterie of girls who formed their entourage.

The whole gang of us used to get together every Friday night at a Hungarian restaurant just off Baker Street called the Duna Cafe. I can still remember the taste of the pork fillets, large chunks of succulent meat surrounded by the very best mini baked potatoes and a spectacular mushroom sauce, all for about 45p in new money – those were the days.

At one evening gathering in 1963, when there were about ten of us carrying out our weekly review of the world, we sat in stunned silence at the news of JFK's assassination. He was a hero figure of ours – spectacularly easy to relate to and impossible not to admire. The memory of that moment on that evening is unbelievably vivid and seemed to all of us to be a massively tragic event which we took personally.

CHAPTER 6

1961

At SH Benson my role changed over the years. I spent some time in each of the departments of the agency, ranging from sales promotion through direct marketing and television production but I finally found a home in research and marketing. This was an early attempt to carry out some of the things that planning departments did later in life after they were invented by Stephen King at JWT and Stanley Pollitt at BMP. I remember one particular project the group of us were put on. At that stage we had a client who produced a product called Delrosa Rosehip Syrup. Today I can't remember the exact use for this long–deceased medicine but as a by-product in manufacture a lot of rosehip seeds were used. We were asked to find a use for the discarded seeds after they had given their life for the creation of the elixir and we came up with a new budgerigar feed. A nice idea but I don't believe any bird food was ever manufactured.

The years that I'd spent in the overseas department didn't lead to a longed for posting in one of the more exotic outposts of the huge Benson Empire. These were still the days of the Raj and the people who made it to the colonies were typically Old Etonian sherry drinkers, more than one of whom passed out consuming this deceptively strong stuff in the Benson bar. Instead it was decided that I should broaden my experience and be treated like a graduate trainee – five or six of whom were appointed every year. So with my degree in street wisdom I joined the other graduates with real degrees. One such new recruit was Adrian Vickers. The son of a doctor from Liverpool, he had an exemplary background and had served in Bavaria in military intelligence, an experience he always spoke about in rather hushed tones. He had a good degree in law from Merton College, Oxford and was much less pompous and self-satisfied than the normal Benson chaps. Adrian joined me in the research and marketing department and early on we were given the task of driving up to the Midlands on behalf of our then client Bernard Matthews Turkeys. Mr Bootifull had bred a small turkey with a very broad breast – no, not Barbara Windsor. His thinking behind this piece of genetic engineering was that he could compete with chickens as a much more frequent meal on the nation's tables. The turkeys who had no choice but to vote for Christmas, I suspect, would have welcomed this life extension.

We were to run an advertising campaign in a test area around Birmingham and its environs just before Easter to see if we could intrigue the public into changing their eating habits for Easter Sunday lunch. So a month before the bank holiday, armed with a list of independent butchers and poulterers, Adrian and I set off in the company Wolseley – a car made by one of Benson's clients, British Leyland – to do our best.

Well, in those days it wasn't called the Black Country for nothing. Two young men from London trying to break the habits of a lifetime for the inhabitants of Wolverhampton did not get a great reception. At least half the turkeys set aside for that particular project spent yet another year in the deep freezers of the Matthews operation in Norfolk. The butchers we met simply weren't interested in talking to a couple of smartly-dressed kids doing market research. In fact we managed to irritate a good number of them as our survey was roundly rejected.

As was Benson's way, we were always encouraged to stay in good hotels because we were ambassadors of one of Britain's biggest advertising agencies. After a weary day of getting nowhere in Coventry (I think one butcher in ten expressed mild interest in the small turkey concept) we decamped in the Leofric Hotel. Virtually brand new, this was four-star luxury. After checking in and having a shower we met in the restaurant. Like a lot of middle-class Oxbridge graduates in those days Adrian believed he was a true socialist. Tucking into Scampi Leofric, the most expensive thing on the menu, Adrian talked enthusiastically about the unfairness of modern society and how wealth should be spread around more liberally and fairly. I found more than a hint of hypocrisy in all this as following the scampi came Baked Alaska. I guess Adrian got his comeuppance because in the middle of night I had a call from Reception saying he'd been violently ill from food poisoning and they'd called a doctor. He recovered quite quickly and messages from the red flag were absent for the rest of the trip. I had made a lifelong friend, a future partner and godfather to my youngest son.

Bensons like all advertising agencies in those days had a licence to print money in the form of the commission system which was operated in conjunction with media owners. It was a very simple system. If somebody outside this quasi-cartel wanted to buy £100 worth of media space or time it cost them £100. Agencies, however, working on a 15% commission under their agreements with both the Independent television contractors and the Newspaper and Periodical Association, took 15% commission on any bookings made through them. So it was pretty simple: we paid £85 and the client was charged £100. Without us the client would have had to pay that amount anyway and so the argument was that our services were costing him nothing.

In addition that 15% agencies made, all production charges from outside suppliers involved in the making of the advertisement would be marked up by 17.65%.

All that meant advertising agencies were immensely profitable. Their management had problems in trying to work out what to do with all the money that was flooding into the coffers. In Benson's case the rather remote board lavished money on buying three stores around the country. The premise was that in order to understand our clients' business and his consumers we should own a small self-service store in Brighton, an early supermarket in Shenfield in Essex and a village store in Meriden in the Midlands. All of us young lads in the marketing Department spent time working in one or other of these retail outlets. These were the early days of self-service and, in keeping with me often drawing the short straw, I was dispatched to the village store in Meridien to stand in for the manager while he was on holiday. With a white coat on I spent my time delivering the groceries in the Centre of England stores van and stacking the shelves in the early evenings with the help of an enthusiastic couple of girls who believed that anyone from London was James Bond. One of my jobs during the two weeks I was in charge was to get rid of some damaged stock which was mostly cans with either small dents or torn labels. Jennie Armstrong's sister lived only a few miles away and after a few of my visits their larder resembled a nuclear shelter's emergency supply.

Benson's other great expenditure was buying the freehold of its building and producing a lavish bar on the directors' floor for their sole use. The board were godlike figures who were never around after lunch as they had decamped to their personal bar for the rest of their day after their full meal. They were rarely seen on any of the working floors and I assume that they maintained top-level contact with the agency's biggest clients but to us mere mortals there was no real indication of this. They were almost deified. Indeed, if you were in a relatively full lift on the ground floor of 129 and the Chairman approached everybody had to leave the lift in order to him to travel up in splendid isolation. It was rumoured that on the short walk from his apartment in Russell Square to the office he did the Times crossword in his head before heading up to the executive floor.

Benson's were responsible for many accounts in those days. A major client was Wills of Bristol. They were manufacturers of cigarettes, the most significant brand of which was Woodbines, the cheapest cigarette you could buy. Unfiltered it was like smoking ground glass. Indeed, rumour has it that new products were researched on the shop floor at their giant Bristol factory which meant every product that was released was extremely strong, rich in tars and all the other toxins that were latterly proven to be deadly dangerous. Around this time Bensons launched a new product for Wills using the recently introduced filter. The brand was called Strand. The advertising campaign used commercials with very moody music featuring a Frank Sinatra lookalike actor drawing heavily on the cigarette. Dressed in a trench coat with the trilby pulled low over his eyes he spent thirty seconds looking moodily at the camera. There were no restrictions on cigarette advertising in those days and so clouds of smoke were everywhere.

The line used in the commercial was, 'You're never alone with a Strand' and the rationale was that you always had a friendly presence in your pocket when you carried a pack of Strand. But this massively backfired. The resulting message which developed like wildfire was that only lonely losers would need to think of twenty cigarettes as a friend. Coupled with the normal throat-burning qualities of any Wills cigarettes the product was doomed to failure and its demise was almost instant. Strand remains, though, a very famous (or perhaps that should be infamous) brand with that generation of smokers.

The problem us employees faced at Bensons was that if you were bad at your job nobody noticed but, frustratingly, if you were any good you didn't come to anybody's attention either. I thought I'd done a pretty decent job in the marketing department but it wasn't at the cutting edge of the agency. Because the creative process was not at the heart of everything the agency did, power resided with the account men, who controlled the agency's relationships with its clients. The role of account men can be neatly summed up as representatives of the agency to the client and representatives of the client to the agency. I had already spent the early part of my career working on accounts in the international department and decided that was the role that I enjoyed most. In a rather desultory way I started to think about my future and decided that I wanted to apply for a transfer back into account handling.

Around this time a couple of major clients fired the agency. This was a very nasty wake-up call to the board. After a root and branch review of all the resources they had at 129 Kingsway, they concluded that they had too many account men, some of whom should be culled together with a number of the ageing creative people. Having announced that I didn't want to be in the marketing department but wanted to be an account man, I was a classic and irresistible candidate for redundancy. There was a day of the long knives at 129 where for the first time in its history Benson's 'let people go'. I was one of the first, joined later in the day by a lady called Helen Bonington, the mother of the soon-to-be world-famous mountaineer Chris Bonington. I can't remember who got rid of me but I know that in Helen's case she was fired by the hawkish head of copy. She responded to the shock of hearing that her services were to be dispensed with by hitting him with her handbag.

CHAPTER 7

1964

I *was 23 years old and had been at Bensons for seven years.* By large they were very good. I'd made some great friends, got a very good grounding in a profession that I'd stumbled into by accident and had dispensed with my Cockney accent. Bensons were pretty generous in recognising my service to the cause and when I left I was given a cheque for £900 which was an absolute fortune in those days, worth around £15,000 today. I still lived at home so my outgoings were relatively few and after I'd come to terms with the trauma of getting the sack I felt very rich which meant I set about finding a new job in a positive, confident frame of mind.

One of Benson's foreign outposts was a group of agencies on the Indian subcontinent called D. J. Keymer and a decade before I joined a London office had been opened for DJK. Soon after that they brought in a man called David Williams who'd had a successful career at another small agency. David was a tall, elegant man who looked uncannily like a very big British film star of the time called Michael Denison. David only ever wore navy blue suits with a white shirt and white tie and every day he had a fresh red carnation in his buttonhole. I don't know how many blue suits or white ties he owned but there was never a mark to be seen on any of them. Like most bosses of that era he was slightly imperious but was always prepared to laugh, albeit rather nervously. Later he became an important influence on my life at a time of great need.

Within a week of leaving Benson's I had an interview at David Williams' offices in Bedford Row, only about 5 minutes as the crow flies from SH Benson itself. I was hired immediately as an account man working on Atora Suet, a very popular ingredient in cookery in those days which subsequently has fallen into obscurity because it is full of harmful saturated fats. Because I'd worked on Johnnie Walker in the past I was also given Lambs Navy Rum to look after. My account director was an avuncular man called Jimmy Kendrick. In fact his name was Tony but the agency had a curious rule that if you arrived with the same Christian name as somebody who was already employed you had to change it, so Tony became Jimmy. Fortunately there were no other Peters at the agency so I was spared the schizophrenic effects of operating under one Christian name during the day and another one in the evening.

I had a really good time at David's agency. Relatively early on we presented for and won the Myers Beds account. Run by three brothers with an ageing factory near Vauxhall Bridge, it was great business to work on. David had won the account himself and asked me to help him directly, thus bypassing the hierarchy. I don't believe this went down very well with Tony Kendrick but David's word was law. I vividly remember one career-threatening meeting we had with the Myers brothers at their offices. David had just acquired a new car – a deep blue second-hand Rolls-Royce. He was enormously proud of it and decided for this particular meeting he would dispense with his chauffeur and drive me down to the back streets of south London himself. During the journey he regaled me with stories of the greatness of Rolls-Royce playing back the famous Ogilvy line, 'The loudest thing in a Rolls-Royce is the ticking of the clock'. These were the days before electric windows and I was rather warm because of the combination of the car's efficient heating system and my own nerves which were in overdrive, so I asked David if I could open the passenger door window slightly. To my dismay as I wound down the window the handle came away my hand. Despite him saying it was of no consequence the look of horror on his face suggested otherwise.

I followed David rather shakily into the Myers offices. Anxious to make up for the sullying of his beloved car, I kept wishing the three brothers Happy Easter. As it was two days before Good Friday I was surprised to receive no response. I tried the greeting again only for it to be returned by rather blank and slightly irritated faces. So I gave up. It was only when we were returning to the agency in the crippled Rolls-Royce the David gently told me that they were Orthodox Jews and to wish them Happy Easter was not the most appropriate thing to do.

During that period I made many trips to Acton for meetings at the giant complex which housed the Atora brand group. They were big clients, buying colour pages in every issue of almost all the numerous women's magazines that were published in those days. In the main these ads featured recipes for classic suet dishes. One starred Spotted Dick, a dessert of overwhelming heaviness much favoured at public schools as healthy comfort food. We ran this particular advertisement in a number of issues until a frantic telephone call from the client suggested that something was wrong. In the list of ingredients outlined in the ad the sultanas, which were the spotted part of the recipe, had been omitted. So if the recipe was followed to the letter all that would come out of the steamer at the end of the process would be a large lump of white stuff. I was the man who presented the work to the client so it was quite clear that responsibility for this disaster rested with me and so my job was in jeopardy. In fact, I am certain that a more brutal regime would have fired me. But David had a soft spot for me and that helped enormously because after I had a sleepless night he told me that financial compensation to the client had been agreed and I would keep my job but that as a special treat I should take the marketing director out to dinner with his wife. There was a belief in advertising at that stage that any problem could be solved by a large meal coupled with some other entertainment. This was obviously also a great outcome for me from what could have been a disastrous situation.

The film of *My Fair Lady* had just been premiered at the Warner Brothers cinema in Leicester Square. I booked four of the best tickets and, with Jennie acting as my consort for the evening, I sat through the film entranced by Audrey Hepburn. The show ended and I told our guests where we were going for dinner at this relatively late hour. The marketing director immediately dismissed my suggested restaurant and asked where else we could go. I was at a loss for ideas so we cruised down the Kings Road and just before World's End found a nice little French restaurant where two things happened. First, after ordering a desert to follow two very large courses which were dispatched with unseemly haste, he looked slightly green and excused himself. While he was away his wife innocently explained that they rarely ate out and that as she wasn't such a great cook beans on toast were the staple diet in his household. He returned looking very pale and explained that he just thrown up in the loo. I said that under those circumstances I should cancel our desserts and go straight to coffee. He held up a restraining hand and said he would feel better in a minute and subsequently devoured an enormous plateful of a meringue concoction doused in fresh cream.

He was the same client who at a lunch a couple of months later asked for 'client privilege'. I'd never heard this expression before so he explained that this entailed the choosing of the wine. In no position to refuse, I allowed him this request and he chose an unbelievably expensive claret which he tried himself after downing a brimming plate of bouillabaisse. He pronounced it to be wonderful and with a taste to die for. As the bouillabaisse had been swimming in garlic there was absolutely no chance that his taste buds could have discerned anything at all, let alone the delicacy of the vintage claret.

That bottle of wine exemplified a hugely important lesson for an advertising man like me. The wine itself tasted good – it was obviously a cut above Mateus Rose – but the difference in taste was, in my opinion, far from enough to justify the enormous cost of the bottle. But it was the romance of the label – the vineyard where the wine originated – and what it represented as an item of luxury and aspiration which was as important as any of its physical characteristics, such as its flavour. The lesson is that the same principle applies to any product: selling something successfully is about far more than its physical characteristics.

I enjoyed my time at David's agency. Because of my relationship with him I was allowed to punch well above my rank in the hierarchy. Best of all I made some enduring friends – Peter Campbell, the son of a life peer who subsequently shared a flat with me, Judy Urwin, Kay Hughes and by far the most important of all, Susie Smith who was my first real girlfriend. During a long relationship Susie and I lived together in Marylebone and spent lots of holidays together. I'm fortunate enough still to count her as a close friend. We grew up together.

Amongst the many people that I'd met as a result of my friendship with the Sherman brothers were a really great couple, Pam and Ian Hayton. Ian, the son of a famous showbiz couple, was from Liverpool. Although he'd spent some time pursuing a reasonably successful career in advertising he was an entrepreneur at heart. When I first met him he and Pam, a beautiful

Australian model, lived in a flat above David Sherman in Paddington Street in Marylebone. He was selling small cigars through classified ads in the *Sunday Times* but then went on to start his own leasing company and moved to a wonderful house in Sunninghill in the golf triangle of Wentworth, Sunningdale and The Berkshire. Like the man who turned down the Beatles, Ian passed on the opportunity to start a European venture for a new American company called Holiday Inn. However, the motel bug had bitten him.

He came up with an idea of going round the country and talking to people who owned land adjacent to main highways. The proposition was that he would go to the landowners offer to build a 100-room motel on their property and have an operating contract to run the motel and split the profits on a formula basis. We spent many hours discussing and refining the plan. After one very long meeting following Sunday lunch in Sunninghill he asked me to join him in this venture. He outlined a very attractive proposal where I might even get a small share of the equity and a company car. I was really intrigued and really perked up when he suggested that the company car could be a Ford Cortina GT, the trendy car of the moment. Having spent a little time thinking about this career change of direction I agreed and resigned with some regret from David Williams. In my month's notice period, having had a leaving party and helped find my replacement, the day of joining Ian grew ever closer. At the same time I told my parents that I would be moving out finally from our flat in Peckham. I had been given the chance of renting, at a favourable rate, a nice but small mansion flat in St John's Wood. As working-class boys usually only left home to get married this caused my parents some distress but they understood.

This was happening at the time of the 1966 World Cup. My father hadn't been well for a while and was plagued with a series of very bad bouts of bronchitis, the legacy of years of smoking two packs of cigarettes a day. After one especially bad period the news from Guys Hospital was not good: his heart had been affected and he was ordered to rest. He seemed to be recovering and during what I thought were to be my last few days living at home I loved sitting with him watching England's tortuous progress through the early rounds of the football tournament. He was absolutely convinced that England would win the World Cup and got very excited when our team ground out victory after victory and progressed to the semi-final. We all went to bed the night before the match hugely excited about the following day.

At three o'clock in the morning my mother rushed in and said that dad was having a heart attack. I went into the bedroom and saw that he was lying ominously still. We telephoned for an ambulance and while we waited we attempted mouth-to-mouth resuscitation but to no avail. Before the ambulance arrived he was dead. The worst job I've ever had in my life was to drive to his elderly mother's at five o'clock in the morning to tell her that her baby boy was gone.

Dad's death was devastating. My mother had dedicated her life to looking after him and us and was lost. I was bereft at not having had the chance to tell him how much I loved him and regretted intensely that I had not been more inclusive with him in my life. Our relationship was a typical father/son one of the era. It existed in strict parameters with him unable to express his feelings of pride, interest or anything like that, because in south east London in the post-war years, that just wasn't what fathers did. He might have boasted about me in the pub but I would never know about it. I was stunned. It was 1966 and I was 26 years old.

As we tidied up his papers we found a small cutting in his wallet from *Advertisers Weekly* announcing my move to David Williams. This was the only thing that had been written about me up until that time.

CHAPTER 8

1966

Although *my father's company*, The West End and District Window Cleaning Company, had generated enough to support my parents there was no spare cash in his bank account. Indeed when we sorted out all his affairs there was just enough money to pay for his funeral. In the midst of the family grief I had to reappraise all my great plans. Having a job as speculative as the one Ian was suggesting was no longer an option. I could not run the risk of having no income for months on end until the motel operation took off. The government of the day had made it even more difficult to achieve our objectives by capping capital expenditure on buildings which meant, in the short term at least, Ian's business plan could not be achieved.

My move to St John's Wood, which I had looked forward to so much, was also now a non-starter. I had to stay at home to comfort my mother who was inconsolable for a while. Having helped David Williams find and train my replacement there was no way I could return to my old job so Mum and I carried on trying to keep the window cleaning business running. The two guys who had worked for the company were sympathetic but thought that the business should pass to them as there was no added value to come from us. We resisted this for as long as possible to ensure that some income to

Mum continued to supplement what she earned from her part-time job at Boots near Waterloo. She had worked there for many years and was horrified to find that she would be allowed the day of the funeral off on full pay but was expected back the following day otherwise her pay would be docked. I would imagine that such insensitivity would make Jesse Boot turn in his grave.

I frantically started writing to advertising agencies to get a job and as luck would have it I heard a rumour that the hottest agency at that time, Collett Dickinson and Pearce, had a vacancy in its account handling department. An old friend, David Puttnam, had been a star at the agency but was leaving to pursue a new career representing the very best photographers of the day. I managed to get an interview and I went through the process of meeting the whole of the top management of CDP. I appeared to be doing okay although I suspect that my slight desperation did shine through. I had my final meeting with Ronnie Dickinson and we had a very interesting discussion about advertising campaigns they were doing at that time. There was one campaign that was personality-led by a controversial figure of the time. When Dickinson asked me what I thought about that particular campaign I said I was surprised they were using a personality who was roundly disliked by what I estimated as half the population. He concurred with this assessment that said that the other half loved him to bits and that delivering that intensity of loyalty was worth alienating those who disliked him.

We came to the defining moment in the last meeting I was to have at CDP. Dickinson asked how much money I was looking for. I swallowed hard and said that I didn't think I could take a new job paying anything less than £3250 a year. Taken aback he told me that this particular post was going to be advertised at £4500 a year. It might have been the first time but it was certainly not the last time I undervalued my potential contribution to an employer. Two days later I got the letter which told me that although I was very close they didn't feel that I was absolutely right for the vacant post. I never managed to talk to Ronnie Dickinson subsequently but I'm sure the fact that I asked for so little money decided my fate.

I had always wanted to work for CDP, they did great creative ads and were absolutely on the crest of the wave. The other hot agency in town was a brand-new one called Kingsley Manton and Palmer. These three had broken away from two big agencies in London. Kingsley and Manton were account men who joined from a big American operation called Benton and Bowles. Brian Palmer, the creative man in the trio, was a member of the Young's brewing dynasty but was obviously a black sheep and had gone into advertising at an agency called Young and Rubicam. His claim to fame was that he had written the first commercial ever to be aired on the new medium, commercial television. It was for a toothpaste called Gibbs SR which showed the pack embedded in a block of ice. After some initial success the three of them had taken a floor in a building called Thorn House in St Martin's Lane literally across the road from the Ivy, years before it enjoyed a renaissance as a seriously fashionable restaurant.

I can't remember how I got an introduction for an interview or indeed if it was a response to one of the many cold letters that I'd started sending out in desperation but in any event, I got a letter from David Kingsley asking me to go for an interview in the late afternoon. I arrived at Thorn House and went up to the high floor that housed the agency. It was quite an avant-garde building with concrete stilts on four sides creating a double-height reception. It made that part of St Martin's Lane a wind trap and on particularly inclement days you had the impression that mini tornadoes were swirling round the base of the building. Thus I arrived at KMP's reception for my interview with hair that looked like Doc, the mad professor in the film *Back to the Future*.

The agency was an early adopter of the new fashion of open plan offices. Custom-built furniture and thick carpets accommodated the 40 or so staff on one side of the vast Partners' office with the 25 or so creative people settled in at the rear of the floor. Although open plan was much beloved by management in those days because you could cram more people into the available space, the people who worked in it were slightly less enthusiastic. I was shown into the Partners' office immediately, where the four of them had desks fashioned into a large square. The fourth partner was a man called Len Heath who had a very good career in marketing and joined the three founders from Bird's Eye where he had been marketing director.

There was a seating area furnished with Herman Miller chrome and black leather settees and that's where David Kingsley and I sat for this critical interview. David was a very charismatic man with steel grey hair who looked very much like Harold Wilson, or at least a younger and more energetic version. He had piercing blue eyes that Paul Newman or Steve McQueen would have been proud of. His manner, although very professional, made me feel at ease and we spent half an hour talking about ads, agencies and me. He said he would like me to meet with Michael Manton and I should arrange the appointment for as soon as possible.

My meeting with Michael was fixed for two days later and I arrived at the designated time. I was shown into the seating area in the Partners' room where I waited for Michael to finish a meeting in the creative department. From my seat saw on the coffee table between the sofas a copy of my letter to David Kingsley on which he had written, 'I think this guy is very good, Michael. You should see him as soon as possible'. Michael was much more enigmatic than David. He was beautifully dressed, tall and elegant, but also slightly menacing. As almost always happens in interviews, I had little idea at the end of it how well it had gone. Michael said they would be writing to me over the next few days with their decision.

I could hardly sleep during the period between the interview and the letter arriving at 20 Collinson House. I had been out of work for two months and my family's financial situation was becoming difficult. My mother needed me to get this job. I remember my hands shaking as I opened the envelope with the KMP logo on. Thank God they decided to employ me at a salary which was exactly halfway between what I'd asked CDP for and the sum that the job I never got was being advertised at.

The founders of KMP surrounded themselves with a number of very bright young men. The three senior guys in the media department were then in their mid to late twenties and all went on to start their own agencies or media companies. Of the account men, two of them again started on their own. I suspect that KMP had spotted in all of us an entrepreneurial streak which reflected their own instincts. Their agency had created a lot interest by being the first real major breakaway which was started from scratch. By the time I arrived, which was almost immediately after I was offered the job, new business was flooding in. The Regent petrol brand (which subsequently was renamed Texaco) had given them the opportunity to do high profile advertising using a rather scantily clad girl toting a petrol pump handle like a pistol and urging people to get out of town fast. It was unlike any other advertising in the sector.

I sat down with David on my first day and he told me that I would be working on two newly acquired pieces of business which were the Salvation Army and White Horse Whisky. They were both in his view chances to do some arresting creative advertising. He always had a very highly developed sense of social responsibility so the Salvation Army in particular was something he felt very strongly about and he would be the lead partner on the account. White Horse Whisky would be supervised by Len Heath so very early on I had a chance to work with two of the four partners. I was also asked to work on a pitch for Wrigley's chewing gum, a giant piece of business that everybody was very excited about. We invented the slogan 'unwrap a bit' and produced lots of collateral material including a deckchair with the support canvas printed as a giant pack. We didn't get the business but the pitch involved a life-changing event for reasons I discussed earlier.

Around that time we pitched for and won some business from Gallaher. It was for their loose tobacco brand called Old Holborn, the largest brand in the hand-rolled cigarette business alongside Golden Virginia from Imperial Tobacco. It was a very interesting brand to work on. We discovered an interesting thing about our users: during the week they rolled their own but at weekends they bought Benson & Hedges gold box, the most expensive cigarette on the market. It was just like the famous Volkswagen Beetle ads of the sixties. One in particular showed a Beetle alongside a flashy American car with the headline which said something like, 'Guess what does all the work during the week and doesn't go to the parties at the weekend?' The meaning is roughly the same but I'm sure the headline on the actual ad was much more elegant.

Working on this piece of business meant that I had a chance to report into Michael Manton. Although he sported a rather indifferent style of management at times, he was very good to me. My father's death continued to affect me badly. My lifelong hypochondria started around that time, coupled with depression which Michael, who I suspect was familiar with the concept of depression, recognised. One day he asked me in for a cup of tea and expressed concern about my well-being. He suggested that I should go away for a week to a health farm, get lots of sleep and maybe even lose some weight. He said the company would bear the cost of a week at Shrublands near Ipswich. This was an institution made famous by Sean Connery as

James Bond in *Thunderball*. It was where he locked a protagonist in a steam cabinet.

I arrived at Shrublands to be greeted by the duty sister who asked me if I wanted to start my diet immediately or would I like an orange. I had a full medical the following day with an earnest young doctor who told me that I was in such a state mentally and physically that if I didn't change my lifestyle completely and find a much less stressful job I wouldn't last much beyond another five years. I will always be grateful to Michael for that week. I did in fact lose ten pounds on a diet of three glasses of hot water with a slice of lemon daily which meant that I did actually sleep a lot, largely because I had no energy to do anything else. I thought then that one could get used to wandering around all day in a fluffy white robe in a beautiful country house surrounded by women dressed similarly.

Refreshed, I returned to Thorne House determined to repay both David and Michael for two real acts of kindness. All my accounts were fresh to the agency and had new campaigns to be prepared so there was plenty of work for me to do. For Old Holborn we found a rather disturbing fact in research, which was that as well as splashing out on weekends on expensive ready-made cigarettes many of its customers couldn't read. So in an unashamed rip-off of the world-famous Marlboro cowboy campaign we spent all our money on posters featuring a man's man in masculine situations smoking a rolled-up cigarette with a headline 'ROLLUP Old Holborn'.

Obviously the choice of model was critical. After a search with various casting agents we decided that Eric, the company's chauffeur, fitted the bill better than anybody else we'd seen. So from then on twice a year we would send a photographer and Eric out to find themselves some craggy situations where they could take that season's shot. There was one famous occasion when we presented the work to the Gallaher general manager in charge of the brand. He had the temerity to say to Michael that he wasn't quite sure that the composition on the latest set of shots was quite right. Michael responded in a way that only somebody who owns their own advertising agency can. He said, 'I didn't know that you had studied photography Roland,' to which the hapless client replied that he hadn't. Michael replied, 'In that case keep your opinions to yourself – the photographs were taken by a professional.' Blood drained from the client's face but he wasn't about to take on the fearsome Manton on that occasion.

Working on that account was useful because it got me into a relationship with Eric, the chauffeur who also had responsibility for allocating car parking spaces in the underground car park at Thorn House. Almost every day one of the partners was not using his space and Eric, my new friend, would tip me the wink and I would be able to drive up from Peckham and park for free.

The Salvation Army campaign presented a much more exacting creative task. Our two clients from this most admired of institutions were majors in the Army. Ken Nutty and Will Pratt were in charge of running the relationship with KMP. Despite their names, which together sounded like a couple of characters from a pantomime, they were wonderful people to work with. Like the Salvation Army itself, they never attempted to ram religion down our throats or anybody else's if it comes to that. The Army went about its daily business of helping almost anyone in need. From the hostels and soup kitchens in London's East End to the counselling services they had for children in trouble, their work was exemplary but they needed a major injection of funds to widen their ever-increasing need to supply help and comfort.

The agency produced a campaign that I'm as proud of as any I've been associated with over the decades. A very talented art director called David Holmes came up with the idea of asking the world's best photographers to go out and take appropriate shots of people in trouble, for no fee. The accompanying text outlining the subject's dilemma was set using a John Bull printing outfit which added enormously to the drama of the words. Each ad finished with the imperative, 'For God's sake give us a pound'. David himself invented the Salvation Army bond which was sent in return to everyone who filled in the coupon in the ad and sent it in with an appropriate donation. It was a very powerful campaign and people like Richard Avedon, David Bailey and Terence Donovan sent in their photographs to be used. The most prolific of all the photographers was a man who specialised in taking pictures of the stars. His name was David Steen and he was relentless in his pursuits of subjects for his camera that would best illustrate our campaign.

The day arrived when David and I went down to Queen Victoria Street where the Army were based and presented the work to the General of the Army, who had the ultimate say over what appeared. He was uncomfortable at the obvious blasphemy but accepted that a real impact had to be made in order to reach our target of £1 million. As he was trying to come to terms with the religious discomfort that the slogan engendered outside the skies darkened and there was a clap of thunder. From that day to this it was the only time I saw David Kingsley disconcerted. He immediately said that we should add to the slogan to obtain the greater authority's approval. From then on our campaign message was 'For God's sake care, give us a pound'. We raised our million pounds.

I was so impressed by what the Army had achieved that I suggested to Ken and Will that I should leave advertising and become a Salvationist. They very kindly said to me that they thought I would make a great Salvation Army officer but would be of infinitely more use to them as a communicator. On reflection they were absolutely right. They were as professional as any client I've worked with since.

The campaign provided me with my first brush with celebrity. Quite apart from rubbing shoulders with the world's best photographers, I met David Frost who kindly agreed to write an introduction to the book of the campaign that we produced. Another great side benefit was that I got to take out on a few dates the beautiful Indian doctor who had won the Miss World beauty competition that particular year. But it didn't do my ego any good as whenever we went to a premiere or out to dinner I could hear people saying, 'Isn't that Miss World over there?' followed swiftly by, 'Who is that strange looking bloke she is with?' Unlike the leading players in 'Slumdog Millionaire' many years later romance did not blossom between us.

The other campaign was for White Horse Whisky. The campaign finally produced was based on a premise that 'you can take a white horse anywhere'. Obviously the thinking behind this positioning was that White Horse would be the whisky of choice for any occasion. This was to be brought to life by having a live horse photographed in a number of unexpected situations. The first two treatments featured the horse in a pub and a bathroom. We felt this was a campaign that could run and run using different scenarios. Unfortunately we discovered after the first two photographic sessions that in real life you can't actually take a white horse anywhere. Our pale white thoroughbred had a disconcerting habit of evacuating his bowels within half an hour of appearing on set. He also disconcertingly went to sleep while standing up. Although the campaign continued it never quite worked and perhaps not surprisingly it never won any awards for KMP.

Around this time I was dating a really nice lady who had her own elegant apartment in Basil Street just behind Harrods. In there she had a drinks tray stocked with every conceivable alcoholic beverage. Every so often I would take a bottle Of White Horse Whisky round to replenish her stock. One evening I arrived clutching my gift early for our dinner date. She let me in with her hair in rollers told me to make myself at home and said that her flatmate was also preparing to go out to dinner with an American who I should let in and entertain if he was to arrive before they were both ready. Sure enough the bell rang soon after and I answered the door to be greeted by an extremely well-turned out American gentleman. Rather proudly I showed him into the sitting-room and offered him a drink. He produced a bottle of 100 Pipers Whisky as his gift for the drinks tray. Using my extensive knowledge of the golden Scottish liquid I told him that we had White Horse Whisky and it was a much superior product. Much to my surprise he thanked me and said that he preferred 100 Pipers. Later that evening at dinner I asked my date who that strange American was who didn't appear to know much about whisky. She said his name was Edgar Bronfman and he was the billionaire chairman of Seagrams – the biggest drinks company in the world and distillers of 100 Pipers and a multitude of other brands. I was more than a little embarrassed and that encounter taught me a lesson never to exaggerate a knowledge of anything of which I had very limited experience.

I enjoyed working for David, Michael, Len and the others. David's remarkable energy, boundless enthusiasm and razor sharp intellect meant that you had to be on your toes on any business reporting to him. In the days before electronic keyboards or any other handheld devices he had reams and reams of thin green paper over which his pen travelled at remarkable speed, spewing out strategy documents, marketing plans and creative briefs. I worked briefly with another account man at the agency called Richard Head, a name imposed on him by his unsuspecting parents who can't have realised that the alternate of his first name in conjunction with the family name would cause more than a hint of embarrassment in the years to come.

On many occasions, because I loved the place, I would go out to dinner with a girlfriend, drop her off at her flat and then come back to work deep into the night. I did so because I wanted to, not because I was afraid of my impressive but benign bosses. But in the midst of all this I started feeling unsettled, in common with some of the other young Turks of the open plan floor in Thorn House.

The fact that the partnership had employed young gentleman with entrepreneurial ambitions carried its own problems. All of us became restless and looked for advancement. Anxious about my own future, I had a chat one day with Len Heath and asked what I had to do to get ahead of the pack. His response was that I just had to get older. As you can imagine this did not satisfy my desire to get on and climb the ladder. The premise in football that if you're good enough you're old enough applies equally well to any form of commercial endeavour. One by one the enormously talented second layer at KMP who should have carried the agency forward successfully left. After a stint of working on other pieces of business I decided that I needed to know more about creative side of advertising and began to look around.

CHAPTER 9

1968

In the 1960s the American firm Doyle Dane Bernbach was the most famous advertising agency in
the world. Until DDB appeared on the scene, American advertising was
known for its blunt, even bullying tone. The classic USP (unique selling
proposition) approach favoured by Rosser Reeves at Ted Bates had been
carrying all before it for decades. The theory was that you would find something unique and original to say about a product and then say it relentlessly,
almost beating people over the head with that message in the hope that it
would lead them to buy the product.

But DDB changed all that. It used charm and humour to get over powerful selling messages and quickly became the talk of Madison Avenue. As I
began to look around I was aware that I had a lot to learn about this alternative and creative approach to advertising. Somebody gave me an introduction and I went for an interview at their offices at 62-64 Baker Street, now
the site of a fashionable French restaurant called Galvin's.

Some years before, DDB's American office ran a campaign for the
Jamaican Tourist Board which was unlike any other destination advertising
that had been done before. Beautiful shots of Jamaica coupled with elegant,
persuasive copy proved enormously successful with upmarket vacation-

ing Americans. This was all brought about by a man called John Pringle, a member of one of the founding families of Jamaica whose fortunes were made on sugar plantations. John himself opened Roundhill which was the first hotel complex to be based on a central facility with accommodation scattered around in villas and apartments. Legend has it that on a flight from Kingston to New York, where he was going to try to raise money to complete his avant-garde hotel, Pringle sat next to Bob Hope. By the end of the trip he had persuaded Mr Hope to front a golf tournament on the property in return for a complimentary extended stay at one of the villas in the grounds.

The hotel was so successful the Jamaican Government persuaded John to become Minister of Tourism. He knew that he needed to change the image Jamaica had in the holiday business and he had heard of the revolution Bill Bernbach was presiding over in New York and so he invited him down to persuade him to take on the account. John greeted Mr and Mrs Bernbach at the airport in an open top limousine and he was busy explaining to them that Jamaica's reputation for lawlessness was a thing of the past when somebody removed the gold watch that Bill had on his left wrist. John was the kind of person for whom something like that was only a minor problem and it was quickly brushed aside. Soon after that DDB took on the assignment.

A few years later Bernbach, impatient at the slow progress of his newly opened London office, asked Pringle to become its Chairman and Chief Executive – a massively adventurous step as John had never worked in advertising before. Bernbach thought he needed a showman to sell the unique DDB style in London's conservative advertising marketplace. John's first action on his arrival in London was to spend a fortune on creating very stylish offices in Baker Street and it was in these offices I had an interview which was to be a turning point in my life.

Amazingly, after what I thought was a poor interview with a rather stuffy head of Client Services, I was offered a job as an account manager on the two of the most famous DDB worldwide clients. They were Volkswagen and Chivas Regal, both multi-award winners for the unique advertising created for them by the New York office. For me this situation was mildly embarrassing because Chivas Regal was owned by Seagrams which was run by the man I'd made such a fool of myself in front of some time before in Basil Street – Edgar Bronfman. But it was an irresistible offer – the chance to become a member of the DDB family was way too good to turn down for me. The new job gave me a chance to get involved in real creative advertising and led me to a life-changing meeting with David Abbott, who was to play such a central role in my life, as well as the rest of my advertising career.

But it was with a heavy heart that I had to tell David Kingsley I was resigning because up until that point he was easily the most influential boss I'd had. As David had left his previous employer to start his own agency and had surrounded himself with a cadre of ambitious young men, it didn't exactly come as a surprise to him that some of us were restless. Indeed, he had deliberately created the environment where we were trained to believe in ourselves and that anything was possible. When I told him I was leaving he was typically gracious and understood that the offer to join the gold standard of creative advertising was too good to turn down. In some senses I felt my job there had been done: we had raised our £1 million for the Salvation Army, White Horse Whisky was selling well and Old Holborn had taken over from Golden Virginia as the preferred choice for do-it-yourself cigarettes. But none of that prevented me from feeling very sad about leaving a company that had instilled in me some of the operating principles and beliefs that I still use today.

I said my goodbyes to Mike Gold, the hugely talented Head of Media at KMP, and Neville Cruttenden, a fellow account handler, both of whom would play roles in my future. My other friend was Richard French, a dynamic and energetic account man who would also cross my path on a number of occasions on my advertising journey. I remain convinced to this day that David Kingsley and his partners, together with CDP, blazed a trail through British advertising and changed London in some ways as profoundly as Bill and his partners had shaken up New York.

By moving employers I also swapped the fringes of Covent Garden for the rather more genteel surroundings of Baker Street in Marylebone, where I was destined to spend most of the rest of my advertising career. Baker Street, itself famous for its Sherlock Holmes associations, was also home to the big American agency FCB, a stone's throw away from the new kid in town and on a street dominated by the giant Marks & Spencer's head office building on the other side of the road.

The mid to late sixties was a very exciting time to be in London. Carnaby Street and the fashion revolution had started, the Beatles and the Stones had redefined popular music and Mario and Franco had transformed eating out with their Italian food revolution. It was the perfect time to be in the most stimulating place in British advertising. There was a general can-do atmosphere pervading everything.

DDB had gathered a who's who of creative people to drive the place forward. The creative department itself was launched by John Withers and now had a slim, prematurely silver-haired copywriter in charge. His name was David Abbott. David had spent time with DDB on Madison Avenue and was truly one of those famous, or infamous, Mad Men, immortalised decades later by the series on television. Married with four children under six, he dominated the department not by fear but by pure talent and a very easy style. When I joined he was already Creative Director at the age of only 28 and was to be Managing Director before he hit 30. He got along very well with John Pringle and coached the ebullient Pringle through the basics of advertising while doing some great work himself.

John, although completely out of his depth, had never been troubled by a lack of self-belief. The term 'silver spoon' might have been invented to describe his upbringing and he was about as different as any other agency chairman in town as you can imagine. Indeed, soon after I joined he got the whole agency together for a pep talk. He said somewhat plaintively that he'd been stranded in New York at the age of 17 with just £15,000 to his name. This was a fortune in those days, the equivalent of just under £500,000 today. He also justified his penchant for expensive handmade shoes from Lobb in Jermyn Street by saying that non-tailored, shop bought shoes hurt his feet. But what he lacked in knowledge, he made up for in unbelievable enthusiasm. He also had a very beautiful wife Liz who was the famous American photographer Richard Avedon's favourite model. In the world of British advertising Pringle and Abbott were a formidable combination.

Somebody forgot to tell the office supremo Mike Waters about me joining. So when I turned up on my first day I was shown to a store cupboard which someone had hastily stuffed a desk into. There were no windows and I had to go outside to borrow somebody else's telephone to make calls for the first couple of weeks. Ultimately I was given a small office with a sliding door next to Laurence Isaacson, who was the account man on London Weekend Television, a newly acquired client. Sitting immediately outside Laurence's office was his secretary, Lynda McDonnell, who was to become my first wife and who played an important role in my life for around 10 years. Laurence himself was never particularly comfortable in the advertising business and subsequently left to become a restaurateur and did very well, owning Scotts, Chez Gerard and Chutney Mary among other successful places. He was instrumental in developing the chain model in catering.

It was made quite clear from day one that the role of the account managers at the agency was to handle clients with one aim in mind – to sell the output of the creative department. Bernbach's philosophy of putting creative work above everything ruled the day in Baker Street and it was a point of view that I've always felt very comfortable with. The creative people were the geese that laid the golden eggs, the rest of us were around to build a nest and make sure that those eggs hatched. This pecking order meant that the relationship between us account men and the creative department was always slightly fractious. They had a true superiority complex which led them to refer to us as 'bag carriers' on more than one occasion.

I started work on the two key accounts, Chivas and VW, who both had very successful US advertising campaigns that had been running for quite a while. I worked with two of the most irascible but brilliant copywriters in Baker Street, Dawson Yeoman on VW, who was also head of copy, and Tony Brignull, the most awarded copywriter of all time, on Chivas. Both of them decided that although the American work and style of campaign in each case was very celebrated, they would do their own thing. Dawson decided to ignore the very simple layout style, large product photographs and cleanly presented, shortish copy for a completely different look which entailed a small shot of the Beetle, VW's hugely successful small car, and reams of copy. Where the famous American launch ad used 'Lemon' as the sole headline, Dawson wrote 'Slow, Noisy, Ugly and Expensive' as his introductory banner. The ad looked very different from what VW had come to expect. Equally, on Chivas, Tony decided that he would ditch the urbane lifestyle advertising for the 12-year-old whisky and substitute a campaign thought

231

and tagline which read, 'Chivas, the non-throat burning whisky'.

This created mayhem at DDB, so much so that Mr Bernbach himself had to fly over and gently persuade both our star copywriters to adopt the American advertising style. I'd been quite vociferous in my belief that the campaign should stick to the American style which didn't make me very popular, particularly with Dawson. At one famous meeting with VW as he sat brooding at my side, I was making a point about his copy and said, 'I feel very strongly about this, I think.' He found this mild contradiction in terms hilarious and sent a note to everybody in the agency outlining what had happened in the meeting, using my quote to illustrate my 'strong stand'.

One of my other early jobs was to present to VW UK a new letterhead that the agency had designed for the company. I went to the meeting with a box which contained 135 different designs, all printed as samples and most completely inadequate for the task because they were in dark green which meant any black type was unreadable. Presenting some of those to Alan Dix, the powerful head of VW, was not an easy task. I also had to present the bill for the final work which was a king's ransom – printing every single design didn't come cheap.

After my early baptism of fire I was much encouraged when I heard that Arthur Taylor, one of the American art directors imported from Madison Avenue, had gone home and said to his wife about me, 'At last we've got an account man who cares about creative work.'

Arthur was right. I also saw that any new account man at DDB who didn't subscribe to this view of the world had a bad time. The creative line-up in Baker Street, as well as being full of talent, was populated by some pretty powerful and sizeable egos. The ethos of the organisation, following the creative revolution in New York, was very clear: as David Ogilvy once said, 'we sell or else' and the same applied to us bag carriers. We were expected to take the creative pearls down to clients and woe betide us if we came back with any changes at all to the work. They'd all forgotten that Bill Bernbach had once said, 'When you go to a client meeting have an imaginary piece of paper in your pocket on which the words "maybe he's right" are written.' It would have been all right for Mr Bernbach to come back from a creative presentation confessing that the client had changes that made sense but none of us young account men would have dared to return and impart this news to the terrifying bunch on the second floor.

I learnt an enormous amount about the creative process by being exposed every day to some of the very best copywriters and art directors in Europe. Dawson and Tony B accepted the American advertising template for Volkswagen and Chivas Regal and produced brilliant ad after brilliant ad for me to take down to Purley in Surrey for Volkswagen and St James's to Seagrams and sell their work. David Abbott recognised that Volkswagen needed a slightly more sympathetic tone than had been portrayed by the harder edged Dawson and produced some masterpieces of his own. I remember going down to present one of his pieces of work on the day that Bobby Kennedy had been assassinated. I heard the news en route on my car radio and, ashen faced, said to one of the senior executives at VW how terrible it was. His response was that 'the bastard deserved it'. I have rarely been more shocked by anything anyone has said before or since as I was by his reaction that day in sunny Surrey.

My portfolio of accounts was extended to include an Italian publisher called Fabbri who had produced a series on classical music called The Great Musicians. It was a weekly offering of a recording of one of the great composers' most famous works together with a book outlining biographical details. Until then my musical tastes had been totally mainstream and I found it fascinating to learn the Beethoven was deaf when he wrote many of his great pieces, Mozart died in relative penury and one of the other greats died of syphilis. The creative team on the business did some very elegant press ads and television commercials but towards the end of the production of the first campaign the client asked for an ad which catalogued every benefit the product gave, a sort of catch-all. The team flatly refused to do it and in desperation I went to David Abbott to explain this perfectly legitimate request from the client and their reluctance to comply. Rather than have a scene with the team, David simply sat down and wrote the ad in about 30 minutes – it was a great reminder that the very best can turn their hand to almost anything.

My relationship with John Pringle continued to get closer. He felt that I was his 'man of the people' and he also knew that he could beat me at backgammon, which meant we spent a good number of hours in his office in the late afternoons and early evenings where he would triumph over me in game after game. This was an echo of my role at David Kingsley's flat on some Friday evenings, except there it was Scrabble, not backgammon and I was the only person who would lose to his mother-in-law. I was almost unbeatable at Monopoly, though.

One evening with John, as I was exhausted after yet another round of defeats, he came up with a favour that he required of me. I had already become his acolyte at office parties where I was instructed to stay very close to him as we approached any member of staff. My job was to surreptitiously whisper the name of that person in his ear so that he could greet them with easy familiarity. Having carried out this function for a while he asked me if I would go to the pub where everybody hung out in the evenings and check for him the mood of the agency. He specifically said that I was never to name names but he would like me to come have breakfast with him every Sunday morning at his mansion in Montpellier Square and report any issues that he needed to address to make sure that everybody was happy and contented in the office. He clearly understood that I was not to be a whistle-blower or a quisling but would just let him know the things that he needed to do to keep the rank and file happy. There was a time when I was deputed to ask John to sign off a request for kit from the newly formed DDB cricket team. He, like most of us, had taken a dislike to one of the creatives, who had turned lip-curling nastiness into an art form, and John's response to my request for kit money from the agency was that if we could guarantee contact between a very hard cricket ball and Mr Unpleasant's genitalia, he would pay for the equipment himself.

Around that time I was working for a wonderful Irish account director called James McMenemy on Volkswagen. He came to me one day and said that he had been offered a big job at Bensons, my old agency, and he would like me to join him there. My close relationship with John had not endeared me to the American managing director at DDB who I suspected was slightly envious. It seemed to me that my career at DDB was on hold and I had learned as much about creative work as I was likely to. Although I was aware of the perceived wisdom of never going back, I'd already had one brush with this as a concept. After I'd been at DDB for about two months KMP rang me and said they were opening a new recruitment advertising division and would like me to be its managing director. I was then 27 years old and was totally bowled over by the prospect. They, very smartly, had some letter-head produced for the new company showing me as its managing director. I resigned from DDB and opened a small office in Bond Street to house the new venture. The final clincher was my own parking space at a multi-storey in Savile Row. But after two weeks of sitting on my own with just a secretary for company and no business at all I realised I'd made a terrible mistake.

With David and John's help, I was welcomed back to Baker Street and learnt a valuable lesson that in commerce, as in life, all that glistens is not gold.

So it was with very mixed emotions that I resigned for the second time and returned to Kingsway to join James and the team working on the giant British Leyland account. My time at DDB together with the time that I'd spent at KMP was incredibly useful. The way that KMP treated us and allowed us to flourish together with the concentration of importance on the creative work at DDB laid down a blueprint in my mind for the perfect advertising agency. I had already resolved to start on my own but felt that I needed a couple of years working on really big business to complete my advertising education.

I was sad to be leaving John and he expressed regret at my departure but couldn't get involved in the details of it. He said he wanted to remain friends and later in my career he bought shares in AMV and championed us publicly. He was even closer to David – they were a very good team. I enjoyed working for him and I admired his relaxed, friendly management style.

John was very popular and successful at DDB. He created an environment where we believed anything was possible. He had no self-doubt and that was incredibly infectious among his staff. His extraordinary presence drove them on, empowering them to do better and better rather than bossing them around. He made people proud of their work and their employer and remarkable things were achieved because of that. When it came to starting AMV and establishing the kind of working environment and culture we wanted to create, the lessons I learned from John were very important.

On the first day of my second stint at S H Benson I entered through the front doors of 129 Kingsway, rather than via the Despatch Department at Kingsway Hall, as I had when I started there for the first time. At roughly the same time as moving back to Bensons I moved from the estate in Peckham to a ground floor flat in the rather more elegant St John's Wood, so it was a time of great change in my life.

The move into my own flat was exciting but nowhere near as momentous as our family's move from Southwark to Peckham a few years earlier. In those days young men usually only moved out of the family home if they were getting married so I was a rarity, even though by this time I was 29 years old. In terms of my own life, moving to St John's Wood was an amazing step forward. My mother was sad about me leaving but she was philosophical. Like any good mother, she understood that I had to do it. But my life wasn't entirely independent – she and my aunts used to come to my flat and clean it and I would still take my washing home on Saturdays. I still needed her and that made her happy.

I rejoined Bensons as an account manager (there were many fewer titles in those days: the hierarchy on any piece of business would be account director, account manager and various account executives). Just before I started the account director on British Leyland had left to join the client as marketing director and was creating havoc with his successor at the agency. He moved up to the giant manufacturing facility at Longbridge near Birmingham and rented a house in one of the really pretty little villages close by. Having spent all his prior business life in advertising, after leaving the East African Rifles in Kenya where he was a serving officer, he thought he knew everything about the business and was determined that none of us should get away with many of the little tricks that he'd perfected as an agency man.

I was also given British Leyland Europe to work on. They were based in Lausanne and the European marketing director was a really nice, smart man. He fervently believed in long-term relationships and my predecessor on the business as account manager had developed a good working rapport with him. When the managing director of the agency wrote to him and told him that I was taking over, as my predecessor had been promoted, the client immediately wrote back protesting that he was very happy with the status quo and did not want a new man, i.e. me, to take over. Our MD responded by asking him to give me three months grace to change his mind – if I hadn't managed to do this he would replace me with the original incumbent on the business. It was a glorious account to work on. I had to fly to Geneva at least once a fortnight, rent a car and then drive the full length of the lake between Geneva and Lausanne. Every one of these trips necessitated an overnight stay in Geneva because the Palace Hotel in Lausanne, was way outside my expense bracket. I managed to convert the client almost immediately and we became really good friends and quite often I would say overnight with him at his home in Lausanne so that we could make an early start the following day on our European strategy.

As well as visits to Switzerland, I spent most of my time on an aeroplane visiting the British Leyland agencies in all the capital cities of Europe. I got to know most of them very well and had varying degrees of success in trying to persuade them to use centrally produced work for each of the marques. It was always a hard job and I was massively sympathetic with the argument that I met everywhere which was that the image of say Jaguar and Mini in Paris was very different to the way British motorists viewed them. I had small victories in each market through selling photography produced in the UK, but which was always retouched to move the steering wheel to the other side of the car for their campaigns. British Leyland at its core was a sales-dominated company. Customer preference and a strategy for each of the brands was not high on the agenda of the inhabitants of the Kremlin, as the headquarters buildings in Longbridge were known. Their approach was led first by engineering and then by sales. They did no market research into what people wanted before making something new and that made our job harder because it was very difficult for us to sell really creative advertising to them.

I particularly enjoyed going to Copenhagen, where British Leyland were well represented by some of their less exciting models. Luckily for me the Danish marketing director was an extremely pretty woman and she and I got along very well. The relationship developed to a point where she invited me to her apartment just off the centre of Copenhagen one evening, offering to cook me dinner and to see how the evening developed from there. I arrived in a high state of anticipation only to be met at the door of her flat by her flatmate: the biggest, coldest-looking Doberman I'd ever seen. Every time I try to get even mildly physical with his owner a growl from deep in his throat instantly stopped me in my tracks.

Around this time James, my account director, who I'd left DDB to work with, started complaining of bad headaches and blurred vision. An inoperable brain tumour was diagnosed and although the prognosis was that he had only about 18 months to live, he insisted on coming to work on the basis that being at home would only mean that he would focus on his horrifying condition all the time. He became more and more eccentric and following the hit single 'Something in the Air' by an artist called Thunderclap Newman he adopted Mr Newman's Christian name and called himself Thunderclap McMenemy. This caused a great deal of consternation amongst the rather staid gentleman who ran the agency. I always liked him. He was a big bluff, hard-drinking and very smart Irishman. A great guy of whom I have very fond memories.

In my early days back at Bensons I still had my white Lotus sports car and argued persuasively to the management that I should drive a British Leyland car instead. The only sports models available were the Triumph TR6 and the MG models, both of which were too small for me to get into. The Lotus finally went during a period in Longbridge where we were doing big presentations to launch the new Mini Clubman range. I was in charge of the presentation itself and decided that I should be in control of the electric curtains which would sweep aside and reveal Lord Stokes, the then chairman of the company. But just before the big moment I managed to break the control unit which meant Lord Stokes, who by now was fuming, had to wait behind curtains that wouldn't open and then, to top it all off, an electrical fault meant they caught fire. After this calamity I managed to convince the managing director of Bensons to let me have a company Jaguar E Type so as not to blot my copybook even further by being seen driving anything other than a British Leyland product. To anybody who asked I argued that this change of car was commercially sensible rather than massively self-indulgent. I'm not sure I convinced them.

The sales and marketing director at British Leyland, an ex-Ford manager called Filmer Melvin Paradise, was one of those American executives who viewed advertising people as being slightly lower than a dung beetle in evolutionary terms and took every opportunity to heap humiliation on us smart suited young men from London. His idea of fun was to call a nine o'clock meeting in Longbridge on Monday mornings which meant that we had to be up at dawn, if not before. Having raced there to be on time, he would then keep us cooling our heels in reception for at least an hour and sometimes longer. On one particular occasion I was stopped for speeding in Leamington by a traffic policeman who told me rather proudly that I was the first E Type that he'd ever pulled over. James and I still managed to arrive at Longbridge at the appropriate time and made ourselves comfortable in reception in preparation for the usual long wait. But after 45 minutes James strode to the reception desk and told the receptionist that Thunderclap McMenemy had spent enough of his unbelievably precious remaining time waiting and was returning to London forthwith. I carried on waiting for a further half an hour until a furious Mr Paradise demanded an explanation. Unfortunately there was none.

In the UK we worked on the Austin/Morris brands. The portfolio included an array of not very exciting cars with the massive exception of the Mini, which revolutionised small car design. Legend has it that at the end of the Second World War, Morris were offered the Volkswagen factory as part of the reparation treaties. The people who ran Morris turned it down believing the quirky Beetle would never have any appeal outside Germany. Yet another great decision from those people who gave you the Morris Minor!

British Leyland had tried to capitalise on the Mini's excellent suspension and transverse engine designs by using them on bigger cars but without a great deal of success. The marketing department under Mr Paradise – all ex-Ford – were obsessed by market share in relation to their previous employer. By and large they were not marketing men at all, but salesmen by trade and background. They believed that advertising was a sort of tap that you could turn off and on, with immediate effect.

I remember one Sunday morning after the ex-Benson marketing director woke me up at seven in the morning complaining about the reproduction of our latest Mini ad in *The Sunday Times*. I got a call at around 11 o'clock from Filmer Melvin himself, saying he was in the office and had looked at the storage car park through his window and it was full of Minis. He wanted a large campaign to start the following day to 'shift metal' and he was not interested in my protestations that advertising didn't work like that so the agency troops were scrambled to accede to his request. This was another brick in the wall that would be my own agency: the ability to be much more assertive with clients who had daft ideas.

There were two major launches that we had to look after. The first was the Austin Maxi. As the name suggests, this was a model that the wise men in Longbridge thought could take on all the best features of the Mini. Not a bad market positioning but unfortunately the car was rubbish. One reviewer described it as having a gear change that was like moving a rusty stick around in a bowl of marbles. It didn't look great either, so the advertising creative problem was a tricky one. The team and I spent quite a lot of time trying to work out what we could say about this metal monster. One of the senior creative guys was Brendan Nolan, who if I remember correctly was a copywriter. Although good, he wasn't a star but there was obviously a great deal of creativity in his genes because his son is Christopher Nolan of Hollywood's *Dark Knight* and *Inception* fame and one of the truly creative film directors of his time. But back to the Maxi. We jointly came up with a line which I remember playing quite a large role in creating: 'The Maxi – the car for people with more sense than money.' The car did reasonably well but would not appear in any automobile Hall of Fame.

But if the Maxi was a bit of a dog the next model dreamt up by the new product people was one of the pigs of all time. This one did get into Clarkson's all-time Hall of Shame – it went under the Morris label and was called the Marina. It is appropriate that one of the worst names of any car was saved for one of the worst cars of all time. I guess on reflection it was an appropriate name because it drove like a boat. At this time because the account was so large we shared it with another agency in London called Dorlands. Because Filmer and the boys felt that the Marina would be a breakthrough car with enormous volumes they decided that a competitive pitch was required. They briefed both of the agencies well in advance of the car appearing in metal flesh. In those days creative pitches were really expensive, glossy affairs. Tons of thick white card carrying possible advertising routes were produced. Words had to be written, pictures taken and everything put together on the expensive card as if it was the finished advertisement.

As the dynamic new model was not even in production we were briefed by Longbridge to use a Mustang in our dummy photography. Dozens of people were mobilised as this was going to be a big launch. Creative teams and photographers were despatched to America to shoot moody images of the Mustang for the print ads and a dummy commercial was shot for the TV campaign. Tens of thousands of pounds were spent on material that even in the event of our winning the contest could never be used.

This was the heyday of the finished art external studio and the most successful in town was run by a man called Brian Norman who got a lot of Bensons work. He also got a lot of Dorlands work so before the final pitch for both agencies was put together his studio just off Regent Street was producing work for both of us. His version of a Chinese wall was to put a large sheet across the middle of his massive studio with Bensons work on one side and Dorlands work on the other side, with a very large bouncer to prevent either of us taking a sneak preview at the other's efforts.

Armed with all this material we set off up the M1 quickly (no speed limits on motorways in those days). We presented to the then Chief Executive in the executive office building – the Kremlin. Surrounded by his marketing and sales team, he reviewed our work with the air of somebody who felt he had more important things to do than listen to a bunch of soft southerners with half a hundredweight of cardboard and a couple of reels of television commercials. As was often the case in those days, nobody expressed an opinion about anything before he made his views known. It really did feel like being in the Forum where the senators would not open their mouths until Caesar had opined. His disinterest only lessened when we got to the media schedule, where the *Daily Mirror* featured. I always had a problem with this medium because of its role in my early days as an Andrex substitute. He asked why the Mirror was on our media schedule because he thought that it had ceased publication. I tentatively told him that it had a daily circulation well into the millions but it was not aimed at him. He rather aggressively asked if I believed he was anything other than a normal working man. As he arrived for work every day in a helicopter which landed on the Kremlin's roof, having flown from his estate in a very leafy part of Warwickshire, the absurdity of this question was obvious. I, of course, immediately concurred that he was a man of the people and that his newsagent must have made a mistake by not delivering 'The Voice of the People' to him on a regular basis.

Back down the M1 we stopped at the Watford Gap service station to have the inevitable inquest into how the meeting had gone. Those of you have who experienced the soul-draining experience of putting together a major pitch for a piece of new business will recognise the terrible feeling of anti-climax when it's over and be familiar with the almost linear split which appears between those optimists who thought the meeting had gone very well and the pessimists who thought it was a disaster.

In this particular instance both were wrong. We got a call two days later from our friendly marketing director saying that the exercise had resulted in a dead heat. Dorlands' work had more strategic merit while our offering was more creative. They would like us to go again with Dorlands injecting more creativity into their stuff and us paying more attention to the strategic routes. We had to start all over again, with tens of thousands of pounds of more non-recoverable money being spent on adjusting all the work we'd done over and above the hundred thousand pounds that was already on the books. Many years later I can't even remember who won after the second round but certainly both agencies had burnt the net profit on this account on the pitches. The car was roundly vilified by one and all and the hoped-for assault on the market share of Ford's enormously successful Cortina never materialised.

If that exercise was dispiriting there were some rays of sunshine. The relationship with British Leyland Europe continued to strengthen, although the Doberman meant that I spent less time in Copenhagen than before.

In those days motor shows were a great jolly for all concerned and were much less about attracting potential consumers to our stands than they were about having a good time chatting up the eight or ten models who, in common with all other stands, were draped, scantily clad, across the bonnets of our hopefully world-beating cars. Bensons took their entertaining obligations very seriously at motor show time. When it was London's turn I was told to rent the biggest penthouse suite at the London Hilton Hotel and be on call 24/7 to wine and dine any member of the client organisation who felt like skiving off from Earls Court to central London for copious wine and smoked salmon. The expenditure was enormous and I always used to put on at least half a stone during the London Motor Show Week.

I don't know how we did it but one year in Paris we managed to get a pre-release version of the Beatles' White album to use on our stands at the French show. This meant we had overwhelming interest, although sadly not in the cars. Our stand was heaving from morning till night with people wandering around trying to take in the whole album which was a double LP, while pretending to engage with perspiring salesman who were trying to get them interested in the Mini and Maxi. Like the rest of us, they had already given up on trying to persuade anybody to be interested in the Marina.

I had become increasingly appalled at the way our relationships with our clients worked because our function seemed to be to give them what they wanted rather than what they needed. Long before the odious term 'supplier' was applied to advertising agencies, Bensons, in those days, was indeed nothing other than a supplier. Coupled with that, my rotund account director had done a yearly review of me which culminated in the words, 'He will never be anything more than an average account director, at best.' Not surprisingly I took great offence at this and began to make my plans to work elsewhere.

This coincided with financial predators casting their eyes over advertising agencies. Although they made every attempt to spend the vast amount of revenue that was coming in from the commission system, agencies were very profitable. By and large, though, they were badly run in a normal business sense. Dorlands itself fell and Bensons was being looked at very seriously by a property asset stripper who worked out that the lease or freehold of 129 Kingsway was worth a lot of money. Although the board who ran the business when I'd been at Bensons before had been replaced by slightly more savvy Americans – a result of a working relationship with a big Chicago agency called Needham Harper – they had no idea of the great value of their mortar and glass palace.

As a defensive measure, a merger with the large Ogilvy & Mather agency, founded by the great David Ogilvy himself, was hurriedly cobbled together. Plans were rushed through to vacate 129 Kingsway and take a new building in Jermyn Street to house the new Ogilvy, Benson & Mather entity. It was a long time ago and I can't remember who got the benefit of the lease in Holborn but I do know it went to someone external.

One of the account directors at Bensons had decided to set up his own agency and asked James McMenemy to join him. At this time James was in a very poor way. He was suffering almost constant headaches and must have known that the cancer in his brain had taken a terminal grip. As a defiant gesture and a refusal to accept the inevitable, he resigned from Bensons. The then managing director Simon Bryan refused to accept his resignation, thus leaving in place the enormously generous medical and life insurance benefits that James enjoyed. Within weeks James passed away but his family were looked after because of Simon's great gesture.

With James gone it was obvious that my career at the agency was about to hit a very low glass ceiling. The place was riddled with politics and the anti-McMenemy faction had prevailed. Although I had done a pretty good job on the British Leyland account, my route to the higher echelons of the agency was blocked. This all happened at the same time as my real desire to strike out on my own intensified. My ambition to leave was hastened when one of our senior clients rang and asked that we should rent for him a Jensen Interceptor, a very expensive sports coupe, for the weekend and also supply a leather desk set from Asprey's as the British Leyland standard issue plastic set was beneath contempt. I passed this request up the line with a firm recommendation that it should be refused. The recommendation was ignored and I was told to comply with these outrageous demands.

The merger and the move meant that people were distracted and maybe would acquiesce to what in other times might seem way over the top. I chanced my arm with a very decent man called Bob Swanson who was running the agency as the Needham Harper representative and asked if I could leave with no restrictive covenants and keep my Jaguar E type as a farewell goodwill gesture. To my astonishment and eternal gratitude he agreed and that was the last time for decades that I worked for anybody other than companies that had my name in the title.

CHAPTER 11

1971

By 1971, a whole series of events had conspired to bring me to the point of starting out on my own. There was no precedent of any Mead family members starting a successful business from scratch. Even my father had inherited the West End & District Window Cleaning Company from the man he had worked with for some 10 years. He had been dead for five years when I embarked on what was considered among my immediate family to be a somewhat foolhardy venture. I was reminded of a book one of the great creative people of the *Mad Men* era had written, which was called *George Be Careful*. The man in question was George Lois, a member of the elite group who made up Doyle Dane Bernbach in the 60s. When he told his mother he was leaving she berated him, saying that nice Mr Bernbach had paid him a lot of money and looked after him and what was to be gained by doing it himself? After he carefully explained his burning desire to try and change his particular world she did indeed say, 'George, be careful'.

My mother felt pretty much the same. She had seen me fly around Europe, drive an exotic motorcar and always appear to have money in my pocket. Indeed, I had flown the nest and now lived in St John's Wood, a highly desirable part of town. Like George, I tried to explain to her that there was a real opportunity to start up my own business. There was nowhere else I wanted to work – Collett's had already turned me down some years earlier.

You didn't need much money to start an advertising agency in those days and as I began to plan and work things out, I was reminded of one of my favourite old ads which Ernest Shackleton ran in the *Daily Telegraph* trying to recruit people for yet another Antarctic expedition. The copy, to paraphrase it, asked for volunteers for a hazardous journey in which the likelihood of failure was high but success would bring fame, recognition and rewards.

At roughly this time I met an inventor called Eddie Leshik. He told me how he had spent years developing a portable music system. It was based around a mini cassette, not unlike those used in dictating machines, and a battery driven player. This coupled with a pair of small headphones meant that a music hungry populace could play the latest single release on the move. His concept was a good 10 years in advance of Sony developing the Walkman and was very seductive. Although he never actually produced a working model he maintained it was only a matter of time before his device would make all of us very rich. He needed marketing advice and believed that advertising for his wonder machine was absolutely essential. He was constantly searching for capital to turn his dreams into reality and was always reassuring about a queue of people looking seriously at his magic project. So the first client was sitting there waiting for the Mead project to see the light of day.

I had for a while been encouraged by a couple of wealthy potential backers to start up. I'd calculated that I needed just enough capital to finance the business for six months without any income from clients. This would obviously mean myself and my partners working for nothing during the initial start-up phase. Being single with no commitments other than to look after my mother's modest needs meant that this was a no-brainer for me. I thought the ideal setup for our new company would be a copywriter and art director, a media man and another account man to help me trawl for new business.

The two agencies that had been very formative in my life to that point were KMP and DDB. The second account man and the media man, Neville Cruttenden and Mike Osborne respectively came from KMP and, despite both being family men, counted themselves in instantly when I broached the subject with them. The creative team had to come from DDB and I knew exactly who I wanted. David Abbott by then had been made Managing Director or even Chairman at the hothouse in Baker Street. He had spent the last few years working with Brian Byfield as his art director and they had produced a really impressive body of work, particularly on Volkswagen. But no matter how hard I tried I couldn't persuade David to come with me. It wasn't difficult to understand his reluctance. He was doing extraordinarily well at DDB and had four kids under the age of ten to provide for. Although passing on this particular opportunity he was very useful in helping me to persuade Brian Byfield to join me. After lengthy meetings in my flat in Grove End Gardens and the recruitment of Paul Whelan, one of the really good, if somewhat intense, writers at DDB our new venture was born.

The absence of David was a major blow but I figured that Brian had a stellar enough reputation to create a stir in the marketplace. We decided that democracy would be the guiding management philosophy for our fledgling company. This was epitomised by the name we chose. The agency was to be called Byfield, Cruttenden and Mead. I remember the meeting when this was decided we had some letterhead dummied up and found ourselves an office just above the Post Office in Baker Street. With the money put in by my chums as backers we secured the lease and everybody gave in their notice at their respective companies. Although I had raised all of the money and was I guess the driving force behind the new company, I gave away 67% of the equity to my four partners. Before we started Byfield, Whelan and Osborne decided to oppose the name of the company and poor old Neville was removed from the letterhead. So Byfield Mead it was.

We had a great time in those early days, with the combined fear of failure driving us all on and within a week had a lead for our second piece of business – Mr Leshik and his miracle box being our founding account. Brian's aunt worked for a company called Medway Builders. Based in Rochester in Kent they were healthy competitors to the dominant company in portable office space at the time – Portakabin. She told us that she had been serving tea at a board meeting when she overheard that they were looking for a new advertising agency. Excited by this we rushed off a letter to the managing director of the company and to our astonishment got a reply asking us to go down to the busy Kent town and present our credentials. We were halfway through this exercise in front of the whole board of Medway when the door opened and tea lady came in. It wasn't Brian's aunt but her best friend at the company. When she'd dispensed cups to everybody she turned to the chairman of the company and asked if he minded if she spoke to Brian. Mortified, the two of us stood there while she said, 'Brian your auntie May said when you finished maybe you'd pop into her flat on the way home for some tea and cake.' She then pushed her trolley out and left us believing that our chances of winning this piece of business had disappeared.

Astonishingly, this wasn't the case and we were appointed virtually immediately. Paul did some great ads, I wrote a headline, Brian got a great artist called Alan Aldridge to do some spectacular illustrations and we had our first double page spreads in colour in *The Sunday Times Magazine*. We were off and running. Our very first ads won creative awards at the following year's design and art direction competition. We were creating interest and we had found a window of opportunity where few new advertising businesses were starting up.

I had written to the heads of all the major agencies in London announcing our existence and slightly begging for any crumbs that came their way – accounts that were too small for them could make all the difference to us. *The Financial Times* did a small piece at the time of our launch under the headline, 'Byfield Mead Minus Frills.' I'm still not sure what they meant but the publicity gave us all a warm glow.

Sadly we were brought up very short by Eddie Leshik getting into financial difficulties. We had spent about 10% of our precious capital developing a campaign for him and his product for which were never going to get paid. The buccaneering spirit of my partners, particularly Paul, evaporated almost overnight. I tried really hard to reassure everybody that things would be fine but it was a struggle and they were pretty dark days. A week or so later I was sitting in my office after another uncomfortable session with the brooding copywriter when I got a call saying we had a chance to pitch to a company called United Rum Merchants which my old friend Peter Campbell was connected to – his father was the chairman. We were briefed on a project called Santigo which was yet another attempt to unseat Bacardi. The pitch was to look at the project from top to bottom. We designed the label and the shape of the bottle itself, together with a raft of advertising. We were competing against URM's other agency, FCB, who were situated just across the road from us in Baker Street. While they pitched in the morning we were on at three o'clock the same day.

When our meeting began the sales and marketing director entered in a state of high dudgeon. He was outraged that on his arrival at FCB he had been given a cup of coffee in a paper cup. He found this both offensive and disrespectful. He told me of this story while sipping from our Rosenthal china cups. At the end of our presentation he told me that we were to be appointed and to this day I'm sure we won because of FCB's paper cups. This was early autumn and around Christmas time, at the lunch the client gave for both its agencies, the three FCB representatives made things even worse by ordering gin and tonics at the bar. Despite a very extensive repertoire of spirits, gin was the one product not in URM's portfolio. Not surprisingly the three of us ordered Santigo and tonic. A sensible gesture, but it tasted disgusting.

Our first year in business flew by. We appointed a number of really good people but always ran the business conservatively to ensure that we could repay our initial backers and never had to use an overdraft. We won a couple of other small pieces of business including a hi-fi company called Eagle International who were a competitor of Alan Sugar's Amstrad brand. The flaws of running as a full democracy amongst the five of us were beginning to emerge. Decision-making was tortuous and every small move forward had to be discussed and negotiated at length between the five of us. In addition, the UK economy was worsening, leading to a reduction in advertising budgets and a clients having a more cautious view of moving their business to a small agency. Also, all of us had worked on major pieces of business in our past agencies and felt that we were not being stretched either strategically or creatively on the accounts that we'd acquired. We needed a really significant advertiser to both enhance our reputation and give us a bigger canvas on which to paint.

Almost on cue came a telephone call which transformed our little agency. The sales director at British Leyland was a man called Michael Hellas. He'd left the Longbridge giant and unbeknown to me had joined Thomas Tilling, a conglomerate who had the franchise to market Mercedes cars in the UK. He said they were looking for an agency and asked if I was interested. Barely able to contain my excitement, I said we'd be happy to go down and have a chat to see there was any way we might work together.

All of us turned up for a two-hour meeting at the Mercedes headquarters on the Great West Road. It went very well and we could hardly believe that there was every possibility that the great German carmaker would be our first major client. Mike told me that they had another agency to see but that I shouldn't worry as they really liked what we had to say. But the following afternoon I got a call saying that it was bad news. The other agency had produced creative work which they quite liked so they were inclined to give them the business. Brian and I were devastated but it occurred to me that Michael had behaved in an uncharacteristic way. So within half an hour of receiving his call I rang him back and asked if he told the other agency that they'd won. He said he hadn't but planned to do so imminently. I said I thought he'd behaved rather unfairly in that we didn't have the opportunity to show we could do for him creatively. He pondered for a moment and agreed that we could have 10 days to produce creative work so at least if they still chose the other agency the whole exercise would have happened on a level playing field. We all worked every hour for the next week or so, particularly Brian and Paul, and produced a raft of really great ideas. After our presentation Mike took me aside and said we had the business. Although none of us were heavy drinkers we made an exception that night. We were off and running towards the big league – it was a wonderful feeling.

Since the beginning we had been banking with the Royal Bank of Scotland and our initial capital injection meant our early expenditure was all covered. Even with Eddie's bad debt we had not had to call on them for any financial help and with the acquisition of the Mercedes account we were making a slight monthly profit. To raise the capital to start the agency all of us had got rid of our smart motorcars and were driving around in a motley selection of old bangers. As Thomas Tilling also owned the Audi franchise we decided we would purchase Audis for the partners as those were the days when company cars were an integral part of anybody's package. This would entail a short-term loan of some £10,000. I went to see our bank manager in Burlington Gardens and put forward this as a proposition. It was immediately turned down.

Since the early days of the agency a man called Jonathan Agnew had been chairman. He owned a tiny amount of the equity and was from the Agnew art dealing family. An old Etonian, he worked for a major merchant bank called Hill Samuel who had just started a retail operation based in very elegant offices on the corner of St James's Square. When he heard of our shabby treatment at the hands of RBS he suggested that we go along to see a man called Ted Emerson who ran the first Hill Samuel retail branch. Within half an hour of meeting Ted we had secured a loan for the Audis and had switched our business totally to his bank. Coupled with the appointment of Arthur Andersen as our auditors and Lewis Silkin as our lawyers we had put together a very respectable line up of advisers. In the decades that followed Ted Emerson played a central role in my life for which I'll be eternally grateful.

Despite being very different agencies, the combined cultures of KMP and DDB bound us together. We were early supporters of a new company called The Advertising Agency Register. Set up by a very energetic nice lady called Lindy Payne, who I'd known from my Benson days, it allowed clients to secretly look at agency offerings from the central register that the AAR had compiled. It proved very useful for us and a relatively steady stream of new business came in to see us. Our conversion rate was about 50% and within a couple of years we found ourselves working for not only Mercedes and Medway builders but for Canada Dry and Standard Brands who had a new margarine product called Fresh Fields, together with a quasi-government appointment – the Milton Keynes Development Corporation. This quango was overseeing the creation of a new town just off the M1. The highly ambitious concept was to pull together a number of villages around a huge central complex, not unsurprisingly called Central Milton Keynes. The vision was to have great infrastructure, in particular a road system that was easy to use and understand.

For a while it was a curious account because we were asked to spend money on advertising but as the concept had been so readily adopted we were told that the advertising should not attract either potential residents or industry. The Chief Executive of the Development Corporation was a great man called Fred Lloyd Roche. Not only was he faced with the enormity of creating a big new town, but he had to combat an enormous amount of local hostility. As each new spoke of the road system was built he planted saplings everywhere – Milton Keynes was eventually going to be a city of trees, he told me. Quite often the saplings were vandalised almost immediately after being planted but Fred was never deterred and planted a new lot every time which were again vandalised. Around the fifth time, when a whole new consignment of baby trees were ready for planting, I questioned whether it was worth doing and asked if he would ever give up. He said that ultimately the vandals would get tired, the trees would begin to grow and that once they started growing the vandals would become their guardians. I thought he was crazy but as it turned out he was right: the trees grew and the very people who had torn up their predecessors became custodians of the rapidly emerging tree population.

Jennie Armstrong, who I'd known for a number of years since I met her at Benson's, had become emotionally involved with a man called Peter Mayle. At that stage, along with David Abbott, he was viewed as one of the star copywriters in British advertising. Like David he was good-looking, urbane and very charismatic. He had started the UK operation of a hot US creative agency called PKL. This had been acquired by BBDO London, one of the offshoots of the New York-based American operation. Peter was creative director of the enlarged entity but after a couple of years decided that turning the operation around would take too long and that great idea would be to buy Byfield Mead to inject new energy and allow us to work together. Although the five founders of our small agency were getting on well enough, hairline cracks were beginning to show and the promise of being part of a much bigger operation appealed to us, largely because of the extra security we would have. BBDO were prepared to offer just something short of £250,000 for our agency, an enormous amount of money for a business in its infancy. I flew to New York to meet with Bruce Crawford, the legendary head of BBDO Worldwide and we seemed to get along fine.

But an element of greed set in and we collectively decided that we would push for another £50,000 and deputed Jonathan Agnew to negotiate directly with Bruce Crawford. This really was chalk talking to cheese. Bruce had always thought that the price he was offering was a premium but worth paying because the deal would help him sort out a problem in London and keep Peter Mayle happy. He didn't appreciate Jonathan's negotiating style and the deal died. On reflection, this moment was the beginning of the end of the agency. Even though a deal was not struck, during the negotiations people had already started emotionally spending the money they thought was coming their way. The hairline cracks in the relationships between the five of us started to become fissures and discontent started stalking the floors of our offices in Baker Street.

Around this time relationships between the government and trade unions was at an all-time low, resulting in a number of strikes and leading to the slightly surreal situation of businesses only being allocated enough energy to operate three days a week. We continually had to decamp to the Churchill Hotel in Portman Square to carry on trying to grow the business. At the same time, we were bursting out of Baker Street offices and found a great site 500 yards away for our new premises. They backed onto a park diagonally across from what became AMV's offices years later. New business came in but the discontent, for which we were all responsible, grew. Brian and I pitched for an old piece of business that I had worked on previously – White Horse Whisky. It was truly one of the worst presentations that he and I had ever done together and on the way back in the taxi following the pitch we berated one another for the awfulness of our performance. When I got back to my desk there was a message waiting for me from the marketing director saying that they were blown away and the business was ours. It was a reminder of something that I learnt many times over the years: that it was almost impossible to judge the result of a competitive pitch in advance of the decision being made.

We moved to our new office and for a while things settled down. We still had fractious board meetings. Every decision, no matter how small, had to be decided on a vote and factions emerged. The trouble was that the following board meeting factions emerged again but were differently aligned. Nonetheless, we carried on winning the odd piece of business, the agency's reputation grew and nobody had left us since the start. We'd also never had an overdraft.

The final nail in the coffin of Byfield Mead came with BBDO approaching us again with a view to merging. I had a call from the then CEO of the London office asking for a meeting. By then Peter had left to go to New York with Jennie where he was working on clients like Gillette in the agency's Sixth Avenue offices. The London CEO, a man called Mike McLoughlin, explained that he would like us to join him to once again try to revitalise their London operation. The British economy had worsened substantially since the offer of two years before and the new suggestion was to acquire us for 30% less than the figure which had been at the heart of our earlier negotiations. We had just been put on a shortlist by our first million-pound account and I took the view that this meant we had broken through the awareness barrier and were developing a reputation amongst London's agencies that might result in relatively spectacular growth. This view was shared by one of my partners but the other three had had enough and instructed me to try to negotiate the best deal that I could. My heart wasn't in the negotiations and my opposition only served to exacerbate the widening gulf between the partners.

After a protracted and unpleasant period of negotiations with both BBDO and internally among the partners, the cracks became chasms. I became the lightning rod for the pent-up frustrations and anger of the partnership and it was decided I should leave. Writing this many years later I fully accept my share of responsibility for the breakdown of the relationships between the five of us. The manner of our parting left an enormous amount to be desired, and the enforced acquisition of my 33% shareholding for £11,250 was, I still believe, derisory and unfair. The agency that I had conceived and founded had a modicum of success over the next few years but never became a major force. It was eventually gobbled up by another London group and disappeared without trace.

CHAPTER 12

1975

I took quite some time to recover from the brutality of my departure from the agency. Some people were wonderfully supportive, such as Susie Gold, a long-time dear friend who started and still runs the very elegant West End dress store called Wardrobe, who came over as soon as she heard. Not for the first, or indeed the last time, David Abbott took me out to lunch at the fashionable Meridiana in Fulham Road and said he would do anything he could to help. Curiously enough, he'd left Doyle Dane Bernbach about a year after we started Byfield Mead and he joined two of my mates from KMP, Mike Gold and Richard French. French Gold Abbott was proving to be really successful and David seemed relaxed.

Although stunned by the chain of events I was determined to try again. There is a song in the musical *South Pacific* with the lyric, 'There's nothing to put on a clean white suit for.' I've always believed, and still do, that life is about having something to put on a clean white suit for. So even though I had nowhere to go, I got up every morning, dressed for the office and made my plans. One of the sad things about my departure was that I couldn't use the advisers who I'd employed at the agency. It was really galling not to be able to turn for legal advice to Roger Alexander, the lawyer who set up

Byfield Mead for me. I'd met him four years before at Heathrow when we were both returning from family holidays and he had been a wonderfully calming and wise counsel, a role he carried out for me for decades until he retired a few years ago. So in my fight with my erstwhile partners I had to use an unknown law firm. The antagonism which caused the breakup continued in negotiations which dragged on endlessly.

But there was one ray of sunshine. Gerd Hoffman, the then Chief Executive of Mercedes in the UK, had sought me out and said he was disinclined to stay with Byfield Mead beyond the end of the year and if I got an agency together when their business was put up for re-pitch he would make sure I was included on the list. He was an elderly, steely-haired German of the old school in that he had a highly developed sense of fairness. I still remember presenting ads to him. In one piece of copy the first line was 'Nothing in a Mercedes-Benz is the whim of an engineer', and although his English was good he said to me, 'Vas is vhim?' Good question, I thought, as I tried to explain the meaning of this literally whimsical word.

In addition, Gerry Adler and David Harris, his marketing director at Eagle International, said they would join me any time I set up the new agency. It was a pretty exciting thought. Mercedes spent enough and were prestigious enough to get any new agency off the ground. My only problem was that I had no money, no partners and no premises. I racked my brains to think of the potential backer for Peter Mead & Partners – a catchy name, I thought – and kept returning to David Williams, the man who'd been so kind a few years before when I had desecrated his beloved Rolls-Royce. In advance of seeing him I spent a lot of time thinking of who I would ask to join me in this new venture. I needed a creative team and a good account man.

At the time, Collett Dickinson and Pearce under Colin Millward and Frank Lowe were carrying all before them creatively. They produced a series of great commercials for a cigar brand from Benson & Hedges. Beautifully written and shot, they were devised by the team of Alec Wignall and Lyndon Mallett. There was also very languid account director called Jonathan White who I thought would add style and class to back up my industry and tenacity. After a series of meetings in my newly rented Sussex Gardens flat in Paddington, which went on over a period of months they agreed to join me. The time was right to talk to David Williams. I arranged an appointment with him in the offices where I'd spent a couple of happy years. He had been bought out by an American operation called Ketchum International which many years later would be acquired by Omnicom – small world. My proposition to David was that he should buy 25% of the company for £35,000. He asked me to wait while he called his American partners. Twenty minutes later he came out of his office and told me we had a deal. This was an amazing leap of faith on his part and I will be forever grateful for his support at a time when I really needed it.

The agency was on its way but time was passing and we didn't have an office. French Gold Abbott had been growing fast and had outstripped the very nice offices they had in Soho at 66 Frith Street. David said that our little operation could use the office until they found a new tenant, a process which would certainly take three or four months. The great joy was that these offices had housed an advertising agency and the tiny band of us moved in and felt at home immediately.

Unfortunately we didn't do great work for the Mercedes pitch and although I know that Gerd would have liked us to handle the account, he couldn't in all conscience give us the business. It was sad not to get the business but I knew that without the Mercedes dynamic giving us that early momentum it would have been much more difficult for me to start again. The early days became a long, hard slog and we moved into a first-floor office in Bond Street with a porter who appeared to have the same affliction as the hero of *The Singing Detective* – bits of his face seemed to be falling off on a daily basis. Eagle International came in, as they'd promised, and we had our first client but we were not moving quickly enough for my other three partners. They decided to look elsewhere and I still remember Jonathan White kindly saying that he did not want to keep his 10% equity stake as it wouldn't ever be worth anything. A trifle hasty of him given the value AMV achieved many years later.

In both my attempts to start an agency I had believed that Adrian Vickers would make a wonderful partner. He was a thoroughly decent and smart man who'd had a very reasonable career to that point. He'd been with one agency pretty much ever since he left Bensons. They had fallen on hard times, though, and decided that he and they should part company. This was absolutely perfect timing. I seem to remember in the first instance Adrian joined me to give him somewhere to go while he looked for a proper job. Fortunately, although he claimed never to have had an entrepreneurial bone in his body he took to working for himself almost immediately. To help us with creative work we had Peter Mayle who was true to his word when said that he would help in any way. In addition to writing some stuff for us he also cajoled some of his old creative colleagues who were 'resting' to come in and help out. One of those was Rick Cook. Another disciple from Collett Dickinson and Pearce, he was a true delight. One of the funniest men I'd ever met he helped lighten what was a pretty depressing grind in those days.

Our other recruit was a highly talented and well thought of planner. No agency starting in the 70s could be without a planning department – quality of research and thought was argued by the planners to be at least as important as good creative work. Guy Davis had recently been at the mother of planning, BMP, and the trouble was that his talent came at a price. He was wilfully acerbic and had little time for anybody who he perceived to be intellectually inferior. He didn't have much time for account men, whose role he thought was to deliver his massive pearls of wisdom to clients without contributing any of their own largely unworthy observations.

Life is, I guess, full of defining moments and we three youngish men in Bond Street stumbled across one very fortuitously. I can't remember how we met but we came across a man called Gill Foster who was the marketing director of a Spanish company called Williams and Humbert. They were in the sherry business, indeed their headquarters was in the fabled Spanish town of Jerez. They had a pretty successful product called Dry Sack which partly lived up to its name in that it was dispensed in a small canvas sack. Rather more importantly, however, it wasn't a dry sherry (the most desirable of the variants) but a medium Amontillado. It was much darker and sweeter than the dry Fino sherry which was much loved by the smart set.

Adrian and I hit it off with Gill immediately and he promised us an opportunity to pitch for his business against one of the giants of British advertising. He thought he needed wild creative work to break out of the rather middle-aged imagery that sherry, particularly sweet sherry, had slumped into. He planned to spend a lot of money on revitalising the brand and also had a unique way of ensuring he got distribution for his product through a commando sales force. So the enticing proposition was that not only would we do the advertising but would be a surrogate marketing department handling relationships with the large independent distributor Food Brokers.

No matter how hard Adrian and I tried, Guy insisted on doing a massive survey of the market and its consumers and when the day of the pitch dawned the planning bit of the presentation comprised 126 separate charts.

Gill was both devastated and angry. He expected us to have off-the-wall creative ideas but they were overshadowed by Guy's massive brainpower and market modelling, a brilliant piece of work which, however, demanded a lot more attention than Gill was prepared to give. We didn't get the account which was a body blow. The agency now had the rather more bulky title of Mead Davies and Vickers. Fortunately the big agency that had won the business attempted to reposition Dry Sack as a trendy drink. This route failed completely, largely because the drink looked like a sherry, smelt like a sherry and tasted like a sherry.

So we got another bite of the cherry – or should I say sherry. We had converted a few pieces of business and with the wonderful Ted Emerson's help and David Williams' support managed to keep our overdraft down to manageable proportions. We decided we should have a receptionist/telephonist and when we were down to a shortlist of two the vote was split. Fortunately, Guy and Adrian prevailed and we appointed the lady who subsequently became my wife – Sammy.

In truth, the job of receptionist at our tiny agency in the beginning was not life-enhancing employment. In the absence of many clients or, to be honest, a great deal of interest in our fledgling operation, her days were pretty boring. The tedium was only broken by the endless games of carpet bowls played in the long corridor of our tatty office in Bond Street.

Sam was certainly a child of the late sixties and early seventies. Having left home in Devon at 17, she enjoyed the fun place that was London to the full. She came from farming stock and from her early childhood was a great horsewoman, winning many three-day event competitions. Beautiful and vivacious, she had no trouble at all in attracting a multitude of male followers. One day she came to me and said that she was going to decamp to the South of France with her new boyfriend, an American from one of the dynastic banking families. He had bought a yacht and they planned to live on it just outside Cannes and operate charters throughout the Mediterranean. In those days I'd managed to get a membership of the Ladbroke Club in Hill Street. This was the flagship casino of the Ladbroke organisation and, as with all gambling operations, the food was both really good and very cheap. Although I rarely, if ever, ventured onto the gaming floor, I developed a relationship with the people who ran the restaurant which meant two or three times a week I ate spectacularly well there for very little money. I took Sam to lunch to try to persuade her not to go to France and instead to stick with our company, which I was sure would be a success. If I found it difficult to persuade myself of this eventuality, I failed totally with her and she left with our best wishes to pursue an idyllic life on the Cote D'Azur.

The year following, her departure was momentous as far as I was concerned. My first marriage ended but a new one with David and Adrian took its place. About nine months after she went to live in France Sam rang one day to ask a favour. She and her boyfriend were planning to visit the States for an extended holiday and she had an opportunity to train with the American three-day eventing team in South Carolina. She was finding it difficult to get a visa as she apparently had no job to come back to here in the UK so she asked if I would be prepared to write her a letter stating that I would employ her six months later at the agency. She hurriedly added that this was just a strategy and she had no desire to resume a career as a receptionist. I agreed to this immediately.

Almost exactly six months later I came back from lunch and my secretary told me that Sam had been on the phone asking to buy me a drink to say thank you for having written the letter. She had asked that we would meet at the Polo Bar at the Westbury Hotel just off Bond Street at 5.30pm.

I already had an appointment that evening with my then girlfriend, the actress who played Leonard Rossiter's daughter in the sitcom 'The Fall & Rise of Reginald Perrin'. I said that we should try and rearrange the drink but was told that it was impossible to get hold of Sam as she was going to be out all afternoon shopping prior to our drink. Mobile telephones had not been invented so there was no way of reaching her before the appointed hour at the Westbury.

Reluctantly, I made my excuses to my other friend and turned up for the drink which changed my life. Sam was much more beautiful than I remembered and 5'4" with deep brown eyes and a shock of light brown hair. She was also elegantly tanned from her days in the South of France. After drinks at the Westbury, we went to dinner at Burke's, a fashionable dining club just around the corner. From there, totally uncharacteristically, we went dancing at Mario and Franco's club in the Kings Road. At the end of the evening I asked Sam if she would like to come back to my flat in Fulham to watch a movie. Being a gadget freak from those early radiogram days, I had the first Philips video player and somehow had got hold of a copy of a very hot film called 'Klute'. It starred Jane Fonda playing a hooker with Donald Sutherland as the love interest. In those days there were no films on television, indeed television itself finished at 10.45pm with the national anthem and a tiny white spot on the screen. Sam decided to come back to carry on the non-stop conversation we'd been having all evening.

As things transpired, we magically connected she moved in that night and 36 years later we're still together. Fiercely independent, she decided a while later that she would start her own company and, after hearing a film director friend of ours bemoaning the quality of catering on film location shoots, she set up a company called The Mobile Mouthful. Within three weeks of the decision, she had bought a second-hand catering van and, having persuaded her brother to join her, six months later was feeding the cast and crew of Ridley Scott's iconic film 'Blade Runner'. For the 20 years or so that she ran her company it was universally acknowledged as the best in the business.

Before all this, Sam's appointment marked the moment when we began really looking more like a proper company. We even let a few people who had nowhere else to go and run their own small operations from our offices to give us a feeling of scale. Second time round with Dry Sack it was hardly a re-pitch because as I remember it Gill as good gave us the business on the spot. We decided we would splash out and celebrate. Ted Emerson had appointed one of his deputies at the bank to look after us and we thought he and his wife should be included in the celebrations. We took the private room at Meridiana. Over coffee Gill and I had what appeared to be a terminal argument when he accused us of behaving badly. I think he was enraged by copious amounts of Italian red wine. I angrily stormed out of the restaurant after telling Gill what he should do with his account. On reflection, this was rather unwise of me.

Fortunately the wonderful Adrian played the peacemaker and calmed Gill down by spending most of the night pouring oil (and large amounts of Chianti) on troubled waters and driving Gill to the airport for him to return to Jerez the following morning. By the time he arrived back in his office we were all friends again and to his credit he apologised, an apology I accepted with supersonic alacrity. After these conversations had taken place I suddenly remembered that Mr and Mrs Bank Manager had been at the dinner. They had arrived in full leathers after their trip on a motorbike to be with us – eccentricity was a major part of his make-up. He took my call and explanation with scarce concealed relief that he could report to Ted that serious income would be coming our way.

We had our first television commercials to produce. Food Brokers were doing a good job in getting distribution for Dry Sack and in those early days I spent at least a day a week down at their vast warehouse complex where the thousands of cases of Dry Sack took up a tiny portion of their storage facility. Delivery vehicles were leaving the warehouses every few minutes stacked with the products they represented in their role as a sales force. Peter Mayle was in his element with us – he was one of the great writers of amusing and stylish commercials. Jennie, before she went off with Peter, was one of the most influential producers in London and between them they enlisted the services of a very hot director. Peter brought Williams and Humbert to life with characters played by a seasoned character actor called Jonathan Elsome and a spear carrier from the Royal Shakespeare Company called Charles Dance who went on to very big things indeed. Peter created a fictional board meeting where the chairman was suggesting a name for their new sherry – 'The name Dry Sack has been suggested' – when Jonathan in his role as Mr Williams protested, 'But who could think Dry Sack an appropriate name for a medium sherry?' The chairman's response was, 'The name was put forward by my lady wife,' and the enthusiastic response from the board was, 'Dry Sack it is.'

The 15% commission system was still operating in those days and with the Dry Sack account spending hundreds of thousands of pounds we were suddenly feeling flush and decamped to a stylish little office in Bruton Place, opposite the exclusive Guinea Grill and a strip club. We then won a couple of new pieces of business in quick succession. The big German haircare company Wella came on board and the northern sweet company Tavener Rutledge gave us their business too. An enormously successful television series called *Kojak* had been running for a few years and the main character played by Telly Savalas was the epitome of cool. When he wasn't smoking slim cigars he was always sucking a lollipop, all the while solving unspeakable crimes. The series was beautifully written by one of the early great American scriptwriters called Abbey Mann. Somehow Tavener Rutledge had got the UK franchise for Kojakpops, which were pretty run-of-the-mill multi-flavoured sugar lollipops but vested with the cool New York detective's imagery were really sought after.

They had a few years of enormous sales but it was felt a successor was required, something to rejuvenate the market. We were given the task of creating that successor. At that time Laurel and Hardy were having a very surprising renaissance. The chattering classes had taken to their quirky humour and acting genius with a fervour no one predicted. And so we invented Ollie's Lollies. Not for the first or last time I had my doubts about my chosen profession when at a sales conference I stood up and extolled the virtues of this new brand. I assured the sales force sitting expectantly in front of me that Ollie's Lollies would rule the lollipop market for the next decade. I'm glad I didn't have any kids to go home to who might have asked me what I did at work that day.

The other side benefit of Tavener Rutledge was they delivered unbelievable amounts of their other products for us to try. Buttered brazils, sherbet lemons, caramel whirls, coconut ice and many other sweet delicacies jammed the storage cupboards in our small reception. With my weakness for such things I was once again pitched into a ferocious battle against the twin scourges of obesity and tooth decay.

CHAPTER 13

1977

Over *dinner one evening Adrian and I decided that if our agency was going to reach* the next stage of its development we needed a really heavy weight creative partner, even though Peter Mayle was doing a great job, particularly on Dry Sack. By this time Peter and Jennie were living in the South of France and coming over sporadically and staying with me in my new Fulham flat which meant they couldn't be fully engaged in the business. And so we drew up a list of people we would like to approach.

David Abbott was at the top of our list. He was a friend of both of us, with me from DDB and Millwall and with Adrian from their time together at Merton College, Oxford. He was also the biggest star in British advertising. The idea that he might join us was a bit like Millwall deciding Lionel Messi would be the answer to their goal scoring problems and then making a bid for him. But having been emboldened at our dinner by the odd glass of wine, we thought we would give David a crack. We were, however, realistic enough to expect we would have to get to number 10 on our list before we met with any success.

As luck would have it, three days later Adrian was having one of his occasional lunches with David, where they would catch up and chew over old times. Adrian and I agreed that he should approach David at this informal gathering because I had previously badgered him unsuccessfully to join me at Byfield Mead. Since then David had done extremely well. Despite his partner Mr French moving on, the agency bearing the Abbott name was pretty successful. Through a succession of mergers they now had a rich American parent company, the board of which idolised David and had great plans to move him to New York to run their worldwide operation in the not too distant future. So it was with neither hope nor expectation that Adrian set off for his lunch in Soho.

While he was with David I hardly gave their meeting a second thought. I really did think David would turn him down. But Adrian returned flushed and excited. He said that David was interested and wanted to talk more. I was astonished because it was an outrageous thought that David would even consider joining us. I do not exaggerate when I say at that time he was a man who could have got any job in advertising, anywhere in the world. He was the hottest property in the business and I could hardly believe he was taking the prospect of joining us seriously.

The one weapon in our armoury was that the three of us were really good friends. On the rare occasions we met up we always finished up helpless with laughter over all sorts of inconsequential issues. But that was friendship. This was business and David quite properly agonised over the wisdom of joining our small operation and discussions went on for quite a while. He finally rang me one Saturday morning when I was at home in Fulham. I was already feeling rather gloomy for a multitude of reasons and David added to my bad mood by saying he couldn't come. I asked why and he replied that it just didn't feel right. I told him that I couldn't do anything about that feeling. If he instinctively felt that he couldn't be on board I understood that but I left him in no doubt that I was deeply sorry. We agreed to have lunch in two or three weeks when the dust had settled. It was a huge disappointment and I had a very miserable Saturday - Millwall lost as well.

The following morning David's wife Eve rang me and asked how I was feeling. I explained my sadness but said that I understood why he had made that decision. She then told me to be at Bianchi's, a lovely little Italian restaurant in Soho run by a famous restaurateur called Eleanor, the following day. I turned up believing that lunch would be a consolation prize, an explanation of how he couldn't overrule his instinctive emotions that the move wasn't quite right. I was astonished when he said that he had changed his mind and would be joining us after all. He explained that it was my response to his announcement that he wasn't coming that made him believe that it was the right thing to do. David was characteristically fair about his level of equity in our venture. He and I were to be equal partners with Adrian next and the remainder for our other partner Guy Davies. Overcome with emotion, I almost choked on a piece of chicken but couldn't wait to race back and tell Adrian and Guy the great news. And so Abbott Mead Davies and Vickers was born.

It's fair to say that the news stunned the advertising world. The big American magazine Advertising Age ran the headline 'British advertising's answer to Robert Redford joins small shop'. David immediately asked Ron Brown, one of London's very best art directors to join us. The two of them worked together until the day David retired and produced campaign after campaign of stunning brilliance. Another man from David's past agency called Ken New, a great media director, also joined. The top floor of Bruton Place became the creative sanctum for a while – David and Ron used the table tennis table we'd put out there for recreation to write some great new ads for Wella and for Austinsuite, a large UK furniture manufacturer who rang up and appointed us on the day we announced David was joining. When they weren't working they played a version of seated table tennis using their office chairs to zoom around on.

Our new business relationship was tested almost immediately. Before David arrived, Adrian and I had narrowly averted a bad debt with a toy company called Condor. We had had the account for a little while and managed to do some decent work created by Rick Cook. The business was run by a Cuban from a warehouse just outside Luton. The head office of Condor was based in Puerto Rico and the only address we had out there was a PO Box. Some debts were building up and in those days agencies were responsible if a client defaulted because we acted as principles with the media companies we purchased time and space from. Not surprisingly, we found it relatively difficult (impossible!) to get credit insurance on a company with a PO address on the other side of the world.

Adrian and I went up to Luton and had a very cordial discussion with our Cuban client and we both felt reassured on the drive back down the M1. The clincher, I seem to remember, was me saying to Adrian that he must be all right and rich because he was wearing a gold Rolex on each wrist. Naïveté and desperation were to blame – we wanted to believe that everything would turn out all right, and in this instance it did. We were lucky.

We also had another account called Video Master. Atari had enjoyed enormous success with a very rudimentary electronic game called Pong. Video Master had a couple of very interesting variants in production, or so they told us. They talked about very high levels of expenditure on advertising and that they might even be prepared to give us a small equity stake.

For me, it was shades of Eddie Leshik because about three or four weeks after David had joined us, Adrian came white-faced to my office and said that our potential Apple rival had gone into liquidation leaving us about

£60,000 in the hole. The chances of us getting any of this back were zero and in the short term this would have serious implications for our cash flow. I thought it best to break the news to Ted Emerson at the bank before we outlined this major setback to David. After mildly berating me over lunch in Langans, Ted said that he would support our position. This was yet another occasion in the history of the company where he proved to be a true friend and supporter. Many years later when I discussed this issue with him during a trip down memory lane he said that he always had faith that even if things had gone bad we would have repaid the money somehow – he was right.

After a rather uncomfortable couple of hours with David explaining this little financial problem he told us that he had ambitious plans to speed up awareness of the agency. He said that he found it curious that advertising agencies didn't appear to believe in advertising. Only a tiny number of them had ever spent any time or money on advertising themselves. We all agreed that we would take a number of double page spreads in Campaign magazine. The very first was a picture of the five of us (Abbott, Mead and Vickers with Mayle and Davies) and a headline which read 'Watch out Collets we're only £35 million behind you'. This was a great example of David's unerring ability to find the right positioning for products, in this case us.

We were excited by a call a few days later from Subaru who said that they would like to come in and talk to us. This excitement was tempered slightly a day later when we discover that their shortlist was 60 agencies long. We decided not to take part in this pantomime. We announced David's arrival in early December with the Campaign spread and some good editorial features. In a rush, Christmas was upon us but in our state of high excitement we resented the fact that the world seemed to stop for the festivities. Momentum was growing and we wanted to carry on working. But the tiny group of us found time for the first AMD&V Christmas lunch at the

Mykonos, a friendly Greek restaurant in Soho which, until we outgrew it, was our Christmas lunch venue of choice.

Early in January we had a much more significant call. The management board at Volvo UK (a concession held by Lex) had undergone a shakeup. The new boss was a man called Jim Maxmin, a devoted and long-term admirer of David's work at his past agency. Jim wanted David and me to go down and meet with him to discuss moving the business our way. David was much less excited than the rest of us. He explained that he'd been writing ads for Volvo for a number of years and that it had become a brand that had lost its way in terms of its image. Maybe, he said, we should hang on and land another car account. Despite his misgivings we went down to Volvo's Marlow offices, close to where I live now, and Jim reassured him that he wanted to return to core values for the brand and he couldn't think of anybody better than David to achieve that. Soon after, Volvo became a client.

That was a very important moment in the history of the agency. A really major advertiser had joined us, or to be frank joined David, and it marked the start of an enormously productive relationship. Sir Trevor Chinn, the boss of Lex, became a great friend of the agency.

Even before David joined us we were bursting out of our bijou little office in Bruton Place and we had been looking around for a little while to try and find a great deal on a new office. At that stage Charles and Maurice Saatchi had an amazing edifice in Lower Regent Street for their Saatchi & Saatchi agency. However, the rump of space ran back to a little mews off Jermyn Street called Babmaes Street. It was essentially the back entrance of the grand Saatchi front office. I think they had already sold the lease on that to Cunard and so we set about making a main entrance from a back entrance. As an aside we were positioned immediately opposite the back of the Libyan embassy and a few years later some of our people swore that they saw machine guns there. Curiously, at that stage Martin Sorrell was the finance director of Saatchi's. They retained the head lease so I had to negotiate with Martin over the terms of the sublease that we were to take on. He initially suggested that as part of the consideration for the offices they will be prepared to take an equity stake in our agency. Cheap rent was tempting but we resisted and they remained our landlords for our stay.

We did our best on the limited funds we had available at that stage to make the offices look nice and reception, particularly, looked pretty good when we'd finished. One of my abiding memories was on the morning of a particular pitch the sight of David Abbott on his knees using a brown magic marker to touch up the worn stair carpet leading up to the conference room. David had come from FGA's stylish offices near Paddington Station and showed remarkable tolerance for our rather tatty accommodation. On a visit to the premises before we signed the lease we spotted a couple of mice enjoying a reflective moment in what was to be our reception area. Luckily that didn't put David off joining us.

A few days before we were due to move in Adrian came in to see me with a slightly grim look on his face. He had been pursuing a new piece of business for us called Marshall Cavendish, the major player in the part works industry. Part works companies had a simple business plan: they took a subject of broad interest and undertook to publish 156 weekly parts on that subject. They then spent a fortune on advertising and promoting Part One. Adrian told me that the marketing director was keen to appoint as but had one proviso – he didn't want me involved in any part of his business. Despite being a little upset about this – nobody likes rejection – I had absolutely no problem with accepting this as a condition of winning the business. We always felt with new clients that if they didn't like me they would like

David, if they didn't like David they would like Adrian and if they didn't like Adrian they might like me. Sure enough, we signed up the giant publisher and they played an enormous part in supplying early profit to allow us to grow the business. After a while I became very friendly with the marketing director but was quite pleased that his initial requirement meant that I didn't have to handle the account because it was the kind I didn't like – it was all about conveying information to people, such as whether there was a record or a book or membership to a club included and there was very little creativity involved. Accounts like this one, riddled with details and primarily factual, are, to use a book metaphor, more like manuals than novels and I definitely prefer novels.

Within two years we resigned the business because we felt it was doing nothing for our creative reputation and stopping us pitching on more creatively rewarding pieces of business. Indeed, the whole creative department at one stage were overrun by Marshall Cavendish titles ranging from cooking, home, craft, sewing and sex to motor mechanics. The account represented about 130% of our profit at that time and so it seemed like a brave if not foolhardy decision. But we believe we had the potential to more than make up for the loss of the account. Before we finally did part company, David wrote a quote for one of the cookery part works which said: 'Your eyes taste the food before your tongue' which was the first of his many innovations in food advertising.

In those days if people who started UK advertising agencies wanted to capitalise on their efforts, there was only one exit strategy for them. At an appropriate time when the business was running well and making a profit they would typically sell to an American operation looking for British and/ or European representation. I had already experienced some of this at

Byfield Mead with the BBDO adventures and was soon to be involved for a second time.

Early in 1979 a major player in American advertising, Ed McCabe of Scali, McCabe, Sloves (SMS), came to London to deliver a lecture at the IPA. He was the youngest copywriter ever to be inducted into the American Copywriting Hall of Fame and one of his main claims to that fame was his work on Volvo. David and Ron at that stage had produced some award-winning work in the press and on posters for the brand in here in the UK. David knew Ed slightly so we arranged to have dinner while he was in town. David had a worldwide reputation and he, Ed and I got along famously.

SMS had recently been acquired by the worldwide Ogilvy Group and had been charged with developing an alternative 'global network with creativity at its heart'. SMS would own those agencies and in turn Ogilvy would own SMS. Ed talked to us over dinner about the possibilities of us joining this network. Fallon in Minneapolis was already part of this growing group of agencies, as was the Martin agency in Richmond, Virginia. Both of these were doing great work and we were intrigued. However, we'd only been going for 18 months and we were gaining traction quite quickly in the UK advertising market so we felt it was far too early to sell a part of our business. Ed reported back to his boss Marvin Sloves that we were absolutely the sort of partners they should have in the UK.

Marvin was a man of great style who reminded me immediately of Orson Welles (before the great director swelled up like barrage balloon) in his style and voice. I also loved his quote when he sold his agency to Ogilvy. He was asked what the main difference was between SMS before and after the Ogilvy sale and he replied that before the sale the partners did not have a pot to pee in but after they spent the money they got from the sale, they would have 26 bathrooms between them.

Marvin, being the master of grand gestures, sent two Concorde return tickets to New York for David and me. It was irresistible. We flew over a week or so later and met with Marvin, Ed and their partners over dinner at the Four Seasons in New York. The stylish Sloves had his own table in the beautiful Pool Room at the power restaurant in the Seagram building, designed by Mies van der Rohe on Park Avenue. They argued persuasively that because we both worked on Volvo and creativity was at the heart of both our offerings, they would be the ideal parents for us. They said that it was inevitable that we would finish up with American partners one day and there would be nobody who we'd like to be more involved with than them.

They were right, of course. There was an immediate bonding and the start of lifelong friendships – both Marvin and one of his partners, Alan Pesky, became godfathers to two of my sons and to this day David and Eve often holiday with Joan and Sam Scali. David and I both loved the mercurial McCabe. During the negotiations, at an evening out at the Ritz Casino in London's Piccadilly, we really bonded as a trio when Ed disconcerted the rather po-faced staff by demanding that they acquire a craps table for him so that he could have a proper gamble. The slightly surreal nature of the evening was compounded by David and me giving Ed a lift back to his hotel. The problem was that David had a Porsche 911 with virtually no carrying space at all and so Ed was jammed in the back doing a passable imitation of Harry Houdini. But from somewhere his right hand appeared – we both shook it and the deal was really on its way.

Despite our misgivings at selling too soon, the benefits of a relationship with this powerhouse New York operation were massively appealing. Very importantly, it also allowed us to buy out Guy Davies's equity because he had not quite gelled with the rest of us. So we did the deal which would remain in place for 10 years. We all got along really well and grew together. The SMS empire expanded.

CHAPTER 14

1985

In the early eighties it was the turn of communications companies to benefit from the wild rush to
market that the Conservatives under Mrs Thatcher had encouraged. As
said elsewhere, up until that point if a group of people started their own
advertising agency and wanted to capitalise on their efforts the only exit
strategy was to sell to an American company at a price of typically eight
times earnings.

But the eighties changed all that and in some senses it was a precursor
to the dotcom boom of the late nineties. By the time it was our turn to go to
the market a number of agencies had already floated with enormous success,
at least initially. Indeed at one stage a PR company had a share price which
carried a profit to earnings ratio or P/E of 89 times. If my memory serves
me correct Saatchi & Saatchi blazed the trail for all other age advertising
agencies. It seemed silly for us not to join the gold rush.

In 1985 the *Financial Times*, reporting on a booming advertising expenditure throughout Europe, said, 'The UK is tipped to enjoy the biggest real
growth, predicted to be 23% between 1983 and 1987.' The Treasury at that
time forecast a 4% growth in consumer expenditure during 1986. As the
song says, those were the days, my friend.

After getting advice from Arthur Andersen, our accountants, we embarked on a beauty parade of some of Britain's more respectable and powerful financial institutions as we looked for help in going public. In our business we constantly had to pitch for new clients and so it was a new experience to be pitched to. Some of them were awful. One famous merchant bank had a presentation outlining their capabilities using an overhead projector where at least half the presentation was missing because somebody had not typed out the cells correctly. The lead presenter also said that he only had fizzy water as refreshment because that's what everybody was drinking those days. It reminded me of paper cups, Byfield Mead and Santigo.

After trawling our way around the City meeting the candidates put up by Andersen's we arrived at Hambros. The presentation was led by a man called John Padovan with Michael Sorkin, one of his fellow directors, doing the presentation itself. In truth most of the stuff that John and Michael talked about went way over our heads but we liked them. The deal was clinched by the arrival of tea with two large tins of Sainsbury's biscuits in attendance. Of all the banks we saw that day only Hambros had done any homework at all. They knew our client list, hence the biscuits.

To go alongside the merchant bank we needed a stockbroker. This was a time before the financial 'big bang' and stockbrokers were independent, very successful and apart from the one we chose, Rowe and Pitman, languid to the point of arrogance. Our main contact at the brokers was Nick Verey, a legend in the City sadly no longer with us, ably assisted by Rory Tapner, who went on to have a major career in financial services and is currently head of Coutts Bank.

So we had a stellar group of advisers and sent about the grinding process of producing an offer for sale document, every word of which had to be verified and overseen by Herbert Smith, one of the more traditional law firms with limitless experience in public offerings. I don't think the senior partner at Herbert Smith had ever dealt with a writer of David's calibre because at one point during the long process of verification he said he found the language in a paragraph David had written a little too racy. David's response was, 'I think we're a little more Hemingway than you, James.'

An offer for sale document is the piece of paper that any potential investor receives to enable him to make up his mind whether to invest or not. I think it's worthwhile repeating the words contained in the introduction to that document:

i.   The agency began with a set of beliefs that are still the cornerstone of the way in which it operates and that are, therefore, as relevant to its future prospects as they are to its past performance.

ii. The principal requirements of clients from agencies is outstanding creative work. Hence all our structures and disciplines are designed to reflect the fact that the creative function is the most important part of our business.

iii. Our clients place great trust in us. We spend large sums on their behalf. We should be honest in our advice, even when it does not serve our own short-term interests. This will earn respect and create long-term relationships.

iv. We value our skills and the service we give. We will work with small growth companies as well as major clients, but we expect a fair return.

v.   The agency should be an agreeable, fair and humane place in which to work. In an industry characterised by a high turnover of staff, the way to retain people is to keep them happy.

vi. Success brings responsibilities as well as rewards. The advertising we produce is in the public eye and should be good mannered and truthful.

We should not create advertising we would not want our own families to see.

Around that time MORI, a respected polling company, conducted a survey of 176 marketing directors about advertising agencies. Their conclusions noted that AMV 'really does seem to be in some way unique and different from all other agencies'.

Endless hours spent verifying resulted in a beautifully written document with a picture of the three of us on the front cover. David and I went to have a meeting with Hambros and Rowe & Pitman to talk about the issue price, the price at which the shares would be sold to the public. These were normally pretty stormy meetings with people in our position wanting the price to be as high as possible and the advisers keeping the price down to a reasonable figure to enable them to make sure that the initial stock offering is successful. We'd heard about this and went prepared. We had a set of playing cards produced with various numbers on them and broke the ice at the meeting by asking them to pick a card. They opened the meeting by saying they would like a price set which equated to 18 times our projected earnings. Remember this was the time when P/E ratios in our sector were anything from 20 times to 50. We said we were rather hopeful that we would do better than 18 and suggested 19. The charade had to go on so with a palpable sigh of relief they asked if they could have 5 minutes alone to ponder. While they were out of the room, David and I agreed that we'd settle for 18.5. When we relayed this information on their return there was a bit of teeth sucking and a nod of agreement with a warning that it could be difficult to get away at that level. The pricing meeting cemented our relationships with our advisers who always went the extra mile for us. Much later they told us that their previous launch of an advertising agency had a price-fixing meeting which lasted for 12 hours. Ours lasted 30 minutes.

Then came the fateful day of the public launch itself. It was at the height of an insatiable demand for stock in almost any company and there was another one going public on exactly the same day as us – the retailer Laura Ashley. The day after the applications closed the *Daily Telegraph* showed a picture of people queuing round the block with plastic bags full of multiple applications for both the Ashley float and our own. Rather shamefacedly, Nick and Michael reported back to us that we were 33 times oversubscribed. What that actually meant was that we were trying to raise a comfortable £6 million but had received applications and cheques to the value of a shade over £200 million. As everybody had their cheques cashed at the same time as their applications, it was only two weeks later that we had to send back something approaching £200 million to the unsuccessful applicants. They were very heady days and the interest on £200 million was a very worthwhile addition to our P&L that year. We somewhat ironically bought presents for all our advisers thanking them for their enormous efforts to make the launch a success.

I remember meeting with one of the most respected young analysts in the sector, an ebullient young man called Richard Dale from the brokers James Capel. He went on to have a stellar career finishing up as European Head of Research at the giant Citigroup. In our first meeting in Aybrook Street, Richard said that he would know when we were in trouble because he wouldn't hear from us. I countered by saying I planned to call him come rain or come shine. He was vital in understanding our business and helping persuade major investors to place their trust in us.

As an aside, on the day James, David and I returned from the City having gone through the painful process of sending all that money back and travelling by Tube because we couldn't get a taxi, I was overcome by dizziness and fell over in Marylebone High Street. That evening, as I lay in bed, the room was spinning around. I went to a doctor who thought it might be an inner ear problem and sent me for tests. I had eight different ones and in the end the neurologist concluded that I had multiple sclerosis, an incurable condition which can cause great damage to the nervous system.

The doctor told Sam first so she could be the one to tell me and she did so in the car on the way home from a dinner. My response was fairly philosophical, which is typical of my personal brand of hypochondria: if I'm inventing health-related things to worry about, I'm rubbish and will flap and fret but if it's a real thing, I'm good, calm and sensible. And that is how I've been with MS, which has had very little impact on my life. I got it fairly late, at the age of 45, so it was unlikely to ever kill me (the earlier you get it, the more likely it is to be fatal) and my symptoms have been limited to occasional extreme tiredness, dizzy spells and slightly dodgy balance from time to time. In fact, the symptoms have been so minor I even tried to get it struck from my medical record but after more tests the doctors refused because I still had scars on my brain, the classic tell-tale sign of MS. I have been very lucky that this deeply unpleasant condition has caused me so few problems.

A year on from the initial launch our share price had doubled and Sam and I had made an offer on a house on Richmond Hill. We were due to exchange contracts two days after the stock market crashed on Black Monday – 19 October 1987. Our share price halved overnight and Sam and I had to tell the vendors we now couldn't proceed with the purchase at the price we'd offered. Apologetically, I said to them we could afford to make an offer which was 15% less than our original one. I said I would understand if they wanted to remarket the house but at least they had a base offer in the future if that remarketing was not a success. But within 12 hours they accepted our revised offer and we moved into Downe House in the middle of Richmond Hill with the great Turner view over the Thames. Not many years later we sold the house to Jerry Hall and Mick Jagger. I think she still lives there today.

Our period as a public company was very enjoyable. We developed great relationships with all our major investors and the analysts who followed the sector. I took the view that we would behave with the 'City' in the same way that we would with a major client, by which I mean we would deliver what we promised and always tell the truth.

For most of that period we were the agency business with the highest profit to earnings ratio, which was the gold standard by which companies were rated. When it came to expanding AMV Group into areas complementary to advertising we took great care. Any discussions were prolonged and we never bought any company where we didn't actually like the people who ran it. It was a given that any acquisition we made had to be best of breed but they also had to share our principles and beliefs and join us in the crusade to create a world-class group.

Following our successful public company launch it became apparent that we needed to expand our executive structure. We took the view that our success or failure in the public arena would depend very largely on the relationships we created with our major shareholders and the way we expanded our group. I believed that our method of operation and our beliefs should not change despite us being more in the public eye than ever before. But after a little over 10 years we needed to refresh our top management. Although we had developed a very strong next layer, we were lacking a standout candidate to take over the day-to-day running of the business while I concentrated on running the public company side. Our relationship with SMS meant we developed a great understanding with the management team of Ogilvy (SMS's American parent company) in the UK. From very early days we had spent a lot of time with Peter Warren, the chairman of Europe and increasingly with Michael Baulk, the chief executive of the London operation and the man widely believed to be the dynamic force behind Ogilvy's great run. Although I had no desire to give up the day-to-day running of the agency (contrary to widespread belief, I really am an advertising man at heart) it seemed sensible to bring in a really heavyweight manager to drive the next stage of the agency's development.

We decided that Michael should be approached to see if joining us was of any interest and I arranged to have dinner with him at Langan's Brassiere. It had become a favourite haunt of both the agency and me personally from our days in Bruton Place, some 500 yards away. As with David 10 years before, I was surprised that Michael, when faced with the prospect of joining us, was very interested. We agreed that we would pursue this course of action although we knew it would be stormy.

Bill Phillips and Ken Roman were the chairman and chief executive respectively of Ogilvy in New York. They had always been very supportive of both SMS and ourselves and were consummate gentleman. But to say they were less than amused by the potential defection of Michael is an understatement. The London office was on the crest of a wave and they were very anxious not to disturb the elements that had contributed to its success. Michael on the other hand, although always mentioning that he did not ever wish to start on his own, felt that being part of the management of a UK public company with a very successful agency at its heart would be a great career move. Despite their irritation and deep opposition, Bill and Ken did not exert any pressure on Michael to try to stop him moving to us even though it would have been absolutely within their power to do so.

So Michael joined us with a new title of Chief Executive of the agency while I took the title of Chief Executive of the group with David remaining as Chairman of both entities. It was a very good time to strengthen our team because creating and servicing our shareholder base was critical to the future of the operation. The advertising business itself was getting tougher and more organisations were springing up to monitor our activities on behalf of clients.

Michael's arrival meant a profound change for me too because while he concentrated on growing the agency business in the face of these new threats, I took some time to learn how to run a public company. Instead of developing relationships with clients I started developing relationships with investors and I was now selling our performance, our strategy and ourselves. I enjoyed this period very much but to this day I miss the involvement with clients and ads that had been a daily part of my life for over 20 years until then.

Within AMV there was some fallout from Michael's appointment. Leslie Butterfield, our valuable head of planning, took the opportunity to start his own agency in light of the fact that his own development had hit a glass ceiling since Michael's arrival. We calculated that this was a likely consequence but on balance felt that Michael's experience in creating and working in a very large agency could only be of benefit to us.

CHAPTER 15

1988

The turbulent times in our business were mirrored by some uncertain times in the world economies. Black Monday had hit us within a year of going public and our share price halved overnight. The days of plenty were coming to a temporary close and we struggled with the blandishments of analysts urging us to buy American agencies one year and then congratulating us on our vision in not getting involved with American agencies the following year. The voracious appetite that the public agency groups had for acquisitions, particularly Saatchi & Saatchi, meant that good companies to acquire were hard to find. We had determined that we would not spend our shareholders' money on a wild shopping spree. So the first few years were quite sparse in terms of acquisitions. Our cautious approach and the relationship we developed with the City ensured our share price held up well.

We still had our relationship with SMS and it was a very good one – they had recovered any money they'd expended on us in the first instance and made a huge profit by releasing some of their shares for our public offering. I was also spending a lot of time in New York exploring the possibility of closer collaboration. They fitted our template very well in that they were people we respected who were at the top of their game and had built an enviable presence in some of the key markets around the world. Over dinner one night, inevitably at Marvin's table at the Four Seasons, we discussed the suggestion that they had put forward of us buying the SMS operation from Ogilvy. The original architect of the deal at Ogilvy which brought SMS into the fold had tragically died and the current management were less enamoured with the idea of a new global network to run alongside the existing one. At that time the American accounting principles made it very attractive for English companies to acquire US operations and so we embarked on a year-long examination of how everything would work in practice.

In successful creative operations such as ours it was inevitable that some pretty large reputations would exist which had to be accommodated and I concentrated on little else except how to do that. The strictures of the public market meant that we had to proceed with the utmost caution and confidentiality. The complex equation of who did what and with what title in the enlarged entity took shape. It was an agonisingly difficult process only made easier by the goodwill that existed amongst the eight or so people whose lives would be affected.

In the middle of these on-going discussions, SMS had a gathering of all their agencies in Venice. Sam went on ahead and was looked after by Pat Fallon who at that stage had become a close friend. I had never been to Venice before and had no idea what to expect, except for a lot of water. As it was a business meeting I calculated that suits and ties were the order of the day and packed accordingly. Arriving in Venice wildly overdressed for the 30° heat, I spend the afternoon with Fallon and Sid Oland, the chief executive of Labatts, the Canadian brewer, trawling round elegant little men's boutiques trying desperately to buy summer apparel. It's fair to say that they did not cater for large English gentlemen. But luckily a combination of some hastily let out trousers and a few summer shirts borrowed from the larger of the worldwide gathering meant that I scraped through without looking too ridiculous.

It was at this meeting that, faced with dressing up for a gala ball at one of the Palazzos that abound in Venice, Sam discovered that she had not brought the body stocking to wear under her antique beaded evening dress. Being Sam and having a really great figure, she wore the dress anyway and was the star of the evening. Many a client had great trouble averting their gaze as they sank a Bellini in the famous Cipriani Hotel.

Eventually we persuaded all our advisers of the desirability of a deal with SMS and even agreed a financial structure with them and SMS. Parallel with this we had to deal with Ogilvy as well because they owned all the equity while SMS owned all the client relationships. Everything was finally put in place, handshakes and letters of intent were exchanged and we were good to go. But about two weeks before we were due to announce the deal to an unsuspecting world Martin Sorrell made a hostile bid for Ogilvy. The level of his offer was irresistible to the Ogilvy shareholders and the deed was quickly done. Despite having agreement from all the participants for our deal we found ourselves starting negotiations all over again with the new owner and I spent a lot of time going to meetings with Martin in his Farm Street offices. The price he had paid for his latest acquisition had massively increased the book value of all its assets, of which SMS was one and despite having relatively cordial exchanges we were unable to agree a formula to go forward and the deal died.

Having reluctantly decided that our dream of an International network with SMS was a non-starter we reviewed the way forward for the agency and the group. A consequence of WPP's takeover of Ogilvy meant that Martin Sorrell was now in control of something approaching 23% of our equity. This made us feel uncomfortable. At the same time we were under increasing pressure to offer our clients International capability. The choices were clear – we could spend the next five years building up a network of offices in key markets either by acquisition or start-up or look for an established partner. The first option, although appealing, would mean that the tiny group of us charged with expanding our successful public company would be stretched to breaking point in trying to create five or six new partners in Europe and beyond. In truth we were all pretty exhausted after the two years that we'd spent trying to bring the SMS deal to fruition.

At that time one of our major competitor in the UK in our terms was BMP. A few years before, they had been caught up in a hostile bid from a French group called BDDP. Martin Boase, the chairman, looked around for a white knight to fend off the unwelcome French attention. He had developed a relationship with Bruce Crawford who, when he was International head of BBDO, had embarked on a crusade to expand into Europe by acquiring or setting up the very best creative talent available. BBDO had been one of the giant Madison Avenue agencies noted for client service but without a particularly distinguished creative reputation. Bruce decided that the acquisition of great creative talent outside the US would most likely drive the home company into raising its creative bar. Following Martin's approach Bruce decided to intercede and do battle with the French to win BMP. By this stage Bruce was chairman of Omnicom – created from a merger of DDB, BBDO and the Chicago agency called Needham Harper and Steers, who had been involved with S. H. Benson when I was there many years before. His plan was, while keeping BMP's identity intact, to twin it with BBDO which had consistently underperformed in the UK. BMP felt that an association with DDB, with its outstanding creative heritage and reputation, would be a much better fit. Bruce acquiesced but it still left him with a BBDO problem to solve in London.

As we were pondering our next move, Martin brokered a discussion between Bruce, David and me to see if there was any possibility of a relationship developing. David and I flew to New York to meet with Bruce who I already knew from my Byfield Mead days. We had dinner at Bruce's favourite restaurant, Lutece. He was very much at home there and over exquisite French cuisine we talked deep into the night about the possibility of an association between our two companies which would solve our international problems and help him with his perennial London issue with BBDO.

Bruce's quest to improve the level of creativity at BBDO New York had borne fruit. Under the creative leadership of Phil Dusenbury the agency had become award-winning and had produced a stunning repertoire of work, particularly on television. Lead by PepsiCo the showreel was as good as any in the States. Even on difficult accounts like Wrigley's the work was much more reminiscent of the good old days of DDB rather than the more institutionalised approach of BBDO in the 80s.

Mentioning Wrigley's reminds me of a meeting we had some years later. We met with William Wrigley Jr to review the first work that we had produced in the UK for his company. At the end of the meeting he said to John Kelly, the creative who produced the work, 'John, I just love your British sense of humour. It's just that I don't want any of it in my advertising.'

Following our dinner, David and I flew back to London and had a series of meetings with our partners to examine our options. There was little appetite to pursue the route of developing our own network around Europe – we were heading into an economic recession and despite our pretty stellar reputation as a public company it would inevitably make the task of raising funds for expansion more difficult. We agreed to review our thoughts over the Christmas period. We had a long-standing commitment to each other that on issues of major importance a consensus was not enough and unanimous agreement had to be achieved. Despite one or two of us having some reservations it was decided that BBDO were the best – indeed the only – major group that we would consider being involved with and we set about making it happen.

After some negotiations with WPP and our advisers, Martin was persuaded to sell his 22.6% stake in us to BBDO. Their London operation was mainly intended to service international clients like PepsiCo, Gillette, Apple, Delta Airlines and Wrigley's. It had a little over 80 employees and there was bound to be duplication that couldn't be accommodated. This meant that our rule of not making anyone redundant would have to be broken. The London management of BBDO calculated the costs of redundancies based on the government rules on such matters, which were more expensive then than they are today. We, however, insisted that a much more generous formula should be applied and this resulted in us paying people in most instances 10 times more than they were legally due. Although nobody welcomed being out of work, many of the people we spoke to were massively comforted by the financial cushion that we supplied. From beginning to end I insisted that the process should not take longer than three weeks. Michael, James and I spoke to every one of the BBDO employees individually and all the legal paperwork for those not staying with us was rushed through.

Inevitably there were some real talents that joined us from the elegant offices in Regents Park. The most famous were Walter Campbell and Tom Carty, a junior-ish creative team who in the following years transformed our television output. Every person who joined us was twinned with an existing AMV staffer to make sure that the integration was as quick and painless as possible. Overnight we had International capability in every important advertising market and Alan Rosenshine, the President of BBDO worldwide, joined our board. Adding a whole bunch of new people to your staff overnight can be traumatic but the integration went very smoothly and within weeks AMV people were working on BBDO business and vice versa.

We were encouraged by our new American partners to expand our group. At the time of our negotiations with Bruce Crawford and Alan Rosenshine we had already agreed to set up Ed McCabe in his New York agency. It was argued that we didn't need a New York presence because of our new partners but we had already given Ed our word and he opened up a business on Madison in the high 60s. We also had a number of flirtations with established companies in the direct marketing/sales promotion arena here in the UK. None of them seemed absolutely right for us but we did come across the opportunity to invest in a start-up.

Two of the brightest young men in the direct marketing business, Simon Hall and Chris Barraclough, opened for business with our financial backing and within a number of years they became the biggest in the country so it was a truly great investment. As far as sales promotion was concerned we acquired a company from BBDO and were offered the chance to buy Clarke Hooper Communications, one of the very best practitioners in their field. They were a public company forced into receivership by injudicious overseas expansion and we had a number of on-going conversations with their management before the bank foreclosed on them. A receiver was appointed who rang us for our best offer. We had already decided that we would not penalise their multitude of small suppliers because they would be critical in ensuring that their business ran smoothly after coming out of receivership – we would pay them rather than walk away from the debts. This meant that the cost to us of acquiring them was much higher than other offers they received from people who had no such compunctions about the way forward. Perhaps unsurprisingly, we were told we'd been outbid but the same evening I got a call from Barry Clarke, one of the founders, saying they did not want to do business with the winning consortium.

The following morning the receiver rang to say our offer had been successful after all. I was aware of Barry and the team's desire to work for us, which was partly motivated by our intention to pay off lots of their small creditors, and so I retracted our first offer and made a much smaller one which was successful. We made good on our intentions to pay the small suppliers but the bank selling the company, the preferred creditor, received less for it.

So in a momentous year we had changed from working with SMS to BBDO and suddenly we were a group of five companies plus the main agency. The share price, buoyed by BBDO's presence and the extra clients that came as a result, meant that in the following 12 months we bought two of our most successful group companies. The first was a customer magazine business called Redwood ran by two ex-BBC publications executives, Christopher Ward and Mike Potter. Although they already had some very big pieces of business, soon after joining us they won the huge Sky magazine account. It was Christopher, the joint CEO of Redwood and at one stage the editor of the *Daily Express*, who one day over breakfast in the Connaught asked me why I thought they would always make their figures. When I was lost for a reply he said it was 'because we never want to let you down'. I will never forget that breakfast.

At roughly the same time we acquired Redwood I was introduced to a dynamic young PR person called Matthew Freud, and we bought his company too. The great-great-grandson of Sigmund, Matthew was extremely impressive and much more importantly, wonderfully likeable. He remains to this day one of my closest friends even though we haven't been in business together for more than a decade. Early in our relationship we were given the task of informing the world that Pepsi were going to change the base colour on their cans to blue. We at AMV did the normal posters and a short television commercial. Matthew, on the other hand, rented a Concorde from Air France, painted it blue, added the Pepsi logo on the side and created huge number of photo opportunities. Astonishingly he also persuaded the Daily Mirror to print on blue paper. It was the first occasion of many when he demonstrated how smart we were to buy him. To this day, however, I still believe that on my first visit to his office he had gathered people in from outside to sit at desks to give me the impression that the organisation was much bigger than it actually was.

There weren't many companies that we set our eyes on and failed to convert. One slightly off-the-wall target that I did fail to acquire was Jennie & Co. Curiously this was a company founded by the very same Jennie Armstrong who I'd known since my very early days in advertising. Her company grew to be a major force in TV production in London. She had long since departed but had left behind a solid business in commercials but intriguingly had two very good commercial directors who had graduated into feature films. One was Terry Bedford, whose career ultimately did not take off in a big way, but the other was Adrian Lyne who having filmed the controversial '9½ Weeks' and 'Flashdance' was obviously on a success trajectory. I reasoned that in the future, because of the promised proliferation of television channels, content would be more important than ever before. I thought if we could get some great directors into the AMV group at this early stage, by the time the demand for content became overwhelming we will be well positioned to take advantage.

Our early discussions went very well but it was obvious that the major talent and the final arbiter on the destination of the company would be Adrian. He was mildly intrigued and one day I got a call asking if I could fly to New York to meet with him. He had just finished shooting 'Fatal Attrac-

tion' and had shown the first cut to a succession of audiences in the Midwest to gauge initial reaction. He was in New York re-cutting the end to make sure that Glenn Close got her just desserts in a way that would satisfy the bloodthirsty cinemagoers of Illinois.

He and I had breakfast at a diner downtown close to the editing suite where he was producing his new cut. He regaled me with great stories about Michael Douglas and Glenn Close. I said I'd just seen a thriller called 'Jagged Edge' which starred Miss Close and Jeff Bridges which I thought was great and was doing good business. I asked if he had the performance of that film in his sights. He dismissed my comparison with a smile and said that initial audience response suggested that 'Fatal Attraction' would be an enormous hit. He was right, of course, and his interest in selling to an advertising group faded away very rapidly.

In the years before BBDO, Marvin Sloves rang me one day and asked if I would meet the deal broker of a very good US agency. So as was my habit, I arranged a meeting over breakfast at the Connaught Hotel in Carlos Place, which runs between two of London's power squares, Grosvenor and Berkeley. Throughout most of the 80s, and a good proportion of the 90s, I would breakfast there at least three days a week. These breakfasts took place before the hotel makeover which in my view changed forever the institution that was breakfast at the Connaught.

Martin Sorrell and Peter Gummer were both regulars and, commendably, always arrived much earlier than me. Breakfast was a pretty formal affair and the staff were a well-oiled machine, dispensing the best bacon, tomato and sausage in town and overseen by a maître d' dressed in full evening wear. There was one morning when, following Marvin's request, I was having breakfast with a lady called Susan Smith who was very high up in a Boston advertising agency called Hill Holiday. The breakfast was to be

our first exploratory meeting to see if there was any basis on which we could acquire the Boston agency, which was known for its high level of creativity. As I walked in I was told that my guest had already arrived and was at my normal table. As I made my way across the dining room I was given a piece of paper by the maître d', I opened it and there were written the words, 'Your flies are undone'. Having introduced myself to Susan, I explained to her that there was, what is now fashionably called a 'wardrobe malfunction' and she should avert her gaze while I corrected it.

Having made my trousers whole again we had a very pleasant breakfast, laughed about my open flies and left promising to meet again soon. A concerned waiter stopped me on the way through asking if my trousers were all right because if not they had a valet standing by with a dressing gown so that one of their tailors could make a repair to the zip. Service from a bygone age!

Having settled in our new influx of BBDO people, we were faced by the worst recession the advertising business had faced for many years. I became president of our industry body, the Institute of Practitioners in Advertising, the IPA, and started my tenure in office by saying publicly, 'Recession? What recession?' My optimistic question quickly received a devastating answer.

My term as the spokesman for our business was characterised by a number of things that I set out to change. In my view the IPA itself had lost a lot of its relevance because membership of the council – the ruling body – had ceased to be of interest to the major players in our business and hardly any of the top 10 agencies were represented. At the same time as this malaise within the IPA was going on, the client representative body ISBA, the Incorporated Society of British Advertisers, had become very militant. As a result relationships between agencies and clients had reached an all-time low. Pummelled by a declining workforce, a substantial drop in client

expenditure and the corporate lack of self-confidence, the business that I spent all my life in was in a sorry state.

During my first year in office I persuaded most of the notable movers and shakers in our business, at least those of them prepared to give up time, to join the IPA Council. Twinned with that I made a conscious effort to improve relationships with ISBA. Fortunately, the President of that organisation newly elected, Graham Robson, sadly no longer with us, was somebody I could do business with. He was the chief executive of a major advertiser, Spillers Foods, and was as concerned as I was that relationships between clients and agencies had plummeted to an all-time low. After a series of meetings we produced a battle plan to get this essential marketing partnership back on track. We managed between us to curb the more belligerent members of his organisation and the firepower our recruiting drive had brought in at our end created more intelligent discussion. At the end of both our terms our councils were stronger and much more prepared for conciliation rather than confrontation. At the heart of this process had been the relationship between Graham and me. This is yet another example of the importance of relationships in business.

The recession went on but at AMV we resisted the temptation to carve a chunk out of our workforce. We had a very tight control over all expenses which didn't affect either the welfare of our people or the service we gave our clients and because of the really good relationship we had with our major investors I was able to sell this to them as a strategy. They were all very supportive over the next couple of years when our profits were either flat or declining. Only one of our major 10 or so institutions felt that we should have been much more ruthless in getting rid of people to reduce costs and they sold their shares but they were quickly snapped up by a combination of our existing holders and one or two new major fund managers. We were

absolutely convinced that our strategy of keeping our production base intact in the face of sharply declining client spend would bear fruit. We calculated that a motivated and secure workforce would not only protect our existing client base but would mean that we would be much more effective at pitching and winning new business. And it worked – we closed the gap in our revenues by winning new major players from our relationship with BBDO and by picking up a whole host of new accounts who had become concerned that the dispirited and depleted workforces at their existing agencies would not be able to service their business.

Following the fateful first trip on Concorde arranged by Marvin Sloves in the late seventies, I was wonderfully fortunate to travel frequently on the flying bullet to New York and back. In those heady days every trip was rewarded by a memento from British Airways. Carefully stored, I have dozens of these Concorde-branded gifts. I suspect that in the decades to come they will be quite valuable. There was one particularly memorable trip in 1994 when I went to New York to meet with Ed McCabe and was planning to stay for just two days. On the day I was due to return I got a call from British Airways saying that my return flight had been cancelled due to mechanical problems and I should turn up at Kennedy the following morning.

After a night at the New York Hilton I arrived at the appointed hour only to be told that because of continuing problems with the aircraft all remaining passengers from New York had already been flown to Washington to pick up the lunchtime Concorde from there. They assured me that everybody had been contacted and that I was the only no-show. I managed to persuade them that I had not been communicated with and I needed to get back to London urgently. They told me apologetically that they did have a newly repaired plane which was returning to London empty. I argued with some passion that it could take me. This was against all airline regulations

because a full menu of food had to be offered to all passengers at all times. Obviously I was prepared to go without food for the lightning fast journey which lasted a shade under four hours. They took pity on me and not only allowed me to fly on an empty Concorde back to Heathrow but actually got a full menu of food to offer me. The journey was wonderful. It felt like I had the world's most expensive private jet at my disposal, even though I still had to go back and sit in row 26 to have a cigarette.

With the enthusiastic support of our new American partners we continued to expand our Group during the nineties. I'd missed being able to participate in the setting up of Fishburn Hedges, a financial PR operation, but acquired them five years later on a deal that was good for both of us and proved we were right to want to be part of them from day one.

In 1994 our profits almost doubled and from that point on for the rest of the decade we rarely looked back. In 1996 and 97 AMV BBDO won Campaign Magazine's Agency of the Year in successive years – a feat never achieved before. It was also the most successful television agency at the British Television Awards for two years during this period, a far cry from the days when we were viewed as just a print agency. We became the biggest agency in the country and I make no apologies for repeating what I said at the time, 'It's amazing how big you can get if you're not worried about how big you can get.' We had strengthened our management substantially when Peter Warren joined us from Ogilvy and, really importantly, Andrew Robertson, the most celebrated of all British advertising's young rising stars, joined us to be managing director of the agency, a mantle he passed on to Cilla Snowball, another ex-Ogilvy star. Andrew subsequently became worldwide head of BBDO. Despite four years of relatively flat profits our share price stood up extremely well and we continued to enjoy the highest

P/E in the sector.

The likelihood of full acquisition by Omnicom was a constant theme throughout the mid-90s. We were neither wholly-owned nor completely independent, although we continued to match up to our obligations to our shareholders as a public company. Indeed, Omnicom backed us as a public company by participating in the various rights issues that we had to undertake to continue to expand the group. There was one particular issue which was especially satisfying. We had worked with our brokers and bankers to raise some millions of pounds to acquire our latest addition and the night before the rights issue was due to take place, James McDanell and I had a long-standing dinner engagement with two of our biggest shareholders. The news of the issue was embargoed but as the evening progressed towards midnight we both began to feel that these shareholders might be unhappy to learn of this event the next morning at the same time as the rest of the world instead of from us over dinner. And so in replying to questions we admitted that the acquisition was in the offing and because the markets were closed and no possibility of any insider trading existed, we explained the mechanics of the operation. After they'd probed the details of the offer, which would be the issue of new shares at a discount to the market price, they both offered more than the price that our bankers and brokers had decided on. At 12:01 we shook hands on the deal. It was a great feeling to ring our merchant bank in the morning telling them not to worry because the issue had been placed at a figure higher than they were expecting. They were mildly disconcerted, especially as their placing fee was no longer payable.

A little later, we finally bowed to the inevitable on media and acquired arguably the best and most thoughtful of the media independents, PHD, and merged it with our own media department and Ken New joined P, H and D in running this new media giant. We had boosted the number of companies in our group to 16 in total, covering most of the communication disciplines. Year-on-year we cemented the agency's number one position in its marketplace. Although unsought, this was a distinction that we began to value on the basis that best and biggest in that order could be valuable bedfellows.

David had quite often mused that he would like to retire at the age of 60. These were musings that I chose to ignore – the prospect of not having my really great friend and partner at my side with his wonderful ability to solve almost any creative problem was far too unpleasant to contemplate. But just past the middle of the decade he decided that he would give up being the Chairman of our public company and concentrate solely on the advertising agency itself and his creative work. It was slightly surreal for me because he and I had always been at the epicentre of all decisions about the public company and I felt lost. I took over the Chairmanship of the group and faced up to the prospect of a business life without him. In 1998 he retired completely and I still miss him immensely.

During this period, Bruce Crawford had decided to stand down as the CEO of Omnicom. His anointed successor was a man called John Wren who built the extraordinarily successful DAS division of Omnicom which stood for Diversified Advertising Services, a conglomeration of all areas of communication outside of pure advertising. This powerhouse division was driving the Omnicom share price upwards and John, who had been with the group for decades, was the obvious choice to take the company forward. He had done a really good job in protecting margins in areas such as direct marketing, sales promotion and increasingly in the new kid in town, digital. John had also been handed the task of cementing the relationship between AMV and BBDO. We had only met John fleetingly at Omnicom gatherings and none of us had had any meaningful conversations with him.

Sam and I went to New York for a short holiday in the middle of 1997. She and I had first met at the Westbury Hotel in London. It had a sister hotel in New York and both of them had been recently acquired by a friend of mine called Elliot Bernerd. He insisted that we stayed in his grand hotel on Madison Avenue and arranged for us to be treated like royalty. On the way over from London I developed a really bad cold and by day two of the trip could barely speak. John arranged for me to have dinner with him at Patroon, just off Madison Avenue and one of many great restaurants in New York. In the heady days before smoking became almost a capital crime in New York, Patroon was an especially sought-after venue for cigar smokers because it boasted a magnificent selection of the best, non-Cuban cigars and on arrival a faint blue tinge pervaded the atmosphere. In those days John sported a luxuriant moustache and was a very imposing figure. I could hardly speak from the effects of the cold, which the air-conditioned luxury of the Westbury had done little to improve, but we clicked almost instantly. We talked deep into the night, finding that we shared similar backgrounds, although he had been a teenage entrepreneur, a calling which came to me much later in life. John dismissed out of hand my idea of the public company selling just the agency to Omnicom – it had owned 25% for a while by this time – and retaining the rest of the group, which at that stage was accounting for some 60% of the profits. John was anxious that his flagship advertising brand BBDO should demonstrate its strength by having a major presence in London.

That evening started a relationship of trust and affection which still exists today. John drove the process forward and towards the end of 1998 finally completed, what was then, the most expensive acquisition in Omnicom's history. I became the first Vice Chairman of Omnicom Group Inc and subsequently took up the role of Chairman of Omnicom Europe.

As the new millennium approached AMV continued to go from strength to strength but with David's departure and the end of our life as an independent public company it was indeed the end of an era. A team of bright, young, home-trained people – Farah Ramzan Golant and Ian Pearman, who had both spent virtually all their professional lives at AMV – took over the agency and not only maintained its leadership position in London but widened the gap year-on-year throughout the next decade. The little agency that the founders had started many years before was now a giant that retained many of the guiding principles and beliefs that we'd put in place at the very beginning. At the time of our deal with Omnicom, Campaign Magazine wrote, 'BBDO now own Abbott Mead Vickers, arguably the most successful UK agency of all time.'

At the time of the agency's 20th birthday, the same magazine also wrote, 'Throughout its history Abbott Mead Vickers BBDO has never pursued size for its own sake, but focused only on achieving excellence. Yet, by concentrating on the latter, it has achieved the former. By hiring the best people and treating them with respect and decency AMV has created a cycle in which virtue brings success. It is hard to see how that virtuous circle could be broken.'

CHAPTER 16

CLIENTS

Over the 35 years of the agency's history we have been blessed to have many great clients and worked for many great individuals who ran those client companies. None of our success would be possible without the support, understanding and courage of those individuals. Each relationship probably deserves a book in itself but that's not possible so here are some thumbnail sketches.

SAINSBURY'S

Soon after we moved to Babmaes Street we got a call from Peter Davis who was the marketing director of Sainsbury's. In the first instance he came in to see David. He explained that although they had successfully countered a major Tesco price initiative he intuitively felt that they were falling behind in quality perceptions against Marks & Spencer. He said it was clear that they had to compete at both levels to maintain and build on their dominant position as a grocery retailer. He said he wanted to run a quality press campaign mainly in the Sunday supplements with all the emphasis being put on quality and innovation.

David and Ron took to this brief like ducks to water. David created an early agreement with Peter pledging to get Sainsbury's into every headline.

The quid pro quo for this was that we wouldn't have to have a giant logo at the bottom of each ad which would interfere with the quality feel of the layout. To his credit, Peter readily agreed and David and Ron embarked on the longest press campaign in grocery advertising history. In order to save money, Ken New bought media in a very disciplined way. He firmly mandated that Sainsbury's would be the first food ad in any issue of any magazine that we appeared in. In order to save money, David and Ken agreed that we would have a single page in colour facing a single page black-and-white. We retained all the impact of a colour double page spread but the cost was significantly less.

In the early days Ron commissioned beautifully lifelike artist's renditions of the food subject matter. He decided quite quickly, however, that this added an unnecessary complication and cost in the production of the ads and discovered a magical food photographer called Martin Thompson who thereafter shot every Sainsbury's colour ad. Probably the most famous ad in the series was shot showing a pack of minced beef with the headline, 'If Sainsbury's don't sell their mince in a day, they don't sell it.' It garnered a host of awards and set the style for hundreds of subsequent mini-masterpieces.

At some stage we were asked to translate our efforts in press to television. This proved quite difficult until one day David said to the account team that he wanted to do recipes. I remember one of them coming to me expressing disappointment that this didn't seem like an earth shattering idea. I slightly agreed but said that we should let David demonstrate what he meant. David was a genius, after all. And I was not disappointed because in my view the campaign he and Ron produced literally changed the face of food advertising on television. They enlisted a director called John Clark, a very successful stills photographer who had turned his hand to directing commercials, and a series of beautifully shot TV ads resulted from this collaboration. The work they did was painstaking, the product of three perfectionists: John might take a day shooting the slicing of a tomato until it was absolutely perfect. The end frame of each commercial had a celebrity endorsing the recipe that had been shot and sales of each of the ingredients skyrocketed. Most of the television commercials we see today are an unashamed copy of David, Ron and John's efforts all those years ago.

Peter's successor, Justin King, has presided over the campaigns that have followed. Both Jamie Oliver's 'Try something new today' and 'Live well for less' have carried on innovation in food retail advertising and many other people at all levels in Sainsbury's have allowed us to carry on producing great work.

YELLOW PAGES

Sainsbury's and Volvo were two of the cornerstones of the early years of Abbott Mead Vickers and they were joined soon after by Yellow Pages. Owned by British Telecom, the enormous directory business was all-powerful in the days before Google came along and changed the world. Millions of copies of the fat books were delivered to households in the UK. For years they had a pneumonic in their television advertising which was the walking fingers and a slogan 'Let your fingers do the walking' and we were approached to pitch for the business against four other big agencies. It was then a massive television advertiser and absolutely of the sort of account we needed at that stage of AMV's development.

The main client contact was a man called John Condron. An impish Northern Irishman he lived and breathed the paper powerhouse. We were comprehensively briefed and told to go away and map out the future. The product itself had been positioned as being something that everybody could turn to in times of emergency. I seem to remember that the most used categories were plumbers, electricians, roofers and the ilk. The business model was very simple: for an extra fee more ambitious tradesmen could buy display advertising to help them stand out from the crowds who had normal listings on a single line of type. Any emergency orientated tradesmen would make sure that they were represented in up to a page of their own advertising.

The pitch team was led by David, myself and Leslie Butterfield, our planning director. We recognised that although Yellow Pages had enormous awareness it had few friends among its consumers. It was seen as something to turn to only at a time of trouble and I remember at the time we compared it to a visit to the dentist. You would only go at a time when the toothache became intolerable. Like Yellow Pages, you would leave the dentist saying, 'I hope to not see you again soon.' We reckoned that if we could turn it into a friend of the family, usage could rocket and our ability to extend the number of people taking display advertising would also go through the roof, if you'll pardon the expression.

Around that time CD players had just been introduced here in the UK. As a lifelong gadget aficionado I was desperate to find one. Despite numerous trips up and down Tottenham Court Road, the electrical gadget centre of London, I had no luck. One day sitting in my office playing with the central London Yellow Pages directory, which was about three inches thick, I turned to the electrical retailer section and started making calls in the hope of tracking down the new breakthrough in music delivery. On my fourth call I found a stockist in the Edgware Road who had one Hitachi player in stock and I asked him if he would keep it for me until I could get to him. Later that day I completed the purchase and I was beside myself with excitement. I relayed this story to David and he thought that the credit I gave Yellow

Pages for making me happy was a pretty potent route to follow.

David wrote two commercials. One featured an old man called JR Hartley looking for a book he had written many years before on European butterflies while the other had a doting dad trying to find a pony as a birthday present for his daughter. David commissioned a very emotional piece of music and enlisted the voice-over talents of Joss Ackland to pronounce the magic words, 'Good old Yellow Pages. We don't just help with the nasty thing in life, like a blocked drain. We're there for the nice things too.' David had to go away so on my birthday, after Leslie had produced a compelling strategic argument for our route forward, I read out the scripts and played the music and voice-over. That was pretty much it for our pitch. We had put all our eggs into one strategic basket which for us showed a lot of promise.

There were 12 people in the room from Yellow Pages. The boss of bosses was a man called Richard Hooper who had a very distinguished subsequent career, made even more famous by his talented son Tom who directed 'The King's Speech' many years later, and Derek Dobie who was John's immediate boss. We finished the presentation and encouraged questions. We were told none would be forthcoming and the decision would be made within the week. On Friday afternoon at around six o'clock I got a call from Derek asking if he and John could come in and see me. It was rare in those days to receive a fee to do a new business pitch but characteristically Derek and John had said that £5000 will be given to every losing agency to cover some of their costs.

They arrived in my office with sombre faces and turned down my offer of tea. Derek started the meeting by reaching into his briefcase and producing a cheque made out to Abbott Mead Vickers for £5000. He made to pass it over but then, like Chris Tarrant on 'Who Wants to Be a Millionaire?' snatched it back before I could take it and said, 'You won't be needing that.

We are giving you the business.' He then reached back into his briefcase and pulled out a bottle of champagne to celebrate. It was a wonderful way to end the week. Changing the JR Hartley commercial from European butterflies to fly fishing and the pony commercial to the purchase of a bike were the only alterations we had to make to the work we put forward at the new business presentation. Many, many years of Yellow Pages commercials were an absolutely carbon copy of the structure of those first two commercials.

I really believed that in our positioning of Yellow Pages as a friend of the family we created a genuine bond not with just our users but our advertisers as well. Every year when renewal time came around for retailers, I think they ticked the box for yet another 12 months of advertising because they felt they had a relationship with the directory. I will always believe that once that link was broken, coupled with the advent of electronic directories, the population's love affair with Yellow Pages ceased.

SMITHS CRISPS

Quite early in the agency's life we won this iconic UK brand. It had fallen into some disrepair and along with Golden Wonder and KP, it found itself being used almost as a commodity brand by the distribution chain. It was owned by Nabisco Foods, a giant American food company. Soon after we acquired the business we were told that the head of Nabisco Canada was being jetted in to add new energy and drive. Although he had worked for Nabisco Canada for a number of years, Stan Heath was a Brit. Almost the first thing he did when he landed on these shores was to ring and ask for a full presentation from us on where we had got to with our market assessment and creative directions.

At the beginning of our presentation he was icily polite and listened attentively although I felt his mind was elsewhere which was obviously worrying for us. At the end of our meeting in the late afternoon I asked him what his plans were for that evening. He said he had nothing on as he was alone in town and so I offered him dinner. We arrived at the restaurant at seven o'clock and left at midnight. Sometime during the evening he told me that he had come up to AMV to fire us. He had quite a lot of experience in dealing with the head of one of the major American agencies in town. He said that he trusted this person and that's the way he operated. He was in a hurry, he said, and he needed an advertising partner who would share his sense of urgency but particularly be someone he could work with. We left the restaurant with him offering a new extended contract to us as long as I would look after him. He was a great bloke so it was not difficult to agree to join him in his adventure.

Stan and I became great personal friends and together we drove his business forward. We were ruthless about the new product program that was underway at the Reading complex, reviewing existing products that could benefit from support as well as new introductions. We relaunched Smiths crisps with a little blue bag of salt to capitalise on the affection that a great swathe of our users had for our products. We launched Smith Square Crisps with a very young Lenny Henry being our spokesman. Stan was a great client and an eager participant in the advertising process.

A particular incident stands out. One day I drove to Reading to present a rough cut of the commercial we'd produced for a product called Potato Tubes. Sadly it was an unmitigated disaster. An idea that looked great in script form just didn't translate into film. Stan asked my opinion and I said we couldn't run the commercial. He raised the question of the cost of the commercial which I said was his call. He responded by saying that he would pay for the commercial if we sacrificed our mark-up. With indecent haste I agreed and asked him why he had been so generous. He said that two things were important. Firstly, we were partners and we had both agreed that it was worth the risk to try and make the idea work in film which meant its failure was down to both of us. Secondly, and much more significantly, he said that creativity was enormously important to him in his product category. If he were to penalise us for being adventurous then the next time a brilliant but off-the-wall idea was suggested at the agency it might get stifled at birth because of the financial risk. He absolutely did not want that to happen.

The upshot of all of this was that every creative man in the agency wanted to work on Smiths. Some great commercials followed and we revitalised the brand. Stan was no pushover but he loved creativity, he always said thank you and absolutely insisted that his team treated our team with respect. Many years later, after his return to Canada, he had a fatal heart attack in his car on the way to the office. He is one of the people who will be remembered most fondly in Abbott Mead Vickers. He became a great personal friend who left us way too soon.

COW & GATE

Another a client for the agency was this West Country-based dairy company. Our particular project was baby foods and our ads would have to navigate carefully around the discussion about the value of breastfeeding against baby foods out of the jar or tin which have been going on since time immemorial. Andy Arghyrou and Chris O'Shea produced one of the most definitive and iconic print ads this category has ever seen. It showed a woman breastfeeding her baby under a headline which said, 'May we suggest liver and bacon to follow?'

Normally you can tell when an exceptional ad was in the frame for an award and the whole agency was pretty excited. On the evening of the most prestigious award scheme a whole series of categories went by without Cow

& Gate getting a mention. It was well after midnight when Chris O'Shea had gone to get his milk train home that the final award of the night was given. It was for the best single advertisement throughout the whole show – Liver and Bacon was the winner.

The chairman of Cow & Gate was a really nice man called Bernard Pendle. One year early in our relationship, he invited Sam and me to join him and some of his friends at the annual Opera Festival that was Glyndebourne. Sam has always been and still is a spectacularly good map reader (I trust her more than GPS) and we set off on our trip to Sussex in plenty of time from our house in Richmond. After we had been driving for an hour she discovered that we had been going in completely the wrong direction on a fast piece of road. We were potentially disastrously late. Part of the Glyndebourne ritual is drinks on the lawn, prior to the performance with dinner during the interval. Driving absolutely as fast as was legally decent (most of the time) we raced towards the complex knowing that we had already missed the pre-drinks but desperately trying to be around for the interval dinner. It's a full evening dress occasion and Sam and I ran from the car park and arrived at the Cow & Gate table just as everybody was sitting down. Bernard accepted our profuse apologies and we had just recovered from our tardiness when it was time to go back and see the second half of Mozart's Idomeneo, an interminable piece, staged very darkly by Trevor Nunn on this occasion.

After the stress of racing down to the Festival I found my eyes closing on a number of occasions. I fought manfully to stay awake but judging by the sound of a number of programs falling to the floor around the auditorium, I wasn't the only member of the audience who succumbed to slumber. When the performance was over Bernard said the journey back to the hotel where we were having a late proper dinner and staying the night was quite complicated. He would be in his Mercedes saloon and would wait for us near the exit to the car park and lead us to a relaxing meal and bed. We started the car and followed the silver Mercedes saloon. After half an hour of driving down a succession of winding country lanes I noticed that on the parcel shelf at the back of the car in front there were two women's hats. I asked Sam if any of the people in Bernard's party had been wearing anything on their head she said no. To our horror we realised we had been following the wrong silver Mercedes for half an hour and at least 20 miles. The whole area is turned into a complex one-way system during the opera season and satnav had still not been invented. We arrived back at the hotel some half an hour later. This time our apologies seemed slightly more hollow and Bernard's acceptance much less warm.

It was only over breakfast the following morning and after an enormous amount of grovelling and small talk from the both of us that diplomatic relationships were restored. It was certainly no laughing matter at the time but in the years that followed Bernard and I had a good few lunches during which he described being the driver of the last Mercedes in the car park waiting for us. We have never been to Glyndebourne again.

BRITISH TELECOM

Along with Sainsbury's and the Economist, BT is the longest client relationship in the agency. We had pitched for the whole telephony business but lost out to J Walter Thompson and their talking animals, although that agency later saw the error of their ways and produced the very famous Maureen Lipman campaign, of which the most famous commercial was Lipman's characters unalloyed joy that her nephew got an 'ology' in his exam results. There came a time, however, when the business was up for review. By that stage we had already won the Yellow Pages business (a direct subsidiary of

British Telecom). After an enormous amount of AMV people pushing and grinding for possible positions on the pitch, David came in one day and said that he thought he had solved the creative problem. It was such an elegant and effective solution that it made sense for him to lead the pitch on his own. The campaign, 'It's good to talk' was brought to life by Bob Hoskins acting as the main player in all the commercials. A particular favourite of mine was the spot which opened with a 30 second silence with Bob looking straight at the camera. The message was consistent throughout – none of us stay in touch as much as we should and a telephone call could transform relationships and people's lives. It was enormously successful and ran for a number of years. We were also lucky enough to win BT's mobile business, Cellnet, which stayed with us until it was floated off separately and became 02.

As in all great relationships we had a client in Stafford Clark who encouraged us to do great work. Sadly he died way too young from cancer. Today we still work with Gavin Patterson and his team producing work that we're both proud of.

GREENS OF BRIGHTON

In the very early days we won this account. Greens was a traditional business in the ready mixed baking sector we had to take on the might of Sara Lee for our market share. The first commercial that was done by David and Ron featured almond slices. It was lovingly shot by John Clark and was the forerunner of the Sainsbury's recipe commercials some years later. The relationship with Bruce Noble, the managing director, was like all our most successful based on a genuine respect and affection.

But at one point in the relationship we were having trouble. We had a series of creative ideas turned down it was proving difficult to make progress. On one of my five daily visits to David's office he bemoaned the fact that we couldn't appear to get anything through and that he thought that we should resign the business. I agreed to make an appointment with Bruce and drive down to Brighton to give him the bad news. I was ushered into Bruce's office and he was as charming as always until I told him that regrettably we had to resign because of creative differences. He astonished me by saying that he refused to accept our resignation of the account. This had never happened to me before, although I have to say I wasn't used to telling clients to go elsewhere either. As I was spluttering and stuttering he asked if David was in the office, I told him I believed he was, and he said that I should return to London with him following behind in his car in close attendance and that the three of us should get together.

Mobile phones had not been invented so was difficult for me to prime David in advance. We arrived at David's office in Babmaes Street and Bruce expressed bewilderment at the decision that we should part based on some creative problems that he could sort out in a heartbeat. After pondering on this, David said that he thought I might have been a bit hasty to resign the business. Over a cup of tea and a shop bought almond slice everybody shook hands and Bruce drove back to Brighton. It wasn't the first or last time the David and I did a good cop, bad cop routine although I usually had more warning when this was going to be the case.

THE LEEDS BUILDING SOCIETY

For many years, financial institutions like building societies had been manna from heaven for advertising agencies. A highly competitive market dominated by three or four giant players meant that each of them were constantly advertising competitive rates for mortgages to satisfy the huge demand that Mrs Thatcher had unleashed. We had in the agency at that time a senior planner called Jackie Boulter who did a great piece of market distillation. She broke down the market not in socio-economic terms but in attitude. There were clearly some people who were up to speed with every single movement of rate changes and any other financial engineering. They would only be interested in the rate itself and cared little about the personality of the company they were dealing with. There are another chunk of people who just couldn't be bothered and renewed their mortgage year in year out based on inertia. The most interesting chunk of people with those who felt they should know more about such matters but found the whole sector impenetrable.

Derek Day and Mick DeVito came up with a great campaign idea using George Cole, a very famous actor who them was at the height of his powers appearing as Arthur Daley in the successful TV series Minder. Other people recognise that Arthur Daley was constantly pushing out the edge of the financial envelope – he knew what he was talking about. In a series of commercials with the endline, 'Laughing all the way to the Leeds', the rather dusty image that the Leeds had was transformed.

George had also done a series of very successful commercials for Olympus cameras. A few years later he kindly invited us to his home and he proudly showed me the two large extensions that he had built – christened Leeds and Olympus respectively. When a few years later the Leeds merged with the Halifax we were unsuccessful in our pitch against the Halifax's agency. Somewhat fortuitously our old friend Peter Davis had just become chief executive of the Prudential and he invited us to pitch for that business which we won, thereby replacing one great relationship with another

CHIVAS REGAL

A few years before we had worked on this iconic whisky brand at DDB.

The campaign consisted of elegant shots of the beautifully designed Chivas bottle with elegant headlines. Early in our new relationship with the giant Seagram organisation David and Ron produced an ad showing an empty bottle of Chivas with a glass at its side. The headline was, 'Chivas Regal is always 12 years old – rarely 13'. I hurried down to Seagram's elegant Mayfair offices to show this to Stuart Kershaw the UK managing director of the American drinks giant. He looked at it quizzically and said he didn't think people would understand it. As gently as I could I said that I thought he was absolutely wrong and it was a simple proposition. He then paid me the ultimate compliment the client can pay to an account man. He asked if I really believed in the ad and its communication. I absolutely did and so it was not difficult to give him the reassurance he was looking for. He told me that although he didn't like it, based on our conversation he would give us permission to run it. The following year it starred in the major award ceremony, winning a Gold for best drinks ad of the year. A great example of the way really good agency/client relationships work – made possible by a great client.

VOLVO

Throughout the many years that we had the Volvo account we were really fortunate in having a succession of leaders at the Swedish car manufacturer who took the Steve Jobs view of the world – that focus was everything. The brand had an enviable reputation for safety and durability. Sexy was not a descriptor anybody would use about their Volvo but the estate car was the absolute vehicle of choice of middle-class mothers. A succession of great print ads and posters flowed. A long remembered poster for the estate car showed a great shot of the car full of parents and children with the headline, 'Always keep your valuables in a safe place'.

Tactical ads based on price were an absolutely essential part of the marketing plan. As always there was nothing vulgar about the way David treated this particular brief. 'For the price of an Escort you could buy a Volvo,' he exhorted. These were early days before television was popular with car manufacturers. A commercial was produced by us with our money which showed an egg box being crushed by hand, catastrophically destroying all the eggs. The voice-over said, 'When you take your family out for a drive you are literally putting all your eggs in one basket. Shouldn't you make sure that the basket is strong enough to protect the eggs? Shouldn't you drive a Volvo?'

This commercial we made for around £500 was the first of many great Volvo commercials that we did culminating in the series done by Walter Campbell and Tom Carty, the star of which was 'Twister'. Many years later after Volvo went through a succession of changes of ownership we reluctantly parted company. But we replaced one great car company with an even greater one – Mercedes-Benz.

THE ECONOMIST

After we had moved to our great offices in Aybrook Street we pitched for this great British magazine. Under its relatively new CEO David Gordon it was making great strides and wanted to substantially increase the readership of each issue. We won the business. A,M and V sat down after Adrian received the call and the three of us decided that it was maybe too small an account for us at that stage in our development after all. Adrian was told to make the call to say, 'Thanks but no thanks.' David Gordon himself intervened and persuaded us to take the business and he was so right. After a series of elegant long copy ads, David produced the first of an incredibly long running series with white type on a red background echoing the magazine's masthead. 'I never read the Economist – management trainee aged 42' was the message. It spawned award winner after award winner and meant that the Economist dominated the poster business for many years.

We've worked with many great clients and great people over the 35 year history of the agency. I hope the above isolated examples illustrate that the agency/client relationship is at its best when the very top management get involved in their campaigns. How they communicate with their customers is a critical part of their business. History is littered with great success stories of chief executives making profound decisions about the message they wanted to put out to the world. From Robert Townsend who approved the DDB campaign, 'Avis – we're number two so we try harder' through to Steve Jobs's 'Think Different', we see that more often than not, great advertising and enlightened heads of organisations go hand-in-hand.

CHAPTER 17

WHERE THE ADVERTISING
BUSINESS IS TODAY

*F*orecasting *what's going to happen next to the business* in which I've spent my whole working life is almost impossible. The speed of change in the way we communicate with our audiences has accelerated unbelievably quickly and the range of choices facing the management of agencies today grows almost by the month. If this were not enough, I believe that our business today is under-valued, under-rewarded and under-appreciated because, fundamentally, we have allowed ourselves to become commoditised. I still remember the sense of outrage I felt when a client first referred to us as a supplier – it was decades ago but heralded a fundamental change in the relationship between agency and client from that of a trusted business adviser to a supplier of a relatively essential commodity.

As an industry, we have failed to affirm the value of the great creative idea. Instead we have allowed ourselves to be side-tracked by the delivery vehicles of the idea, rather than the idea itself. This is being fuelled by people from within, indeed one of advertising's most powerful practitioners was quoted recently as saying that we've reached a point where the medium is more important than the message. In my view this is nonsense. I remember around the turn of the century being told by earnest young men in Silicon Valley that I was a dinosaur, that the business I had spent my life in was dead in the water and that very soon nobody at all would be watching or reading any of the media that had played such a role in my life and career. The world and the word was digital, and the time of the traditional advertising agency was rapidly being consigned to the pages of history.

It is certainly true that the business model that sustained the agency business has probably changed forever. The commission system went the way of all flesh a couple of decades ago, following the advent of the media independent. But it's an interesting fact that there are no longer any major independent planning and buying media operations around. Having split the process away from the major advertising groups, the founders of these companies happily sold their businesses back to the very people they broke away from. This relatively seismic shift in the way our business conducted itself meant that over the last few years, media itself began to wag the creative tail. As my colleague Ian Pearman said in a recent interview, for a while now the media choice has driven the creative choice. Someone else put this way, 'The math men were more important than the mad men.' Both describe a situation in which clients would start with the media plan and then shoehorn the creative idea into that plan – the cart before the horse and all that. There's been a much more liberal attitude recently springing up, the great idea now drives the paid for media which in turn triggers audience participation to liberate the idea across all social media.

In essence what we have now in our agencies is not dissimilar to what happened at the advent of commercial television. Creative people who up until then had only dealt in the written word and still pictures were augmented by a whole new breed who understood the creative opportunities that moving pictures presented. In our best agencies and (with apologies for the advertisement) AMV is helping to set the pace. The best young people who understand the full capability of the communication explosion we have at our fingertips are integrating seamlessly into the agency's operations, and liberating creative people to be much more expansive than ever before as a result.

I'm not a totally slavish devotee of all social media, and to believe that a combination of all of them is more effective than mainstream television is a long way away from being justified. But, excitingly, new young people with complementary skills are joining advertising agencies because we are embracing change so readily. Programme making as opposed to just programme sponsorship is now a reality and the understanding that digital isn't simply the idea in itself, but an unbelievably useful vehicle to place the message in front of people chosen in a more disciplined way than ever before means that the quantifiable effectiveness measurement – the Holy Grail that our businesses have been looking for – is becoming excitingly close

Elsewhere I've talked about one of our major clients educating me on the difference that the creative work we produced for him had made to his business – hundreds of millions of pounds according to him. This client highlighted the difference of creativity can make to a business. We must spread and repeat as often as we can the mantra coined by one of the notables in our business that creativity is one of the last remaining legal ways of gaining an unfair advantage over your competition. There is a feeling still around in some places that creativity is a commodity that has a formulaic value. The truth is the very best creative work is so much more effective than the very worst and we should get to a situation where we can command a premium price for the very best.

I'm amazed that the processes we go through now will approve media expenditure of in some cases millions of pounds but will then spend time arguing at length about the cost of producing the very best piece of creative work to fill that media offering. Sure, the Guinness Surfers commercial could have been made for less money by cutting out some of the special post-production effects. But that saving would have reduced the efficacy of the commercial and turned it into just another piece of film. It's a bit like spending a fortune on the production of two pieces of bread and then skimping on the cost of the filling to go between the slices when as we all know it's the filling which makes the difference between an acceptable sandwich and a great one.

I have already highlighted the value of relationships in business generally. In some senses I worry that we have lost the ability to create great relationships with our clients. These relationships are at the heart of our ability to persuade our client base to trust us in our assessment of what's needed in creative terms to solve problems and create whole new markets. Everywhere in the world there are examples of great creative work making a real difference and it's no accident that most of those have resulted from a close working relationship and mutual respect between client and agency. None more so, I suspect, than the relationship that has endured over the years between Apple and its agency.

The creation of enduring relationships has faced a new threat particularly over the last ten or 15 years. Research has been done recently on the length of tenure of chief marketing officer's and indeed chief executive officers. They are something like two-and-a-half and three-and-a-half years respectively. It can easily take that time to develop a relationship to take the businesses forward and the frequent change in personnel in client organisations has made life very difficult. The building and sustaining of a brand is a long-term operation quite often demanding one step backward before two forward steps can be taken. Beleaguered CEOs are no longer given time to develop their brands. The tyranny of 90-day reporting which the investor base demands means that short-termism becomes the order of the day. We have to recognise and hone our ability to develop relationships more rapidly than ever before.

We should not be afraid to look for inspiration from past masters. There are too few of our young people who are students of our business. There are great lessons to be learnt from the titans of our industry from the last 75 years. In the 60s in the USA it is not fanciful to suggest that the great agencies that sprang up, with DDB leading the way, didn't just change the way advertising was used but actually helped create fundamental societal movements. There is much to be gleaned from examination of the methods principles and beliefs of these past masters.

There is no doubt in my mind that the business I've devoted my life to has a great future. It has given me a wonderful career, way beyond my wildest aspirations. There are few career choices that offer the excitement, diversity and opportunity to make a difference in the way the advertising business does. As long as we revere the magic of the creative idea, constantly examine our operating methods and make the most of the breath-taking speed of innovation, the advertising business will retain and even enhance its essential role in the marketing mix.

****

MEAD & SONS

I've always loved the day to day interaction with clients and the building of businesses from scratch. As my sons grew I used to fantasise that one day we would start a new agency called Mead & Sons where Billy and Ben would be the creative and Harry the account man. Sadly, this is not going to happen – a pity because I think we would have done rather well. The boys, particularly the two oldest ones, have carved out careers elsewhere.

BILLY

From very early days Billy was obsessed by all sport, inheriting this from his grandfather and me. Fiercely competitive, he tried most pastimes but quickly adopted football as his first love. He was given a contract by Millwall as a youth team player at 16 and went on to have a really good junior career, finally being selected by the FA to play for its youth team clad in the England shirt. When he was 20 he decided that he was never going to have real pace, an absolute essential in the modern game so looked elsewhere for a new work path.

After a stint in despatch, he joined the TV support team and learnt his trade doing everything from tape duplication, being camera operator on research shoots and editing mood films. He further honed his skills by being a one-man TV department at a small but highly productive agency finishing by editing a number of commercials for a major car launch. He set up his own editing company just five years ago and has rapidly developed a top ten reputation as an editor, as well as a fast expanding company.

As is described later in the book, he stood at my side during Millwall's troubles, endured endless humiliation as the Chairman's son from envious footballers and kept coming back for more. He has inherited a large part of my father's fearlessness and with Clare, his great wife, has given Sam and me two wonderful grandchildren.

We talk daily on the phone, he lives 10 minutes from us, is passionate about everything he does and he is everything a father could wish for.

BEN

When Ben, my second son, left Bristol University with a degree in Politics, the first Mead ever to get a degree, he was caught up in the pre-Lehmann Brothers financial services euphoria. Having spent some time in New York on an internship at Omnicom, he returned to the UK and through Richard Dale got a serious of introductions to some of the big players in the category. He started out at Citigroup and by all accounts did really well as a trader. I was really proud of him because he totally bought into the 'when in doubt be nice' view of the world while working in an alien universe. Ben became part of a breakaway group and helped start a trading operation at Unicredit (an Italian bank). However, he became disenchanted with the system. The very early starts and being glued to a monitor 12 hours a day began to wear him down, but the main problem was that his work did not play to his great strength, which is a natural talent to develop relationships. As a result the large rewards became increasingly less attractive.

For the last two years or so, having left the City, he, and his now wife Lara, have been successfully property developers and have launched a new brand of ladies' leisurewear called Varley, which is growing rapidly. Ben has been demonstrating great entrepreneurial instincts and talents – I know he will do really well.

Whenever I think of Ben I'm reminded of the eminent film critic who wrote of the epic movie 'Ben Hur', 'Loved Ben. Not wild about Hur.' I couldn't have put it better myself, although I hasten to add that Hur does not refer to Ben's wife Lara – we all love her.

HARRY

Harry is the baby of the family being some seven years younger than our oldest son. From the beginning he was the most equable and gentle of the three boys with a very sunny nature to match. Being the third of three boys meant that he had to put up with, at times, merciless ribbing – an ordeal he endures with a broad smile.

A great animal lover, in his early teens he harboured ambitions to qualify as a vet but after discovering that the length of study time needed in order to qualify exceeded that of a general practitioner he looked elsewhere. After a relatively lengthy hankering to become involved in talent management, he decided in his late teens that it was going to be advertising for him. He has the same entrepreneurial leaning as his brothers as well as an ability to develop relationships at all levels. Although the Mead & Sons fantasy has bitten the dust, in keeping with the current vogue for intriguing names for agencies, maybe Harry & Dad will be on a letterhead one of these days.

Like all the Mead men, Harry is completely in love with film and until recently he and I would hit the cinema a couple of times a month.

Judy Garland had a huge hit in 1939 with a song called 'I'm Just Wild About Harry' – she wasn't a bad judge.

CHAPTER 18

TRAUMAS IN HARLEY STREET – 2008

For almost all of my life I've been an Olympic-standard hypochondriac, and in recent years it has got much worse. This is due to the appearance of the internet, which has added enormously to the amount of information available to fuel my obsession, and Hugh Laurie in his US series 'House', who has presented me with a whole new world of obscure complaints with symptoms I can relate to. After each episode I'm always convinced something important is immediately going to drop off, atrophy or just stop working.

Not surprisingly, my high-level hypochondria has meant that my GP, a New Zealander called Richard Croxson, has become a close friend. Over the years I have been to see Richard to complain of skipped heartbeats, of muscle tremors, undetermined back pain, headaches, toothaches, as well as more exotic symptoms gleaned from a succession of sources ranging from Dr House to the weekly doom-laden Health section in the *Daily Mail*, casual chats with chums or even just a general feeling that something is not quite right. Alongside this, I have constantly believed that there is somewhere a magic pill which would instantly make me feel full of energy, decisive and light of tread – it was simply a matter of finding the right condition to match it.

As I write I can picture Richard's face drop as I describe yet another malaise. This is always followed by him dutifully wading through my inch-thick file and then telling me we looked at that 20 years ago and didn't find anything then but let's check it out again anyway.

A few years ago, in an act of horrendous disloyalty, I went to see another GP in Harley Street and asked for a complete going over. I wanted a second opinion on my vast array of supposed ailments. He saw me two weeks later and, hoping to shake me out of my obsessive hypochondria, told me that he had good news and bad news. He opted to deliver the good news first and said that there was nothing wrong with me. I, dry-mouthed, asked what the bad news was and he replied, 'There's nothing wrong with you.' He understood this was a hammer blow for the hypochondriac.

I have been fighting a battle against my weight ever since the frenetic physical activity of my childhood ended. By my early teens I was living with the legacy of heavily buttered jam sandwiches, beef dripping on toast, and spoonfuls of unbelievably sweet condensed milk straight from the tin. This has always been a subject of humour for my partner David Abbott, who used the occasion of Christmas parties at AMV to tell the world how I was progressing in my constant fight against obesity. He always exaggerated to make a point and when I reached the age of 50 he presented me with a personalised number plate which read F A T 5 0. Obviously this was put together in a way which made people believe it really said FATSO – oh, how they laughed. Another time he mocked a brand new lime green suit I had bought from Jaeger. Admittedly this suit was very 'sudden' in appearance. It was not a subtle colour and the material made pressing unnecessary because the creases in the trousers were sewn in and slightly raised. Yes, it was every bit as bad as you can imagine. The suit caused David to tell the expectant faces of the AMV faithful that one day, while wearing it, I had been overcome with weariness and lay down for a refreshing snooze, only to be woken up by people picnicking on me because they thought I was the Cotswolds. Truly rib-tickling stuff.

Anyway, I digress. Around June 2007 I went for another chat with my medical friend Richard about a general feeling of unease. There wasn't anything specific, I just didn't feel at 100%. Not that I've ever felt 100%, being a heavy smoker as well as overweight, a massive consumer of carbohydrates and, harking back to the days of rationing that haunted my youth, a compulsive consumer of everything that was sweet and sticky (vanilla fudge at every opportunity). On this particular day, Richard wearily went through our normal ritual: after taking blood which, with my recessed blood vessels, was a bit like trying to find gold in the Yukon, he had me going outside to pee into a small bottle and then finally he checked my blood pressure (which had somehow always been pretty good). To my surprise my blood pressure was a bit high and having at least found a symptom that was treatable, Richard reassured me that there was no problem here and a pill every day for the rest of my life would control this common affliction.

I walked out with a slight spring in my step in the way all hypochondriacs do when they actually have something wrong with them. Later I set about educating myself about my newly acquired badge of hypochondriac honour. The most chilling elements of the general research came from chats with David Abbott and John Wren. I can't remember who said which, but one of them told me the blood pressure pills massively affect your libido, while the second said that consumption of the daily pill made his father seriously depressed.

I went back to Richard Croxson and told him that I didn't want to be a miserable eunuch for the rest of my life and so wanted to attack the high blood pressure in a different way. We agreed that the horrible combination of exercise and diet would probably help and that the prize of a nice new Italian wardrobe from Brioni when I reached my target weight would hasten my progress towards 140/80, a perfectly acceptable blood pressure reading for a man of my age.

Two or three times previously I had embarked on a major weight reduction program and I'd been pretty successful at it. I don't think there's much to beat the joy of putting on clothes that you haven't worn for 10 years and finding that they fit, even though fashion had moved on – my extensive collection of flared trousers would never again be acceptable. So I cut out bread before meals, early morning toast and jam and thought it would be worth testing Michael Winner's belief that if you only eat half of what is on your plate weight will begin to drop off. Over the next year the campaign was pretty successful and I went from an elasticated 46 inch waist trouser (yes, really) to a taut 42 with no expandable help.

My spirits were high when I went to see Richard again in June 2008 for a repeat of all the tests which I was convinced would illustrate clearly the progress I'd made. Sure enough, he was very pleased. My blood pressure for a man of my age and height was normal and he was sure that the blood test results when they came back from the laboratory would reflect similar progress on mild problems like cholesterol. And so there was yet another trip to Wimpole Street a week later for the good news. When I arrived Richard had a slightly furrowed brow. This was out of character for him and he hastily reassured me that everything was fine with the minor exception of a measurement that I'd never heard of before – PSA. He explained that this was a way of detecting signs of prostate cancer. Mine was slightly up from a year ago but there was nothing either in the increase or the absolute rate which would suggest I had a big problem. He recommended an advanced form of medical diagnostics called a digital rectal examination which sounded pretty sophisticated to me until I discovered what it involved – you can probably guess.

The medical verdict on the outcome of this examination was 'nothing out of the ordinary' but as we were being so precise and good about looking at every element of my physical condition we thought it might make sense to spend half an hour with an urologist. As this was a member of the medical profession I hadn't met before I was naturally enthusiastic (I'm a hypochondriac, remember) and arranged to see Hugh Whitfield who was based in Harley Street, just around the corner from Richard.

Hugh is a gentle man in every sense. After he had performed another digital rectal examination he calmly assured me that although there was probably nothing to worry about, there was another test available which would totally eliminate any possibility of prostate cancer and it would be sensible for me to do that as well. This test entailed massaging the prostate to shake some cells lose into the bladder, peeing into a bottle and sending it off to Holland for analysis and, I hoped, instant reassurance.

Ten days later Hugh's wife, who was also his receptionist and right arm, rang and asked me to go and see him. I have had dozens of tests over the years and the results of virtually all had been negative so I arrived and sat in his elegant office completely certain I would hear a medical person tell me yet again that I been wasting the time of eminent physicians who could have been treating somebody who was really ill. So it was with surprise verging on astonishment that I receive the news that there was something there – and that a biopsy would be a good idea.

The raised blood pressure had already satisfied my hypochondriac's lust for gratification that week so the news that Hugh gave me wasn't very welcome. He told me there was a chance that I did indeed have prostate cancer even though, apart from the odd journey to the loo in the night, no symptoms had presented themselves. With a slightly heavier step than before, I returned to the office where Sarah, my priceless executive assistant, immediately got to work on the internet to find out more about this potential threat to my well-being.

Following her research, Sarah told me that although it was the biggest killer of men (over 10,000 a year), the likelihood was that I had a mild form that would lay dormant for decades and cause me no discomfort or threat. Indeed, the vast majority of men with prostate cancer die of old age. I was reassured by this but spoke to a couple of friends anyway. Dominic Shorthouse, a really close mate, was concerned to hear of my minor problem and in turn told one of his chums who had suffered from prostate cancer. He rang me back immediately and said that I should go and see the most eminent man in the field at once.

Yet another trip to Marylebone followed. As I sat in the waiting room with four other men of varying ages, I was rather uncomfortable in the knowledge that here were gentlemen almost certainly suffering from the most terrifying of complaints – cancer. The place itself was very impressive, efficient and modern-looking almost to the point of being overly slick. Eventually it was my turn to go in and I sat down in front of a large desk while this world famous physician peered at me from the other side with an air of somebody who knew something that I didn't. Having reviewed all the written evidence, he said it was certain that I did have prostate cancer and that the biopsy I had arranged would only confirm his diagnosis. Hearing I was from advertising he, in my view rather inappropriately, told me that a couple of other famous people in my business had suffered from the complaint. One had gone to the Sloan-Kettering Clinic in New York to have the operation and he'd operated on the other here in London. He told me that it was certain that I would have to have an operation and that he could even fit me in around the end of November, a couple of months later. He told me that I would have to give up smoking immediately and also lose significant weight. I found both of these orders rather hard to take. The immediate discarding of Silk Cut at what was a moment of some stress was difficult enough to contemplate but, much more irritatingly, he'd failed to share my great pride in the amount of weight that I'd lost already. He dispatched me to another anteroom with a DVD and a booklet. I sat and watched some of his success-fully treated patients extolling his virtue through a small screen mounted on the wall and read through the booklet the title of which was something like 'Small But Deadly: A Brief History and Description of Prostate Cancer'.

I decided that if I were to have the operation it would not be with this particular gentleman. I also decided I would wait to have the biopsy which I was sure would negate any need for further action anyway. By a strange chance I'd had lunch a few weeks before with an acquaintance of mine who'd recently had the same biopsy done. He said it was rather uncomfortable but that the most disturbing consequence was that your urine would be stained red with blood for four or five days. This was dramatic but nothing to worry about. I'm really glad that I found out about that in advance.

A couple of days later I went to the Princess Grace Hospital and had a magician carry out the biopsy. She was brilliant both before and after the procedure, telling me that in all probability I had a very low level dose of the disease which would probably mean that I should be monitored every three or four months to ensure that the complaint hadn't progressed. She said that she would send the analysis of the biopsy to Hugh over the next couple of days and he would give me a call.

I was curiously calm throughout the whole process, a calmness that I carried with me when I went for my next appointment with Hugh, my urol-ogist. He very matter-of-factly informed me that the news was not good.

Eight out of the 10 samples taken showed cancer infestation and on closer analysis they belonged to a pretty virulent strain, described on the Gleason scale as being unpleasantly dangerous and requiring urgent attention. I was irritated that Mr Eminent had been right in his diagnosis and I wasn't looking forward to going home and telling Sam that the news wasn't good.

We then began the process of deciding the next course of action. Sarah intensified her research through the web and Sam and I embarked on a visit to an Oncology Centre where the options were laid out. They were very simple – the first was hormone treatment which would precede a course of radiotherapy. The whole process would take about six months.

The oncologist told me that the hormone treatment would have odd side-effects which would equate to the menopause in women: hot flushes, mood swings and all of that. She also said that my nipples would be very sore. Radiotherapy wouldn't be fun either, a six-week daily blast. Not surprisingly, I didn't find this an attractive proposition.

All of this unappealing information was delivered by a powerful, poker-faced woman who was a doctor of oncology. She then went on to tell Sam and me that the only other alternative was a full operation to extract the errant gland. Again this was another member of the medical profession who didn't fill me with confidence, especially as in her follow-up letter to us she suggested in the second paragraph that I had a small prostate but in the third told me that I had a large one.

Throughout all of this process Sam was a tower of strength in the way that she didn't panic and wasn't overly solicitous or gloomy in any way at all. She had always been wonderful at keeping my feet on the ground and whenever there was a chance of me even vaguely beginning to believe my own publicity she quashed it immediately. I really haven't the faintest idea of what I'd do without her.

So the options were pretty clear and not very numerous – very sore nipples were not my idea of a good time but I think the clincher was, as I understood it, that if one embarked on a course of radiotherapy the weakening of the bowel wall caused by the treatment would mean that if the cancer returned in the future an operation would be out of the question.

So here we were deciding to go under the surgeon's knife. Well, not exactly the knife – in reality a succession of small sharp instruments inserted during keyhole surgery and guided by a wizard sitting in front of a screen some 15 feet away. So what we were looking for now was a cross between the brilliant surgeon Christian Barnard and Bill Gates. The instrument used for this process was called the Da Vinci Robot. Inspired by neither Tom Hanks nor Dan Brown, it is a wonderfully sophisticated piece of kit. Each one costs well over £1 million so they were not exactly plentiful on the ground.

Into this process came one of my old friends, Howard Mann. He had had the operation about a year before carried out by the world's best prostate man. Sarah and I had become Marylebone's greatest experts on prostate cancer with the help of Google and so we knew the pitfalls and the consequences of a less than perfect procedure. Although Howard had had his operation in London he did have contacts at the Sloan-Kettering Clinic in New York, by reputation the greatest cancer hospital in the world. He kindly chased his contacts for the names of reputable and good surgeons in the UK. By now I had recognised that my preconceptions about surgeons being equally talented were misjudged. Indeed, I now believe that surgeons are like hairdressers: they can all cut hair but some do it a bloody sight better than others.

When the Sloan-Kettering recommendation came back there were two names on the list – one was the famous gentleman we talked about earlier and the other was a man called Chris Ogden who worked through the Royal

Marsden, London's world-class cancer hospital. I went to see Chris and was massively impressed. He assured me that though I should give up smoking I should not do before the operation because the lungs produce much more mucus once you give up smoking and that would make the anaesthetist's job much more difficult. He also told me that I didn't have to lose any weight because keyhole surgery could slice through the odd pound or two extra that I was carrying. He was a wonderfully calming man, although to my surprise panic had still not set in. He told me that all the specialists at the Marsden had looked at my scans and they believed that the cancer was contained within the prostate area, although the margins were very tight. Although he couldn't guarantee it, he did believe that he could take out the prostate and with it all the cancerous cells. I wanted to believe him and I did.

During the week of the planned operation I was again quite calm and philosophical. Sam and I had already decided that the night before the operation we would go and have dinner close to the Marsden. In Sloane Avenue there is a restaurant called the Poissonnerie. It's a very old restaurant and, as the name suggests, it does specialise in fish. So we booked a table for early on the Friday evening.

On the Wednesday before supper at the Poissonnerie, I decided that it would be really good to have dinner with my sons. Sadly Harry, the youngest, was not around, being a boarder at Wellington College. If I'd have insisted I probably could have prevailed on the headmaster to release him for the evening but, in keeping with the rather low-key attitude with which the whole family had addressed my particular problem, I had a lengthy conversation with him on the phone before my other two sons Bill and Ben (yes, they've heard all the flowerpot men jokes for years now) and I had dinner together.

Although there was no real reason to have dinner within the vicinity of the Marsden they rather characteristically said that they would like to have

343

a big steak with me at the Gaucho Grill, by coincidence again in Sloane Avenue. For those of you haven't been to this particular emporium, the way the food is presented and ordered is pure theatre. Our designated waiter arrived with a whole selection of different cuts of steak from different countries. An evangelical description of the Kobe beef from Japan may have got Bill and Ben's gastric juices working overtime but a sharp look from me, knowing how much this particular piece of meat was going to cost, meant they chose elsewhere. We picked a nice Californian Merlot (perversely a favourite of mine ever since Paul Giamatti was so rude about it in that wonderful film 'Sideways') and set about talking about anything except cancer. We were all very phlegmatic as none of us wanted any element of a 'Last Supper' to intrude on our gathering. After the cheesecake and apple pie pushed our calorie intake off the acceptable scale, we went our separate ways.

Fast forward to Friday and Sam and I sat down for our scampi and sea bass at the Poissonnerie – eating early to make sure we fell within the 'nil by mouth' medical constraints. It had long ago ceased to be a trendy restaurant, but a recent makeover had created a really nice atmosphere. We chomped our way through the meal talking about anything except the following morning and my eight o'clock appointment with Chris Ogden and the Da Vinci robot. After dinner Sam drove very gently down the Fulham Road to the reassuring facade of the Royal Marsden. We checked into the private room section and were reassured by the calm professionalism of everyone we met. We arrived at the room to be greeted by a huge vase full of the most perfect white roses I have ever seen. These miraculous flowers were accompanied by a note which said 'To make sure you awake smelling of roses. With love from all your friends at AMV'. Sam said goodbye, I got into bed and was asleep almost immediately.

The four-hour operation was completed on 28th November 2008. When I came round afterwards, I gather from Sam that I was uncharacteristically both violent and belligerent, of which I remember nothing. Chris did an unbelievable job because the most terrifying potential side effect of the operation – incontinence – has never been a problem. I was one of the lucky ones.

In fact, my luck was even more pronounced than that. Three days before the operation I had been due to go to Mumbai for a meeting and dinner. In the small number of times I've been to this magical city I had always stayed at the Oberoi hotel and was planning to do so again on this occasion. But because of the operation I delayed my trip. It was the night I was due both in the hotel and the restaurant that the carnage in the Oberoi and the Taj Mahal Hotel happened – the terrorist attacks which killed more than 150 people.

Luck was on my side that day. Any man reading this who doesn't know what his PSA reading is should go to his doctor immediately and ask for a blood test. It saved my life – twice.

CHAPTER 19

MILLWALL

When I was growing up and developing an
interest in football, my dad could have taken
me to Stamford Bridge to watch Chelsea, to Highbury to watch Arsenal or
even to White Hart Lane to watch Tottenham Hotspur. But he rejected all
those successful and glamorous clubs and instead introduced me to the love
of his life: Millwall Football Club.

The part of London actually called Millwall is north of the Thames near
the Isle of dogs in the East End of London. But at the turn of the twentieth
century the football club moved away from there and headed south of the
river to its spiritual home, The Den, which sat in rather gloomy surroundings at New Cross in south London, just off the Old Kent Road. Since
long before I was born the club has had levels of recognition and reputation
which far exceed its success on the field. Indeed, 80 years after its move
across the Thames it was one of the very few London clubs that had never
played in the top tier of English football.

But if the producer of any program or film about Jack the Ripper was
looking for a location the narrow, dark backstreets that surrounded The Den
would be perfect. It's been said on many occasions that visiting teams capit-
ulated during the coach ride to get to the ground and nothing on the pitch

could be more intimidating or fearsome. The supporters themselves were tough guys, mainly heavy lifters from the London docks and the club motto of 'We fear no foe' was true as well as appropriate. The road behind the ground gave the stand on the east side of the stadium its name and summed up the hostility of the climate surrounding The Den – it was called Cold Blow Lane. The most vociferous fans stood on the crumbling terraces and before kick-off surrounded the tunnel to hurl abuse at the visiting teams. It was truly gladiatorial stuff imbued with a passion that equalled any other in football. The fans demanded and got no less than 100% commitment from the players who wore the royal blue of Millwall. The club emblem, a rampant lion, together with the colour of the shirt gave away the Scottish ancestry of the workers at a sugar factory on the Isle of Dogs who originally set the club up. It's ironic that the sweetness of sugar was at the heart of this most feared football club.

William Mead had been a supporter since he was seven years old. Although a great fan of Surrey cricket team and England's football team – in fact any English representative in any sport – his overriding passion was the Lions. He travelled everywhere to watch them. Until 2004 (something we'll cover later) the most significant day in the club's history was when they made the semi-final of the 1937 FA Cup, the first third division team ever to do so. Dad regaled me with stories of the day that he went to Sunderland for that game, only to see his team defeated one – nil in front of a crowd of 60,000 people. I know that one of the great joys of his life was that he'd managed to infect both my sister and me with the untreatable Millwall virus. Once it caught hold it would last a lifetime.

In my early days of support he was so passionate that he set up a new supporters' club called the Millwall Social Club (social seems to be a curious adjective when twinned with Millwall) where he became company secretary. In my early years we would gather with other fans at midnight in Grange Road, Bermondsey to board a coach to travel north. For a long time the team yo-yoed between the third and fourth divisions so these trips were not to sophisticated grounds like Old Trafford but much more likely to crumbling edifices in small places like Accrington, Southport and Darlington. These were days before the M1 had been completed so a coach trip north would quite often take up to 12 hours and we always stopped at dawn in Newcastle-under-Lyme for a cup of tea and a bacon sandwich in one of the few transport cafes that welcomed our notorious support. Welcomed is probably an overstatement. Grudgingly allowed us in is probably closer to the mark.

The coaches we travelled in had seen better days and rock hard suspension coupled with ageing seats made for an uncomfortable ride. Dad always insisted on taking the inside seat by the window which allowed him to sleep through the interminable trip, snoring gently. For me sitting on the outside, more than one snooze was disturbed by me toppling onto the floor in the middle of the aisle. Once we made the trip to Boundary Park, the ancestral home of Oldham Athletic which was more than 200 miles away, and arrived 15 minutes before kick-off, just in time. But to our dismay we were marooned inside the coach by a cloudburst of biblical proportions and by the time the rain eased long enough for us to leave the coach and get into the ground, our team was already two goals behind, a deficit which stayed in place until, sodden and miserable, we climbed back on the coach for the dispiriting trip back to London.

After dad died some of my passion for Millwall went with him. It just wasn't the same anymore and the little band of brothers that stood behind the goal at the Ilderton Road end, which included us, gradually disbanded. In truth, my sister Pat had spent more Millwall-related time with father, travelling around the country to away games. Later I met David Abbott and found to my astonishment that he was a Millwall supporter too. He lived in the leafy lanes of Blackheath, an area not exactly riddled with Millwall supporters. As we became friends and more affluent we decided to become members of the executive club at the Den. This bought us seats near the directors' box and tea and biscuits at half-time. We went for quite a few years on this basis and at the end of the game I would follow David home, where his wife Eve would have hot buttered crumpets waiting for us while we huddled around a tiny Sony Trinitron TV to catch the results of other games.

The other people in the Executive Club used to regale us with stories of the old days at The Den. It was said that once a very famous cricketer-cum-footballer called Denis Compton played for Arsenal reserves in a midweek game. In those days even reserve team games got a healthy sprinkling of support. Mr Compton played wide right and was twinkling down the wing before being hit by a large train-like figure playing left back for the Lions. Compton lay motionless following this attack of legal grievous bodily harm when a wit in the crowd was heard to shout, 'Kick him again Harry! He's still breathing!' This summed up the blood-and-thunder style of football which the Millwall crowd loved. They expected then, as they still do, for players to give everything for the club. They will swap technical skill for total commitment any time and a combination of the two would create a hero for life.

Just after we took the agency public in 1985, I was on holiday in Spain and read that Millwall's manager George Graham, who had brought more than a modicum of success to the club in his first managerial position, was leaving to join the Arsenal. His replacement was John Docherty, a little-known figure then managing Brentford. The identity of Graham's successor convinced me that the club had lost all ambition and I decided I would not renew my Executive Club membership. It totally ruined my day.

When we got back to London we went down to a country club in Surrey called Foxhills, owned by my really good friend Ian Hayton whose birthday was the reason for our trip. As was the fashion in those days in a room of six or eight different tables, the seating plan split husbands and wives. As I was sitting chatting to Ian's beautiful wife Pam, my wife was sat next to a man called David Harris, who ran a poster advertising company, knew of AMV and claimed to have met me on a number of occasions. In making light conversation he asked Sam what I did in my spare time. To her subsequent massive regret, she said that I was interested in all sport but football generally and Millwall Football Club in particular

David said he knew the man who had just put a consortium together and had bought Millwall from the chairman Alan Thorne. He asked Sam if I would be interested in meeting this gentleman. Sam said it was almost certain that I would love to and two days later I got a call from Reg Burr, the man who had bought the Club. He asked if I would be interested in joining the board and becoming part of the consortium. He told me 25% of the club would be available for £30,000. AMV had recently gone public and there was a little bit of money floating around and so I found the proposal irresistible. A day later I was the proud owner of 25% of Millwall Football Club. Sadly dad had been dead for a number of years by then but I know he would have been beside himself at the thought of a Mead not only being on the board of his beloved club but owning a chunk of it too.

Reg Burr the newly appointed Chairman of Millwall was a very interesting character. A lifelong Tottenham Hotspur supporter, he had nevertheless been on the board of Luton Town Football Club for a few years alongside Eric Morecambe. These were very formative years in Reg's football education. In fact throughout the 20 years or so that we spent together at Millwall he constantly said, 'When I was at Luton.' Even when Millwall became much more successful in every sense, he still wore his Luton heritage with pride. He came from a wealthy Jewish background and had a colourful business career. Although cleared by a board of trade enquiry, he never really recovered from being a partner in a car insurance operation that went bad. He was devoted to his wife Bernice who sadly was crippled at the time of the birth of their daughter Rosemary. He was unbelievably good in looking after Bernice. Indeed beneath his irascible surface he was a man of enormous kindness. He was not used to having his authority questioned and we clashed on a number of occasions but his fidelity to the Millwall cause was never in question.

Three days after I invested I went to my first game as part proprietor and vice-chairman of the club. I thought I ought to turn up looking smart so wore my best Ralph Lauren jacket over a cashmere polo neck sweater. Having parked in my designated space inside the ground I made my way to the tiny board room and after I received a number of disapproving looks from the opposition directors, Reg gently pointed out that jacket and tie were mandatory for football club directors everywhere.

That first game was against Shrewsbury where a fresh-faced young man of 19 called Michael Marks scored a hat-trick and we won four-nil. After the match the impish little Scot John Docherty joined us in the boardroom. Despite my misgivings in Spain I warmed to John immediately. I was bowled over by his enthusiasm and obvious love of the game. That season John performed miracles. George Graham was not expecting to be made manager of Arsenal and had left in rather a hurry, without securing the services a number of players who were out of contract. By the time John and Reg arrived, the Club was down to its bare bones and we were forced to play lots of the juniors in the first team. One of those was a tall, elegant player called Teddy Sheringham. I learned that George had said that we should accept an offer of £5000 from Aldershot for him. Fortunately this instruction was ignored and Teddy went on to become a Millwall legend and when he left us played for Brian Clough at Nottingham Forest, Tottenham Hotspur, Manchester United and England. Along with Charlie Hurley, who played for Millwall in my early years of support, Teddy became the most successful player in Millwall's history.

We avoided relegation and set about planning for the next season. One Sunday the family were at our home in the Cotswolds when I got the call from Reg saying that John had put together a strategy which he thought would get us promoted to the top division over the next few years. This strategy entailed expenditure way in excess of what Millwall had ever spent on players before. Reg said that John wanted to sign Kevin O'Callaghan from Ipswich, Tony Cascarino from Gillingham, Steve Woods and Terry Hurlock from Reading and George Lawrence from Southampton. By then a very seasoned football superstar who had retired called Frank McLintock had joined John from the Arsenal where he had been skipper of the double winning team and I felt our management team was strong. I expressed real enthusiasm for the plan until Reg said that the only way it would work was if he and I put in £250,000 each as a loan to the club to enable the players to be bought. With some difficulty I cleared this with Sam and then John went ahead with the purchases. Some years later Tony on his own fetched nearly £2 million when we sold him to Aston Villa so it was very good business.

John managed to get every one of his targets and, with the exception of George Lawrence who was injured very early in his Millwall career, they turned out to be brilliant buys. From that moment The Den was a very exciting place. On March 22nd 1988, my birthday, Sam gave me a beautiful

set of cufflinks made by Cartier of the Millwall lion. They were unbelievably lucky charms because we won nine of the next 10 games and went to
Hull virtually sure of promotion to the First Division if we drew and got a
point and with the possibility of going up as champions if we won and got
all three. Nerveless Kevin O'Callaghan scored from the penalty spot and
we won the game one-nil. Millwall were thus promoted for the first time in
the history of the Club to the top rank of English football. Grown men who
had supported Millwall all their lives were in tears on the terraces. In their
hearts they never believed that day would come.

After the season ended we planned for the new campaign with great
excitement, especially when we saw the fixture list. Our trips to Lancashire,
for example, would now see us playing Manchester United instead of Bury.
It was astonishing. The team that John put together to get us promoted he
had always thought would be good enough to keep us in the First Division (it became the Premier League a few years later). Amidst the frenzy
surrounding the stampede for season tickets for the new season, Reg and
I spent a lot of time working on ideas for how we could repair the club's
reputation. We'd suffered years of poor press fuelled by a Panorama programme which we subsequently found out had been largely staged and in
which the average Millwall supporter was portrayed as a cross between the
Taliban and the IRA.

We got very close to our local council, Lewisham, even though part of
our ground was in the neighbouring borough of Southwark. We set up one
of the very first community schemes to operate in our local schools and it
was a resounding success. We opened the first crèche of any football club
anywhere. We blazed the trail in having a family enclosure and we set about
handling the media in a way which would highlight all the good things we
were doing. As I was in communications it was agreed that this would be

one of my areas of responsibility and I wrote to every national newspaper's sports editor. The letter did not disown our past but aimed at communicating the measures that I described above and also attempted to create the golden state of 'the benefit of the doubt'. I had lunch with all the major journalists and Millwall's infamy meant that all of them were curious about this new stance that Reg and I decided would be critical for the future. Despite displaying scepticism at first, all of them were at least prepared to keep an open mind. The behaviour of our fans in the top flight of English football would be central in changing people's perceptions. A few journalists wrote about us sympathetically before the season started and I remember a great football writer called James Lawton writing a really good piece about us in the Daily Express.

The demand for tickets for the new season in the top flight was overwhelming. The fixture list looked good through our eyes although supporters of the major clubs might have been somewhat shocked at the quality of their terraced accommodation when they visited us. To the right of the goal at the Ilderton Road end it was only partially covered and that area also accommodated one of the rather ancient floodlight pylons. Luxurious it certainly wasn't. We worked seriously hard during the summer break and an exhausted Reg disappeared on holiday just before a huge amount of muck hit the proverbial fan.

For a long time the only television coverage of football was on the BBC's 'Match of The Day'. There was virtually no live coverage of matches with the exception of FA Cup ties and the odd league game on a Sunday. While other top clubs in Europe received enormous revenue from television companies for live matches this wasn't the case in the UK. The Spanish and Italian leagues were earning a fortune from TV rights which enabled them to sign the very best foreign players. The wages that were needed to attract the best Latin American and European talent were beyond the means of any of the English clubs. There had been growing unrest about this and the top five or six teams using David Dein, then vice-chairman of Arsenal, as their spokesman started a campaign to strike out on their own and negotiate separately from the Football Association. Greg Dyke, who was then running London Weekend Television and is now ironically Chairman of the FA, saw an opportunity to wrest control of football from the BBC. An integral part of the plan was that the First Division should be reconstituted and that only big clubs would be allowed in. Sadly Millwall was not on anybody's list of candidates for this new super league. Indeed, some of the bigger clubs in the second division were mentioned as founder members of the new top division. After 100 years of striving for it, Millwall's hard-won place amongst the elite was under severe threat. After hours, indeed days of negotiation, the first division obtained an undertaking for a disproportionately large share of the new contract that Greg was trying to negotiate. This meant considerably more money for the big six clubs in particular. LWT offered a massive increase to secure the rights from the BBC.

Reg returned from holiday and added his considerable irascibility to the debate. He was determined that our long-awaited prize would not be snatched from us. In the event LWT lost out to an upstart newcomer in the shape of Rupert Murdoch's new venture Sky Television. Keenly aware that sport and football in particular would drive the subscription-based business model for his new network, Mr Murdoch made an unbelievable offer to make sure that hardened football fans would soon have satellite dishes and access to live top-flight football. It was an enormously brave decision, literally betting the shop on an unproven concept – pay TV. The inevitable consequence was that the FA would lose its total power over the top clubs and the formation of the Premier League came a step closer.

But that was still a few years away and for the time being Millwall had enough to cope with in the First Division. Our first season was successful beyond our wildest dreams. The combination of Sheringham and Cascarino as the spearhead of our attacks took First Division defences by surprise. For a brief moment in September we were top of the division which was truly extraordinary. By March we had settled into third place but shortly after that we ran out of steam and finished in 10th place. Despite dropping a few places everyone connected with Millwall was delighted with this. We were going to get at least another season playing with the elite.

I've often described the daily running of a small football club as being like trying to put out financial forest fires with a tumbler of water. Reg, and subsequently myself, spent a lot of our time pleading with the VAT people for more time to pay. Every year when the annual accounts came in there was a danger of our accountants declaring we were no longer a going concern. We always countered this threat by demonstrating our historical ability to sell home grown players at a large profit – sums which would always allow us to stagger on for another season. Reg had decided that this was a far too uncertain way to run the business and as he had a small issuing house, he persuaded the board that we should go public. This would create a vehicle that he planned to use to buy other companies with a much more stable cash flow than a football club could ever dream of. The novelty of a football club going public with vague promises of affinity marketing opportunities and the recruitment of a whole generation of new fans allied to a hunger for any sort of new issue at that time (something I'd had extensive experience of with AMV) meant that we got the offer away successfully. Both Reg and I converted our loans into stock. He had long discussions with the bookmaking firm of Victor Chandler but never quite persuaded them of the virtue of joining us in the public arena. Despite opening above its offer price this strategy over the long-term didn't succeed, although a rights offer every year was very useful in replenishing our dwindling coffers.

So we embarked on a second season in the top flight as a public company. But this time round nothing went right. Our prolific goal scorers created chance after chance for themselves but failed to convert any of them. Indeed there was one game away at Chelsea where we were three goals down at half-time and the Chelsea chairman Ken Bates said to me we should have had five of our own before Chelsea even scored one.

Despite the novelty of being in the First Division, our fans' expectations ran high and they became restless. After a series of very unlucky defeats the situation was looking bleak and Reg, rather desperately in my view, decided that we would bid for a player called Paul Goddard. We ended up paying £800,000 for him, which I thought was way in excess of his market value. His introduction to the team disturbed the balance between Sheringham and Cascarino and the losing streak continued. The crunch came on a wet and windy evening in Cambridge in a cup game against, ironically the team where John Docherty had made his name, Cambridge United, who were then several divisions below us. We lost 1-0 from an own goal in the dying minutes. In the car coming back, as Reg liberally sprinkled cigar ash over my black carpets, he and Rosemary said that we should change the manager. Never having been a hire-and-fire type of employer myself I thought that this was deeply unfair because our management team had taken us into the First Division for the first time only 12 months earlier.

The rest of the board at that stage consisted of Brian Mitchell, who had had his own PR company, and Jeff Burnige who were also the other members of the original consortium that had bought the club. Jeff's father was a past chairman of the club and a successful property entrepreneur, Burnige Junior had not joined the family firm. The only other member of the board was David Sullivan, a very prominent councillor with Lewisham, who had been extremely helpful in our relationships with the local authority. The board met the day after the Cambridge game and I found myself outvoted four to one in favour of John and Frank being fired. I subsequently resigned from the board but Reg quite properly reminded me of my duties as the vice-chairman of a public company and said that a resignation would be very damaging. I reluctantly agreed to stay on. Bob Pearson the Chief Scout was made temporary manager but after two seasons relegation was inevitable and at the end of the 1989/90 season we dropped down a level.

The next few years saw us trying desperately to get back to the First Division. We made a pretty good fist of it, being in the play-offs on two occasions but not winning the right to play at Wembley in the final either time. At the same time as trying to get the team right on the field, Reg drove forward the project of a new stadium. The Den, the mythical home of Millwall, was literally falling down. Every time we embarked on any sort of refurbishment the lifting of a stone revealed more expensive decay – to rebuild it was a nonstarter. During this time David Sullivan was central in persuading the council to let us have a new site close to the old ground. The sale of The Den to Fairview Homes for housing development enabled us to build a sparkling new stadium – the first in London since Wembley and the first new league ground for 100 years. Seating 20,000 people in comfort with not a single impaired view was an enormous achievement. But revenue from events other than football failed to materialise. This was a hammer blow because we had spent a lot of money preparing the new stadium for concerts and so on.

On reflection, our thinking was fatally flawed because any band big enough to fill The Den would have been big enough to fill Wembley. A smaller attraction would always choose to go to the Wembley Arena, a well-established music venue, above us. We never really recovered financially, although we took an enormous amount of pride in the creation of a ground that will continue to provide football to the Millwall faithful for decades.

The period before the stadium was finished saw personnel come and go, as is the way in football. Reg persuaded Bruce Rioch, somebody he was familiar with from Luton, to join us as manager after an enormously successful term at Middlesbrough where he virtually single-handedly saved the club from financial Armageddon. When Bruce left, Reg and I had breakfast at the Connaught which was a favourite pastime of mine. When he asked who I thought we should try and get, I suggested Brian Clough the legendary manager. Reg laughed and said why would Clough come to Millwall? I responded that if we paid him £250,000 a year that might get his attention. In those days football managers were incredibly poorly paid – always much less than any star player and probably only just on a par with average members of the playing staff. I always found it really strange that the conductor of the orchestra, so to speak, would earn less than any of the musicians. Things changed radically a few years later – I was ahead of my time.

At that time we had playing for us a man called Mick McCarthy. After a distinguished playing career he joined us from Lyon, a French club of some distinction. Mick was an old-style centre-half, fearless and tough, a no-nonsense defender who the Millwall fans took to their hearts very quickly. Reg argued persuasively that Mick had the presence and the respect of the players and the potential to be a very good manager, so we appointed him. Paradoxically, Mick wanted his teams to play good football and for a period was very successful indeed in the season before the new stadium opened – he got us into the play-offs but we fell at the final hurdle yet again.

Reg had worked tirelessly to scramble together the money we needed to finish the stadium. The Fairview Homes deal was a great help but nowhere near enough to cover the cost of Millwall's new home. David Sullivan had performed miracles in Lewisham to get us a very good deal on a piece of land called Senegal Fields no more than half a mile away from The Den. We had employed the very best specialist architects to design us a great new stadium but the fans were in uproar at the move away from their spiritual home. They were also extremely angry at what they viewed as a lack of ambition in building a new venue capable of seating only 20,000 people. They argued that 30,000 minimum should be the capacity of the new ground. However this was totally impossible. We did not have the money to match their lofty ambitions but the stadium was designed so that if unforeseen success followed we could extend to accommodate at least 25,000.

The problems of competing with wealthier clubs than ours to attract really good players to join us intensified. Reg, now approaching his 70s, was expending an enormous amount of energy trying to balance the books, pushing us to get promotion and working hard to keep the Inland Revenue happy as well as handling daily calls from NatWest about the overdraft that kept increasing. Both he and I signed personal guarantees to help the club stay alive and compete. The gap in income between the top clubs and the rest of football widened alarmingly. The contrast between helping to run Millwall with its constant cash demands and being Chief Executive at the very successful public company that was Abbott Mead Vickers could not have been more marked.

The building of the new stadium placed a great strain on the relationship between Reg and the rest of the board. Inevitably the construction phase could not be run democratically and Reg and his nephew, who he had appointed as Finance Director, were making more and more decisions on the run. His view that the new structure should be called 'The New London Stadium' did not go down well with the rest of us and tensions grew. At one of our regular breakfasts Reg made it clear that he would like a couple of years at the new stadium as chairman before handing over to me. If joining the board in the first place was irresistible, the chance to be chairman of Millwall was equally enticing. I wasn't aware then that the term 'poisoned chalice' could have been invented for this particular post at that time.

Our new stadium proved to be a roaring success with the fans. All their misgivings about leaving the crumbling wreck of the old ground evaporated virtually overnight when they found that they could sit and watch their team in comfort, not queue at half-time for the toilets and get some reasonable food and drink. We made some mistakes on the food and drink as well, in particular believing that people would like to eat pizzas and spending a lot of money on half-a-dozen pizza ovens only to sell four slices in the first four matches. I remember showing David Dein of Arsenal around our new stadium and he was very complimentary about what we'd achieved. It was certainly not a blueprint for the new Emirates Stadium but I like to think it gave David a view of the art of the possible.

Our new stadium could have comfortably accommodated 30,000 spectators except that after the horror of Hillsborough in 1989, Mrs Thatcher commissioned Lord Justice Taylor to report on the future of football. Under the stewardship of her diminutive Minister of Sport Colin Moynihan, the final view was that no standing was to be allowed at any stadium after a certain specified date. Although I absolutely understand the requirement for safety, I do still believe it was possible to design football grounds which could have accommodated the standing space so beloved of football supporters who liked to stand with their friends every other Saturday afternoon. But this was a battle I was never likely to win, despite an impassioned plea in *The Times*. It's interesting that the whole subject of fans being allowed to stand up is being revisited now.

Reg finally decided that enough was enough and he would hand over the chairmanship of the club to me. By then things between us had become fraught – we were very different individuals. Reg immediately withdrew his personal guarantees which left me exposed as the sole guarantor for the ailing football club's finances. I developed a relationship with Mick and we went into the new season with some confidence, having signed a couple of strikers including our first player from the German leagues, Uwe Fuchs. An interesting aside was that Mick came to me and said that he'd been offered, I seem to remember, £4,000 by an agent putting the Fuchs deal together to ensure that it happened. Naturally he didn't accept it.

Unfortunately, Uwe rhymed with duvet and from very early in his Millwall career his inclination to go to ground at any opportunity meant Duvet Fuchs became his name. So we started the season with real optimism but it was not our mostly horizontal German striker who turned this optimism into results, it was a renaissance from an ex-Chelsea striker in the twilight of his career. Kerry Dixon, the man who had scored a hat-trick against us during our brief stay in the First Division, was invigorated by wearing Millwall's number nine shirt.

From the start of the season until Christmas results went very well, even if performances did not match them. On many occasions, particularly away from home, having been battered by her opponents we stole the odd goal and got three points where we deserved none. But from September through to early December we were top of the division. I remember an interviewer from Radio Five Live asking me what I would do to ensure our fans behaved themselves following our inevitable promotion to the Premier League. Reg prevailed on me to sign a full-back from Watford who he said in his view would make promotion a near certainty. The club had neither the money nor borrowing capability to enable this transaction to go through so I raided my pension fund and lent the club £400,000. I made a mistake at the time of not charging the club a commercial rate of interest and so later events meant that not only did the pension fund lose all of that money but the revenue disallowed the tax-free element meaning I took a double hit.

Rather disturbingly, in his first game at Blackburn our new recruit did not have the desired effect and our unbeaten run came to an end. Not to worry, we were still clear at the top but as Sir Alex Ferguson put it many years later, it was squeaky bum time. As we approached Christmas the chief executive rang me with exciting news – the then current Russian international pairing of Sergei Yuran and Anatoly Kulkov were available from Spartak Moscow. Sergei was a striker and Anatoly was the international team's playmaker and I checked them out as best I could. George Graham in his autobiography said that these two players destroyed his very powerful Arsenal team when they met Porto in a European Cup Tie. We checked with Sir Bobby Robson who had managed both players during a stint in Portugal and he said as individuals they were as good as gold.

We spent the whole day at the Royal Lancaster Hotel just before Christmas negotiating with the players and the myriad of intermediaries who claimed to represent them. Irritatingly, neither player spoke a word of English. After what seemed like an age we concluded the deal with bits of money disappearing to points all over the world. We signed them for the rest of that season with an option to buy them at £2 million for the following season if we were successful. This was a tiny amount of money for international class players and the signings generated an enormous amount of interest in the next home game against Port Vale. We had our biggest crowd for years turning out to see our glittering new signings.

Sadly we lost the game and the Russians seemed like fish out of water. It was obvious to the rest of the players that the two of them were being paid more than anybody else. I discovered too late that this would not have been a problem if they delivered but their lack of real effective contribution coupled with their inability to communicate with the rest of the team meant that resentment built up and that led to a fearsome destruction of team spirit.

We plummeted down the table. To make matters worse Mick had been approached to take over the managership of Ireland. I found it strange that this man with a very broad Yorkshire accent had played for Ireland in the first place and now he was being touted as their next manager. Being the honourable man that he is – something which meant that we have remained close friends to this day – Mick played the negotiations absolutely straight, asking for my permission to carry on talking to the Irish FA. His last game in charge was at Southend where we played poorly and lost again.

Mick went and we were forced to look elsewhere for a manager to rescue what was turning out to be a disastrous second half of the season. The name of Jimmy Nicholl, then manager of Raith Rovers, was put to me. Jimmy had worked wonders at this small Scottish club, taking them into Europe for the first time in their history and consistenly performing well. Just like the Russians, I had problems communicating with Jimmy who was a Northern Ireland native but it spent decades in Scotland. To my ears his cocktail of accents was about as impenetrable as any could be but Jimmy was a thoroughly decent and nice man, as well as a talented manager. He had had a stellar career at Manchester United before moving to Scotland to play for and become assistant manager at Rangers. He had no experience of the lower leagues in English football but I felt that his track record in Scotland, his obvious enthusiasm and his reputation in the game would cover for his lack of knowledge. He inherited a team disillusioned by the laissez-faire attitude of the Russians which translated into a complete lack of confidence on the field. Even with Jimmy we continued to fall like a stone, although we managed to stay out of the bottom three. A four-nil home victory against

Birmingham, who were flying high at the time, gave us the belief that we could stay up.

However, this was a false dawn and we arrived at the last game of the season in danger of going down. We were away to Ipswich who had a real chance of getting into the play-offs if they could beat us. Our main rivals for relegation, Portsmouth, were playing away at Huddersfield. We all believed that one point would be enough to save us and uncharacteristically Jimmy asked me to have dinner with the team the night before the game to help relax them.

Our best player, Alex Rae, was suspended for this crucial match. Despite a great deal of endeavour and effort, the game ended goalless. This would have been fine but for Portsmouth's massively unexpected win against Huddersfield. It meant we were relegated because they had scored one more goal then us during the season. Goals scored as a method of deciding league places had only been recently introduced and if the old system of goal difference had obtained we would have stayed up. The boardroom at Ipswich was a depressing place that afternoon – they had not secured the three points they needed to get into the play-offs and we had been relegated. Reg had given an interview to the local paper being highly critical of the team, me and the manager, which didn't help relationships between us.

The real disaster of the Ipswich result meant that the financial reconstruction package I'd put in place with NatWest, which was dependent on us staying in the division, fell away. My financial exposure in terms of personal guarantees was getting serious. During the close season Jimmy Nicholl prevailed on me to sign four Scottish footballers. Three were from Raith Rovers and the other one by reputation was going to be Scotland's new wunderkind. The money for this adventure was negotiated with a small private bank who were specialising in making money available for football transfers. Needless to say they wanted some security so my personal commitment swelled by another million pounds.

The financial situation at the club was getting worse by the day. At a social lunch with Derek Wanless, who was then the chief executive of Nat-West, he asked if he could help. I explained the position the club were in and he promised to get involved. My contacts at the bank rang a couple of days later and said they were sending in their intensive care team to have a root-and-branch review of the club and its finances with the aim of helping structure a financial way forward. The bank's representatives arrived with an avuncular smooth gentleman who presented a card suggesting he was a chartered accountant. Five days later he convened a meeting of the board and said there was no alternative but to go into administration and that as a public company we should suspend the shares. He produced another card which suggested that his real role was recovery and restoration and that he was employed outside NatWest. I had little choice but to agree.

The situation we found ourselves in made me feel really strongly that banks should never appoint an investigating accountant employed by another company as an administrator. In my view this creates a massive potential conflict of interest as large fees charged by administrators dwarf those that might be expected to be paid if the exercise is purely aimed at returning the club to financial health. If the investigating accountant is both a) the person who will carry out the administration and will thus benefit from the resulting fees and b) the person who decides whether or not a company should go into administration the potential for a misalignment of priorities is clear. I am not suggesting this is what happened in our case, only that in some cases it could happen or at the very least it could be perceived to have happened. It seems extraordinary to me that no one has thought to legislate to prevent this.

Tragically, as all of this was happening I lost a great friend who would have undoubtedly helped me solve Millwall's financial problems, Matthew Harding. We shared an obsession – football. We met during a famous year in Millwall's history when we played both Arsenal and Chelsea in the FA Cup. Both home games ended in draws so had to be replayed at Highbury and Stamford Bridge respectively. Matthew had become involved with Chelsea not long before we played them the Den. He was vice-chairman and we met over the pre-match meal. We hit it off and agreed that whoever lost would have to buy the winner dinner at Langan's Brasserrie in Mayfair. Millwall finally prevailed after a stormy replay at Stamford Bridge which finally took penalties to resolve. After the dinner, Matthew and I became firm friends. We had lunch quite often and spent some time on holiday in Spain together. He was the founder of a reinsurance company called Benfield and was a multimillionaire. He always boasted that his business of the year was finished on January 2 after frantic negotiations with the European giants in reinsurance. This gave him the ability to spend a lot of time following his beloved Chelsea.

I was in New York one October when I got a call from the hotel reception in the middle of the night asking me to ring home urgently because there had been a terrible accident. Matthew had been at the Chelsea game in Bolton the night before. His team were trounced and I can imagine his irritation and disappointment translating to him insisting to his helicopter pilot that they get back to London that night. In bad weather the helicopter came down and everybody on board was killed. Without any further sleep that night, I got on a plane the following morning to return to London and particularly for a dinner that Sam and I would have with the Abbotts that evening. We were entertaining one of our ex-partners from New York and his wife. We were eating at the fashionable restaurant called Vong at the Berkeley Hotel in Knightsbridge. I ordered crab sticks and virtually immediately found myself unable to breathe. The restaurant called an ambulance and I was carried out on a stretcher and taken to the Chelsea & Westminster Hospital where they gave me adrenaline and told me that I had, for some obscure reason, become allergic to one of my favourite foods. I'm still not totally convinced that my attack that evening in the fashionable fusion eatery was the result of crab consumption. I think it could have been a delayed reaction to the Matthew news or just straightforward tiredness. I haven't put this particular theory to the test by eating crab though since just in case.

For all of us at Millwall the period in administration was horrible. It was announced two or three days before we played Bristol City at home, a game which resulted in another loss. My son Billy, who was by now a YTS player at Millwall, insisted on being at my side in the directors' box. After the game, fans gathered in the car park as a protest and despite being forbidden by the police to go and talk to them, I insisted on doing so. And Billy insisted on coming with me. I spent 25 minutes talking to the fans and as always they ended up treating me fairly. In fact there was a smattering of applause as Billy and I left to go and be interviewed by my friend David Mellor who was hosting 606 on Radio Five at the time. At a time of enormous stress I have never been more proud to be a father. Billy was magnificent.

I had to raise £175,000 in a hurry to guarantee that the club could meet its obligations and we embarked on a horrible few months as we fought to ensure that the club survived. I became a figurehead chairman. I'd never declared anybody redundant in my working career and it was enormously painful to see the carnage that the hatchet-faced gentleman from recovery and restoration wrought on my beloved club. With a day left to complete the rights Issue that would ensure a healthy club would be inherited by the next regime we were still £500,000 short but two of my closest friends agreed to put up that amount of money in return for shares. To my enormous relief they subsequently came out ahead by selling their shares at an appropriate moment.

Theo Paphitis became the new chairman and driving force behind Millwall and I reverted to being a member of the board. I finally agreed a deal with both NatWest and the small merchant bank over my commitments to them. Swathes of my shares in AMV had to be sold prematurely but the most important thing was that Millwall had survived and, despite what has been written since, Theo's regime had a debt-free future to look forward to, along with a £6 million war chest. I had suffered financially but my real regret was that many small people were hurt by the process.

Yet again it was Sammy, my wife, who carried me through this whole painful exercise. Although she had every right to be angry at the way I had put our family finances in jeopardy, she supported me unconditionally. Obviously my work at Millwall was secondary to my main task which was to help manage AMV. That was particularly difficult because my trusted right hand at work, my amazing PA Jo Whyte, had gone on maternity leave.

I struggled through every working day but when I got home Sam had created a sort of cocoon in the living room of our house, with a log fire and comfort food. James Macdanell, my friend and trusted finance man, would join me over chicken pie and mash to dissect the full horror of another day in administration. After we came out of it, I stayed on the board and developed a good relationship with Theo and attempted to rebuild my relationship with Reg, who Theo had asked to return to the board. These were not easy times. Sam, James and I struggled but finally put the family's finances back into order.

Over the years Theo hired and fired a number of managers and the club had a modicum of success. With Mark McGhee in the managerial chair we got promoted back to the division that we had so been relegated from during my first year of chairmanship, the second tier. Good players came and went and although the club was debt-free the financial struggles went on. This time, though, it was Theo who had to try and sort it out through his relationship with the Bank of Cyprus who had taken on the dubious distinction of being Millwall's bank – the hierarchy at NatWest I'm sure had a celebratory party to welcome the baton being passed.

The club's greatest achievement under Theo with Dennis Wise, a famous ex-Chelsea player, as manager was to reach the FA Cup final in 2004. We had had a great season – Tim Cahill, a very talented young Australian player, was scoring goals for fun from midfield and the rest of the team were playing really well. That year we were thought likely to at least get into the play-offs for promotion to the Premier League but at the same time embarked on one of those wonderfully lucky runs in the FA Cup. The truth of the matter is you only have to win six games to get into the Cup Final. Most years if you did well to get through the first couple of rounds you drew a much superior team to yourself and got knocked out. In 2004 the little black balls that were used in the draw were very kind to us. We had a succession of teams to play who were mostly inferior to us. We got through to the semi-finals where the only teams left were ourselves, Sunderland, who were in our division, Arsenal and Manchester United. Miraculously we drew Sunderland and went to Old Trafford to play in the semi-final. It was an amazing day and we beat Sunderland by a goal to nil, scored by Mr Cahill. Sunderland were managed on that day by Mick McCarthy and my great joy in getting through to the final was tinged by more than a hint of regret at seeing him and his great wife Fiona so upset at the final whistle.

As Wembley was not finished we had to play the final against Manchester United, who had dispatched Arsenal in their semi-final, in Cardiff. It

was a massively daunting prospect. United were at the height of their powers. The great Cristiano Ronaldo was playing for them along with ten other
household names. We held our own for about 30 minutes before Ronaldo
scored. We lost three-nil on the day and all of us old Millwall supporters
were sad that we appeared to have gone for damage limitation, which meant
we never had a real go at attacking the mighty Reds. I would have preferred
to have lost five-nil rather than watch the ambition-free containing operation that happened on that day in Cardiff.

We were still favourites to get promotion but after that final our season collapsed. Theo began to talk about retirement, believing quite properly
that we were unlikely to get into a Cup Final again in any of our lifetimes.
Reg and I joined forces to try and find a new chairman who would have
fresh ideas and, importantly, spare cash to invest in the Club. We failed and
Theo installed Jeff Burnige. I really believed that this was a wrong move and
resigned from the board on a fraught evening in a private room at a restaurant just off Regent Street. My time as an unpaid official at Millwall was over.

On reflection my stint at the club gave me enormous pleasure. Of all the
things I've achieved in my lifetime I have no doubt whatsoever that my dad
would have been most proud of my tenure as a director of Millwall. And
there was another wonderful by-product because despite not liking football,
Sam started a local club near our home called Sheen Lions to occupy her
on the Saturdays that I spent away from home. When she retired over 400
boys were being coached every Saturday morning and the five or six teams
that ran out under the Sheen Lions name were phenomenally successful.
League titles, league cups and even county cups were acquired during the
period Sam ran the team.

Both Billy and Ben, my sons, played for the two most successful Sheen
Lions teams. Billy, much against my better judgement, was picked by the

youth coaching operation at Millwall to become a player. He had a good career, playing many times for the reserves – indeed I have a team sheet where he turned out for Millwall reserves against Chelsea for whom John Terry was a substitute. He also played for the FA Youth XI, wearing the England shirt as it was only one rank below the full England youth team. He went on to have a good career in non-league football which was brought to an end by a horrific double fracture of his right leg during a game at Kingstonian.

Mick McCarthy's wife Fiona has said to me on many occasions since that I should never go back into football because I wrongly believed that treating people fairly would work in sport and bring success as it had done in advertising. My sister and her husband carried on as season-ticket holders at Millwall for many years, a run only broken by the untimely death of her husband very recently.

So how do I feel about it all now? The Millwall bug still eats away at me and I accompany my sister to about ten games a season. Over the last five years the unthinkable has happened and Millwall have appeared at Wembley three times. Because of my association with the organisation behind it, I managed to get boxes for our two appearances in the play-off finals for promotion back to the division that I so ignominiously left all those years before. The first occasion ended in disappointment but the following year, 2010, we beat Swindon on the hallowed turf to earn promotion from League One to the Championship – what years before would have been going up from the Third Division to the Second. It was a wonderful day.

Amazingly, in 2013 we managed to get to the semi-finals of the FA Cup, only losing to the eventual winners, Wigan Athletic. Pat and I were there, of course, as were my son Billy and my grandchildren and my youngest son Harry who, although only recently infected with the Millwall virus, shows all the early signs of having the disease for life.

There will be other great days at Millwall and I will be there to share them.

CHAPTER 20

WEMBLEY

One morning in the mid-nineties while sitting in
my office I got a call from an organisation
called London First. At that time we didn't have a London Mayor and this
organisation, which I don't think was government funded, was there to protect the interests of the capital. There had already been a lot of specula-
tion that a new national stadium was necessary because Wembley, probably
the most famous sporting arena in the world, was coming to the end of its
natural life. Behind the twin-towered facade the whole edifice was literally
crumbling. It had been designed decades before seating became mandatory – indeed, 70% of the people who saw football matches at the stadium
refused to sit down primarily because the gradient the stands were pitched
at was designed to accommodate people standing rather than sitting. Coupled with a fan's natural inclination to stand up while watching football, this
meant that the views in the cheaper seats were very poor indeed. Construction techniques had moved on substantially since the iconic venue was built.

London First asked if I would have a meeting with Sir Allen Sheppard,
who was then chairman of the organisation, as well as being chief executive
of GrandMet, one of AMV's biggest clients. I met with Allen in his offices
in St James. He was a very charismatic man of steely determination and was

used to getting his own way. He asked me if I would get involved with the current management at Wembley, which over the previous few years had rescued the public company from a parlous financial state. I very happily agreed to help out. The task represented activity in two of my favourite areas: brands and football. I arranged a meeting with Alan Coppin, the chief executive of Wembley. Alan was and is a smart and charming man who ran the decaying Wembley empire with both precision and style.

We hit it off immediately. Both of us found it inconceivable that any new national stadium should be anywhere except Wembley. In branding terms it was way ahead of any other stadium in the world. As an illustration of its fame, the most famous footballer in the world, Pele, often bemoaned the fact that he'd never played at what he called the 'cathedral of football'. But the threat of another site being chosen was very real. Citing traffic chaos and southern bias, there was quite a head of steam building up for a national stadium to be more accessible to the whole of the UK rather than just London. As funding for the new stadium was to be either government-sourced or at least partly community-funded by the lottery, a competitive pitch outlining the benefits of the various locations had to be put together in a matter of weeks.

I agreed to join the team that Alan had put together to make the case that north-west London should continue to be where we watched our great football occasions. I can't remember which organisation we finally presented to but in my view the worldwide fame of the existing site meant that the decision should have been a shoe-in. In the event we did win, despite having one or two seriously wobbly moments. Alan and I had got along really well during the campaign and he asked me if I'd be interested in joining the board of Wembley to push forward the development of the new stadium. It was pretty much a dream come true. Because of my allegiance to Millwall, my visits to see my team play at that stage had been non-existent but I had been lucky enough on a handful of occasions to see England play on the sacred turf.

It was apparent immediately that the Football Association, being Wembley's most significant customer by far, had their own plans. On the board with me were two giant personalities in Jarvis Astaire, a fabled sporting entrepreneur, and Roger Brooke who was often referred to as the inventor of private equity in the UK through his company Candover. At the same time a new chairman took over Wembley PLC a man called Claes Hultman who had had some significant success running a public company in engineering. Wembley PLC was a mix of businesses ranging from the stadium, the arena and the conference centre on the giant Wembley site through to Keith Prowse, the leaders in sporting hospitality packages as well as the Cavern in Liverpool, the home of the Beatles. In addition we had a number of greyhound racing tracks and gaming concessions in Rhode Island in the US.

The executive branch of the board felt that they had little choice but to acquiesce to the FA and sell them the stadium and the brand. The money generated by this (in excess of £100 million) would enable us to beef up some of our other facilities and pay down debt. Us non-executives on the other hand felt that we should become joint-venture partners with the FA in the development of the new stadium. Despite its age, lack of facilities and obvious shortcomings the stadium was managed and run very well indeed. I believed this should mean that we would be ideally placed to get a long-term management contract from the joint-venture company. Our executive colleagues were much more conscious of the power the FA possessed over a large part of our income. The FA initiative in those days was headed up by Ken Bates, the feisty chairman of Chelsea and a very important player in the FA hierarchy. Ken's plans favoured mirroring what he achieved at Stamford Bridge, where a new hotel would become an integral part of the new stadium development.

At a critical time in deliberations one of our non-executive colleagues was stricken by a stroke while he was on business in the Far East. This meant that only six members of the board remained, Jarvis, Roger and myself on one side and Claes, Alan and Nigel Potter, the finance director, in opposition. The discussions were long, complex, rancorous and bitter. Neither side would back down. After one momentous meeting at Charterhouse, the company's merchant bank, the deadlock was only broken by the chairman using his casting vote – the only time ever in all my career that this state of affairs had occurred. While the executive team produced an offer for sale document for our shareholders, we determined to exercise our right as independent directors to put the counter-argument to the proposed outright sale. So our shareholders were faced with two documents from the same board outlining diametrically opposed views.

In the end a couple of major shareholders, one of whom I knew very well, decided our fate and the three of us were removed from the board very quickly. The deal was done and the FA was faced with raising hundreds of millions of pounds to turn the new Wembley into reality. The whole area surrounding the stadium could have been purchased for some £20 million at the same time. For some inexplicable reason this offer was not taken up and the surrounding areas were sold off to developers.

The remaining bits of Wembley struggled on for quite a while. The company became infamous again a few years later when it was accused of influencing politicians on Rhode Island as it tried to expand its slot machine operations which were very profitable. One of the company's senior executives, was accused of spearheading this move and disastrously was found guilty and spent some time in an American penal institution. The public company limped along for a few years but ultimately ceased trading.

While all of this was happening the FA appointed a new chief executive called Adam Crozier who had been one of the leaders of Saatchi & Saatchi in London. After a series of political battles which Adam had to take on to modernise the institution, he took back for himself total control over the Wembley project. One day, over a game of golf at Wentworth, he asked me if I had any interest in joining the board of the new Wembley which was to be set up as a wholly-owned subsidiary of the FA but with completely independent governance. Poetic and irresistible, I thought, and agreed immediately.

Adam had taken a disciplined view over the composition of the new Wembley board. Members were chosen based on their special knowledge. I was tasked, based on my advertising and marketing background, with ensuring that the Club Wembley element of the stadium was a success. This was important because the financial model created to take the whole stadium project forward was heavily dependent on the sales of 10 year leases on Club Wembley seats and boxes. Although the word debenture was never used, in essence that's what the exercise was about. IMG had been recruited to do the heavy lifting and we on the board, particularly the marketing team at Wembley and myself, were there to provide marketing support and back-up.

It was a pretty heavy task in the early days. The first job we had to do was to try and get the benefit of the doubt from the media. There was some residual resentment about the choice of Wembley as the site of the new national stadium. A stadium of this size and complexity had never been attempted in this country and at that stage was probably unique in Europe. The finance team had been very successful in putting a package together and the construction specialists had nailed down a pretty tight contract with Multiplex, a giant Australian construction company who agreed a fixed price to build the 90,000 seat colossus.

It was apparent from the early designs that retaining the iconic twin towers, for decades the symbol of Wembley, would make the transition easier to swallow. But there was no way that the architects could design a new stadium which kept the crumbling landmarks and so they had to go. We took a heavy beating from the press over this decision. In addition, in the absence of a central stadium the England team had been playing tournament qualifying games around the country including at Old Trafford, the home of Manchester United. This exercise was proving to be enormously popular with the fans and once again the wisdom of a hugely expensive national stadium was constantly debated in the press.

But there was no turning back. The contract for the new stadium's giant steel framework had been signed and the old Wembley was being sold off in chunks. Everything was up for grabs, from pieces of the twin towers through to squares of the famous Wembley turf. Even some of the notoriously uncomfortable seats were sold to smaller football clubs to enable them to catch up with the all-seater stadium requirements.

On a project as big as this it was no surprise that there were constant disputes with the contractor. In addition, the avant-garde design, particularly of the giant Wembley arch, proved troublesome and expensive to turn into reality. The project was delayed by at least 18 months which created a storm of criticism from all sides. Fortunately we were able to run a sustained teaser campaign promising that the wait would be worthwhile because we would have the best stadium in Europe.

As the finishing touches were added to the stadium it was clear that it would match everybody's expectations. I know of no one visiting the stadium for the first time who has not been blown away by its beauty and awesome scale. The sales of Club Wembley contracts accelerated as the opening day grew closer. As this element was absolutely central to the financial strictures imposed by the lenders, we breathed a huge sigh of relief as one after another our targets were reached.

Towards the end of the project Adam Crozier left the FA, quite quickly followed by his successor Mark Palios, who was consumed by allegations published in the *News of The World* which also seriously embarrassed Sven Goran Eriksson. The board was under constant pressure to achieve its targets and became the scene of quite a few fractious meetings particularly involving the removal of the project's chief executive, Michael Cunnah. But the feeling of ownership and pride on the day the stadium finally opened for business was overwhelming. I was very pleased at having successfully carried out the job that Adam had outlined that day at Wentworth. Within the space of 15 years I had been intimately involved in the construction of two new stadiums in London, an achievement I expect is unique.

There was a curious symmetry between the two when Millwall made three appearances at the new stadium. The second trip was successful and my love affair with Wembley peaked that day.

EPILOGUE

So there it is. Inevitably, great chunks of my life did not make it to the buffet table. My experiences with Sir Michael Pickard on the board of the London Docklands Development Corporation, my years as a Vice-Chairman of the NSPCC's Full Stop Appeal, which raised £260 million under the Chairmanship of Prince Andrew, and my time in private equity with Dominic Shorthouse at Englefield. I could write another book about each of those experiences but not even my family would buy a copy!

I could also fill another tome thanking the people who have helped and put up with me over the many decades. I hope and believe they know who they are.

It has been a great joy to create *When In Doubt Be Nice*. I would urge anybody thinking about doing something similar to sit down and start now.

Peter Mead, 2014.

He knows not where he's going
For the ocean will decide –
It's not the destination...
...it's the glory of the ride
'Zen Dog' by Edward Monkton